SLAUGHTER
at Goliad

SLAUGHTER
at Goliad

The Mexican Massacre of 400 Texas Volunteers

Jay A. Stout

NAVAL INSTITUTE PRESS
Annapolis, Maryland

Naval Institute Press
291 Wood Road
Annapolis, MD 21402

Library of Congress Cataloging-in-Publication Data

Stout, Jay A., 1959–
    Slaughter at Goliad : the Mexican massacre of 400 Texas volunteers / Jay A. Stout.
        p. cm.
    Includes bibliographical references and index.
    ISBN 978-1-59114-843-2 (alk. paper)
    1. Goliad Massacre, Goliad, Tex., 1836. 2. Texas—History—Revolution, 1835–1836. I. Title.
F394.G64S76 2008
976.4'123—dc22
                                    2007037974

Printed in the United States of America on acid-free paper ♾

14 13 12 11 10 09 08   9 8 7 6 5 4 3 2
First printing

All maps and photographs in this book are courtesy of the author.

For Monica.
She's a really neat person and pretty to look at.

Contents

Preface

"Everyone's going to think you hate Mexicans—it's too provocative." The title of this book elicited that and several similar responses from friends and family. But I don't hate Mexicans, or anyone else that Americans have fought. I don't hate the British or the Germans or the Japanese, or even the Iraqis who—with some vigor—tried to kill me in 1991. During my life, I've learned that people—regardless of where they live and what language they speak or even what religion they practice—are pretty much the same. All around the world, people are generally good and share the same desires and dreams for themselves and their families. It is only when they are stupidly and viciously led that they commit atrocities. It doesn't matter whether they are Mexican, British, German, Japanese, Iraqi, or even American.

The title is what it is because virtually no one outside the town of Goliad, Texas, knows what happened there. If I were to write about a particular aspect of the Holocaust I could title my book *Horror at Auschwitz*, and a prospective reader would know that I was writing about the Jews and their near extermination by the Germans during World War II. Or, if I were to title a manuscript *Clash at Gettysburg*, the reader would probably know that it dealt with the great Civil War battle.

But today, prior to publication, when I ask people what they know about Goliad they grow a little wide eyed, perhaps fearful that I'll try to educate them. To the broader, ignorant world—certainly outside Texas—Goliad could be anything. I can declare with little risk of being challenged that Goliad was one of the tribal chieftains that Alexander the Great smashed on his way to India, or that it is a river or place in one of Tolkien's tales. Or I could perhaps even pass it off as some sort of medical condition: "Kids, Grandma's in the hospital again—her Goliad's inflamed worse than ever."

So, the title is descriptive and puts the story in context; it tells someone deciding which book to buy that it is about a Mexican slaughter of volunteers for Texas. I won't be disingenuous and pretend that there's not a bit of marketing involved. Texas is our second-most populous state, and Mexicans make up a significant part of our population. Certainly it can't hurt sales to gain the interest of these two huge demographics.

But what about the word "slaughter"? Some of those familiar with the event who are sensitive to the Mexican perspective argue that the killings were an execution rather than a slaughter, or a massacre, or a butchery, but I disagree. An execution is a government-administered capital punishment that is meted out after judicial proceedings. There were no trials at Goliad. The bloody, chaotic carnage of March 27, 1836, was not an execution: it was a killing orgy made possible by deceit and deception. Conversely, some say that the slayings were murder. This viewpoint occupies the opposite end of the spectrum, but it is also difficult to justify. A murder is wholly unjustified and outside the law. As dubious as it was, the Tornel Decree gave Antonio López de Santa Anna a technicality to hide behind. Accordingly, I have stayed away from both words.

The title also asserts that Santa Anna's *soldados* killed four hundred Texas volunteers. There is no precise tally of the exact number of men that were slain while captive on March 27, 1836, and during the days immediately before and after that date, but Harbert Davenport, the eminent Texas historian, was able to account for 342 of these men by name. It is almost certain that—because of the lack of accurate records—there were others he did not discover. Mexican accounts declare that more than four hundred were marched out of the old presidio to be slain, while other Mexican reports describe additional slayings in and around Refugio of thirty or more. While the paucity of records will forever defy an exact count, I do not believe that the number I have chosen is unreasonable.

There are few events—perhaps none—in American history that exceed the Texas Revolution as a study in abysmal leadership. Revolutions and campaigns require competent leadership to succeed. That precept notwithstanding, the fact that the Texas revolutionaries prevailed was hardly due to their exemplary qualities in this regard. Indeed, most of the leaders of the revolution were, despite their ardor, their devotion, and their energy, not just inept, but stunningly inadequate. Most of the men that fashioned themselves into the barely operative revolutionary government were not up to the task, and the majority of the officers they put, or allowed, into the field were likewise untrained and incapable.

Nevertheless, the Texas Revolution had a very strong consideration working in its favor. This factor was the providential (for the Texas revolutionaries) reality that Mexico was somehow even more poorly led—even spectacularly so. The government in Mexico City, which in its short history had never been very effective, was essentially usurped by the dictator Santa Anna in 1833. Nearly all accounts agree that the handsome Santa Anna was remarkably charming, charismatic, and politically astute and persuasive. Yet many of those same accounts reveal that he was also astonishingly corrupt, cruel, and self-serving. His talents as a military commander are perhaps best characterized as uneven.

His leadership failings permeated, with few exceptions, every level of his campaign in Texas. This shortcoming, more than anything else, ensured that Mexico lost Texas. This work, in great part, is a discussion of the leadership failures of both sides.

It is important to explain some of the terminology I use to describe the men who came to fight for Texas. First, I use the term "Tejano" to mean anyone of Hispanic descent who was born in and lived in Texas before Texas became independent. As for the men who came from the United States to fight for Texas, the word "Texan" is commonly seen in other writings, but this usage makes me uncomfortable. First, the word didn't come into common usage until after statehood. "Texian" was a more common term, but many of these men thought of themselves simply as Americans. Next, I had no good criteria for determining what made a person a Texan. Certainly, place of birth was not a good measure, because few of the men who fought the revolution, and probably none who were Anglo, were born in Texas. In fact, at the Battle of San Jacinto, the vast majority of the men who fought had been in Texas for fewer than five years. In the case of the men who were killed at Goliad, most were only a few months removed from the United States and primarily identified with the state they came from, and considered themselves to be, for example, Kentuckians, or Alabamans, or Virginians. They would hardly have considered themselves Texans.

But I couldn't quite get away with calling all of them Americans, because there were Poles, British, Canadians, Germans, and other foreigners among them. I finally settled on the term "volunteers" when discussing the revolution, because they were all volunteers in the cause for Texas, even if some of them were technically part of the regular army. I also use the term "Anglos." This term encompasses the white Americans and Europeans—those who did the bulk of the fighting for the revolution. In fact, there were no Mexican surnames on the list of men who were slain at Goliad. Nevertheless, I do realize that Tejanos served with distinction on the side of independence, but, overwhelmingly, Anglos made up the fighting forces. No slight of the Tejanos is intended by my use of the term Anglos.

In order to put the events at Goliad in context, the book needed to include at least some history of Texas and the events leading up to the revolution. I tried to keep the scope as narrow as possible, while still including enough information for the events at Goliad to make sense. I was tempted to include more—and to chase down some remarkably interesting but only marginally related rabbit holes—but resisted lest the focus of the book become diluted. As for geography, although the borders of the region changed through history, this book does not track the evolution of those demarcations. Thus, I use the term "Texas" throughout to indicate the approximate geographic area of the eastern and southern areas of the present-day state.

People ask why I've spent so much time and energy to write this book. There is no easy answer. I had heard about the massacre during the 1980s when I served as a military pilot in east Texas. As an avid hunter and fisherman, I developed an affinity for the characters as I tramped over much of the same ground. Flying daily over the same region also gave me an appreciation for the geography of the place and the distances involved. I could easily imagine skirmishing back and forth across the area when it was still largely trackless and wild.

The actual sites were interesting to visiting friends and family. The presidio was restored during the 1960s and is a quite accurate representation of the fort as it existed during the 1830s. Today, it is a well-run park that is free of the traffic and mobs that characterize the Alamo. Still, for a long time it was difficult to find a complete account of the historical event itself. This was all the more frustrating because, until the Civil War, the massacre marked one of the largest single-day losses of American fighters in the history of our nation. That it wasn't better known was perplexing and frustrating to me. I not only believed the victims deserved better, but also that the wider public would be fascinated by their story. The result is this book; it is the most comprehensive treatment yet of the slaughter at Goliad.

Introduction

The illegal immigration had to be stopped. An overwhelming influx of Americans into northern Mexico—particularly the region they called Texas—threatened the stability of the region. Accordingly, the Mexican government enacted the Law of April 6, 1830, effectively closing Texas to American immigration

Many have argued that Texas, populated largely with Americans, was inescapably bound to tear itself from Mexico to become part of the United States. The case is compelling. For one, by 1835 Americans made up the majority of the population in Texas by a wide margin: there were approximately thirty thousand Anglo-Americans compared to about four thousand Tejanos. Even the enslaved black Americans that the Anglo-Americans took into Texas—estimated at five thousand in 1835—outnumbered the Tejanos.[1] On the one hand, unlike those Tejanos, the Americans knew democratic government and had practiced it prior to coming to Texas. It was, to their way of thinking, the best and most sophisticated form of governance in existence. On the other hand, Mexico's bloody and abortive attempts to establish and maintain a democracy amid seemingly nonstop coups and revolts did not impress the Anglo Texans.

Another consideration was the fact that the livelihoods and businesses of the settlers were bound to their closest neighbor, the United States. Furthermore, and importantly, the leaders of Mexico were incapable of effectively enforcing the nation's laws so far from the seat of government. In fact, there was little incentive to do so: garrisoning troops on the far reaches of the Texas frontier was expensive and returned no revenue to a national treasury that was bankrupt.

Another factor in the Texas Revolution was the sense of moral, physical, and intellectual superiority that the American settlers typically felt when they compared themselves to their Mexican counterparts. In their view, Mexicans were lazy, poorly educated, mixed-race sluggards who practiced a corrupt religion and who had no appreciation for hard work, business, or industry. Essentially, the Anglo settlers were racists, although they would not have used that word.

General Samuel Houston, an icon in the making of Texas, neatly characterized the attitude of the settlers toward the Mexicans: "The vigor of the descendents of the sturdy north will never mix with the phlegm of the Mexicans."[2] This from a man who chose to live his adolescence and part of his adulthood among the Indians, a race that Anglos widely decried as base and inferior. Even the normally restrained Stephen F. Austin declared that the fight against Mexico was one of a "mongrel Spanish-Indian and Negro race, against civilization and the Anglo-American race."[3]

Arguably, prejudices like this may have been justified in the Anglo settlers' context. After all, the Spanish and the Mexicans—even considering the Catholic missions—had done nothing worthwhile with Texas during the previous two hundred years. Yet they, the Anglos, had already begun to make the wild land produce marketable goods in a very short time. For better or for worse, they had made it into a place worth fighting for.

Nevertheless, it wasn't certain that any fighting would have to be done. Unquestionably, many colonists hoped that the government in Mexico City would take a more pragmatic stance toward the unique situation that existed in Texas. Indeed, rather than revolt, most Anglos put their trust in reconciliation and negotiation. There was also hope that the difficulties with the Mexican government might be rendered moot by an outright acquisition of Texas by the United States. The Andrew Jackson administration had failed in a purchase attempt in 1831, but that failure didn't mean that another overture couldn't be made. In fact, it was realistic to expect the United States to make another attempt to acquire Texas as more and more of its citizens moved to the increasingly troubled region.

Still, as increasing numbers of Anglo-Americans poured into Texas and as the Mexican government continued to resist demands from these new Anglo citizens, a break became increasingly likely. Practically, the Americans had no real connection to Mexico. They lived next to other Americans, they traded with the United States, they corresponded with their families back home in America, they spoke English, and, for the most part, they married other Americans, rarely Mexicans. When they looked around themselves they saw land that had been tamed and buildings that had been built by other Americans. That they should think of joining the nation that had raised them and that they had recently left was not only natural, but also perhaps unavoidable.

Austin characterized this inevitability when he likened the situation in Texas to the natural course that causes fruit to fall from a tree: "Being fully Americanized under the Mexican flag would be the same thing in effect and ultimate result as coming under the United States flag. A gentle breeze shakes off a ripe peach. Can it be supposed that the violent political convulsions of

Mexico will not shake off Texas as soon as it is ripe enough to fall?"[4] By the summer of 1835, the Texas peach was taking on a golden-honeyed hue, and the gentle breeze was becoming a stiff wind.

Of course, it all ultimately led to war, and with that war came savage atrocities. One of the most cruel and unnecessary of these was the Mexican slaughter of approximately four hundred mostly American prisoners outside the presidio at Goliad on Palm Sunday, March 27, 1836. That massacre happened largely because of the decisions of two men—one on each side of the conflict. James Walker Fannin, the incompetent American commander at Goliad, avoided making decisions until it was too late and then made a series of bad decisions that ultimately pitched his men into a battle that they could not win. He surrendered them and they were made captive. Little more than a week later he and his men were brutally slain.

On the Mexican side, Santa Anna insisted on killing the captives and declared that the law—*his* law—demanded it. He did so even in response to a recommendation of clemency by the commander who defeated them. In the end, it was a grotesquerie that occurred because of inept leadership on the side of the Anglos and barbarous cruelty on the behalf of the Mexicans. That it has been largely forgotten is because ineptitude and malice are characteristics that no one embraces or endeavors to memorialize.

CHAPTER 1
Bloody Beginnings

When American frontiersmen and settlers ventured into what is present-day Texas during the late eighteenth and early nineteenth centuries, it had long been home to large numbers of indigenous peoples. In fact, evidence of these natives exists from the end of the last Ice Age, about 10,000 BC. By the early 1800s, the region was populated with many tribes, the most important of which were the Tejas, Karankawa, Comanche, Apache, Tonkawa, Aranama, and Bidais. They ultimately shared the same fate as virtually all natives in North America: their encounters with the European race were variously friendly, neutral, or brutally hostile, but usually, in the end, fatal. Those ends came only after struggles that were a chief factor in shaping the region.

In November 1528, the first Europeans set foot in Texas when a 250-man Spanish expedition traveling from Cuba to Florida went astray and was shipwrecked on the coast near present-day Galveston Island. All but four of the expedition perished—wiped out by Indians, disease, and starvation. The four survivors endured incredible hardships before stumbling into Mexico City after seven years in the harsh and unforgiving wilderness. That tragedy was repeated less than three decades later when Indians killed 250 survivors of a Spanish shipwreck near Padre Island in 1554. Several years later, in 1568, English sailors who had been defeated in a clash with Spanish warships at Veracruz made landfall along the Texas coast. Amazingly, three of their number survived to traverse not only Texas, but also much of the rest of the North American continent, eventually reaching Nova Scotia in late 1569.[1]

European exploration of Texas during the next hundred or so years was limited to survivors' accounts from maritime accidents. Among the European powers, Spain dominated the part of the western hemisphere that included Texas and used the interior of Mexico as a base from which to spread its influence. No other nation maintained such a permanent presence in the region. Accordingly, Spain exercised more influence over the area than any other power and considered it hers.

This claim was tested late in the seventeenth century when word reached Spain that the French had designs on eastern Texas. Actually, the French had set their sights on the Mississippi Valley, particularly as it related to their claims in New France (now Canada), but also extending south to the Gulf of Mexico. It was precisely that terminus—the mouth of the Mississippi River—that the explorer René Robert Cavelier, Sieur de La Salle (1643–1687), sought when he sailed from France in 1684 at the head of an expedition sponsored by Louis XIV. Control of the great river would ensure a southern transportation route for French commerce from New France, and a French colony at its mouth would help deter Spanish expansion into the region.

Rather than making landfall at the Mississippi Delta, however, La Salle and his party missed their mark by several hundred miles and came ashore at present-day Matagorda Bay, on the east Texas coast. During the next two years, La Salle and his men searched in all directions for the Mississippi, but their efforts were fruitless. The expedition progressively disintegrated due to the ravages of disease, malnutrition, and hostile Indians. In the end, La Salle was murdered—not by natives, but by one of his own men. The French effort unraveled.

Although they continued to build their presence in the lower Mississippi, La Salle's disastrous adventure marked the end of serious French activity in Texas. Nevertheless, his expedition had an unexpected consequence: it awakened the Spanish to potential foreign encroachment into territory they claimed as their own and shifted Spain's focus in the region from west Texas to east Texas. With the proven combination of Franciscan missionaries protected and enabled by military detachments, they founded their first mission in east Texas near the Neches River in 1690: Mission San Francisco de los Tejas. Not surprisingly, the harshness of the wilderness and obdurate native resistance to the Roman Catholic religion doomed the effort to failure. Following Indian attacks and other hardships, the Spanish salvaged their supplies, burned the mission to the ground, and abandoned it in 1693.[2]

Despite this early disappointment, the Spanish persisted. In fact, an odd confluence of events and considerations spurred them to build more settlements in east Texas during the next two decades. One of the chief motivations for these settlements involved the French colony of Louisiana, whose governor wanted to establish commerce with Mexico. The colony of Louisiana was foundering financially. The governor, Antoine de La Mothe, Sieur de Cadillac (1658–1730), needed to make Louisiana fiscally solvent, independent of France.

In 1714, Cadillac's emissary traveled west to establish trade relations with the Spanish. That emissary, Louis Juchereau de St. Denis (1674–1744), could not have been more perfect for the job.[3] He was an experienced, energetic, and magnetically charming frontiersman with a profound knowledge of native languages and cultures. After trading with the Tejas Indians in east Texas, St. Denis pushed farther into the region until reaching the presidio at San Juan Bautista on the Rio Grande. The presidio's commander, surprised by the articulate Frenchman who had arrived seemingly out of nowhere, detained St. Denis for a period while waiting for guidance from his superiors in Mexico City. The charismatic Frenchman made good use of his time by wooing the commander's granddaughter and extracting a promise of marriage from her.

A few months after his arrival, the Spanish escorted him to Mexico City, where the viceroy recognized in him a means through which he could strengthen his reach into Texas, engaging him as a commissary and guide. After returning to San Juan Bautista to make good his marriage pact, St. Denis took his place among a group of more than seventy soldiers and missionaries. In April 1716, the column started for eastern Texas. The six or so missions that were established later that same year as a result of this particular expedition became the underpinning for the permanent Spanish presence in the Texas interior. One of these, Mission San Antonio de Valero in the city of San Antonio, would later become famous by its common name: the Alamo.

These new missions hardly enjoyed auspicious beginnings. The same factors that caused the abandonment of San Francisco de los Tejas in 1693 were still in play: the Indians were no more predisposed to give up their own religions for Catholicism than before, and the wilderness had grown no less cruel. In addition, friction between Spain and France had never gone away, and a short war between the two in 1719 caused the Spanish to abandon their new establishments in east Texas, fearful that the French would invade from their colony of Louisiana.

In fact, a six-soldier detachment from the small French fort of Natchitoches in Louisiana did occupy one Spanish mission for a short time, but this was nothing more than a spurious raid. The feared French attack never materialized and the Spanish soon regained their confidence. Spain's first real effort to colonize the region with immigrants from the interior of Mexico took place in 1721, when five hundred men with ten thousand head of livestock moved into east Texas. By 1722, all the abandoned missions had been reestablished and more were being built. The real colonization of Texas had begun.

During the next fifty years, the Spanish colonists engaged in an exhausting struggle against the Indians and nature—and, to a lesser extent, against other European powers. Still, the Spanish were only marginally successful in bringing Catholicism to the natives and civilization to the land. The Indians were especially troublesome, and colonists were under frequent attack from the Comanche and Apache. The dangers from Indian raids effectively limited settlement to those lands that were immediately adjacent to the missions and presidios. However, despite their garrisons and fortifications, even the missions and presidios were not impregnable to the Indians. Mission Santa Cruz de San Sabá near present-day Menard was captured and burned in 1758 by a confederation of Comanche-led tribes. The Comanche subsequently smashed the expedition that was sent to punish them the following year. More than a decade later, the Comanche placed the Alamo under a twenty-two-day siege that nearly succeeded. Clearly, Texas was not going to be settled without either the acquiescence or the destruction of the Indians.[4]

Events abroad continued to affect Texas. Spain and England went to war from 1739 to 1742, at which time the Spanish quickly realized how vulnerable the Texas coast was to English or French military expeditions. Accordingly, the Spanish established nearly forty more towns and missions to counter the perceived threat from English incursions into their territories.

The Treaty of Paris in 1763 that ended the French and Indian War brought more changes that affected the Spanish in North America. Under pressure and unable to make money with their colony of Louisiana, the French ceded all their holdings west of the Mississippi to Spain. As it developed, the Spanish were no better than the French at turning a profit with the territory. Like the French before them, they found Louisiana to be a money pit.

Spain could not effectively rule its holdings in the New World with the resources it had at its disposal. Finally, in a move resembling a modern-day corporate consolidation, Spain's ruler Charles III directed a wide-ranging reorganization that mandated the abandonment of all settlements in east Texas.[5] Because Spain now owned Louisiana, those settlements were no longer needed as a buffer against French expansion. Consequently, rather than spending money to protect the small and vulnerable communities against the depredations of the Indians, it made more sense to consolidate the settlers in San Antonio where a strong garrison and a burgeoning community already existed.

In 1773, the Spanish abandoned east Texas, but that abandonment was short-lived. Bickering between the original townspeople of San Antonio and the displaced settlers from the east was rife. The inhabitants of San Antonio felt put upon, while the newcomers felt shortchanged. Within a year, the settlers applied for and received permission to resettle east Texas. After a false start or two, the Spanish settled Nacogdoches in 1779.

The same sort of mixed success typical of the previous period persisted into the early nineteenth century. More missions were established with considerable focus on the coastal regions where it was hoped that the Karankawa tribe might be induced to embrace the Catholic faith, but progress was fitful. The Indians were more ambivalent than not. Difficulties with the native tribes as a whole continued unabated, and there were few new colonists moving into east Texas from the interior of Mexico. By 1805, there were still fewer than four thousand non-Indian inhabitants in all of east Texas.

External conflicts continued as the French Revolution (1789–1799) and Napoleonic Wars (1804–1815) created havoc in Europe. Nearly all of Spain's New World holdings were at some risk of rebellion at one time or another. The worldwide repercussions from these insurrections meant that there was less money for the development and protection of overseas holdings in the New World. Finally, the financial but strategic millstone that was the colonial territory of Louisiana was passed back to France in 1800 as part of the Third Treaty of Ildefonso. Napoleon, strapped for cash, subsequently sold Louisiana, which at that time made up a large portion of the continent, to the United States in 1803. This sale caused Spain particular consternation: influential persons in the United States, including President Thomas Jefferson, interpreted the deal with the French to include Texas. Spain scrambled to negotiate neutral—albeit temporary—borders with the United States in 1806, but the Americans gave up their claim to Texas only when Spain ceded Florida to them. The Adams-Onis Treaty of 1819 set the border between the United States and Texas at the Sabine River.

The lands and people Spain had conquered were incredibly vast, diverse, and difficult to control. And Mexico—of which Texas was still part—was the most vast, diverse, and difficult to control of all. There was nearly always some small revolt or uprising that needed putting down, but by 1810 a full-blown war for independence from Spain was underway. The fighting was wideranging, with the most important battles taking place outside Texas. That fact aside, the barbarism of the clashes in Texas was especially pronounced. Spanish forces dealt with suspected revolutionaries cruelly and supported themselves on the backs of the people. By 1820, Spain had nearly crushed the rebellion. As strapped for cash and thinly spread as the Spanish armies in Mexico were, they were still better funded—and more importantly, better trained—than their more numerous revolutionary counterparts.

That changed in 1821. Due in part to a military coup in Spain and the potential reforms promised to her colonies in the Americas, prominent Mexican generals and personages who had previously been loyal to the crown switched allegiances and embraced the idea of an independent Mexico. This joining of forces reinvigorated the fight for independence. Except for a few early successes, the previous ten years had been a disaster for the independence fighters; their fortunes changed almost overnight. It took less than a year for the revolutionaries to defeat Spain. The end came in 1821 with the signing of the Treaties of Córdoba, granting Mexico independence from Spain.

Mexico was on its own—and its leaders inherited almost all the problems that the Spanish crown had fought so hard to manage when it was overlord. The making of a nation is no easy undertaking. Much like an adolescent that leaves the protection of home, the leaders of newly independent Mexico struggled to establish their own identity and to flourish on their own.

The last Spanish colonial administrator of Mexico had only a passing familiarity with Antonio López de Santa Anna (1794–1876), more usually known as Santa Anna. Nevertheless, his prediction was so strikingly accurate that it has survived since he uttered these words in the early 1800s: "This young man [Santa Anna] will live to make his country weep."[6] If any single man is the chief villain in the story of the Texas Revolution and in the horror that took place at Goliad, it is Santa Anna. He was a presumptuous, conniving, and cruel man who cared little for anything other than himself. In his defense, those traits were not unusual for a man of his class and type in Mexico at that time. Nevertheless, those characteristics earned him the antagonism of the people of Texas before and long after his death.

Santa Anna was born to a family of moderate wealth in the city of Jalapa, in the state of Veracruz, Mexico, on February 21, 1794. His family was part of the criollo class—an upper caste of New World–born Spaniards. Santa Anna grew to become a cunning, charismatic, savvy, and physically attractive young man, unusually tall for the time and place at five feet ten inches. After entering the army as a cadet in 1810, he saw service as both an infantry and cavalry officer in a number of the provinces, including Texas. He received his first battle wound, an Indian arrow in his arm, in 1811. His service included fighting against American adventurers at Medina in 1813, where he was cited for bravery.

Santa Anna's trademark corruption manifested itself early in his career, although his initial dishonesties were petty compared to the wholesale ransacking to which he would later subject Mexico. Anxious to pay off gambling debts, the young Santa Anna forged signatures of senior officers to draw money against army accounts.[7] He was caught. Although nearly everything he owned was seized and sold to pay off his obligations, whatever other punishment he received was not enough to deter him from similar frauds in the future—nor did it negatively affect his career. His success was largely due to the fact that, aside from his magnetism and intelligence, he was bold and audacious both on and off the battlefield. He apparently was untroubled by even the most basic sense of morality. Principles, loyalties, and ethics seemingly did not burden the budding young oppressor.

Santa Anna's accomplishments during the War of Independence (1810–1821) were noteworthy. As an army officer, he fought with the Spanish Royalists against the Mexican revolutionaries and was decorated for bravery.

But in the spring of 1821, after winning a victory against a noted guerilla, he was surrounded by another revolutionary force. Sensing defeat, Santa Anna switched sides, joined the insurrection, and was promptly promoted to the rank of colonel. He subsequently fought vigorously against the Royalists and led the capture of several major cities.

Paradoxically, after winning their independence from the Spanish crown, the Mexicans sought to install a Spanish prince or other suitable European nobleman as their monarch. As it developed, no suitable royal grandee was found. Ultimately, Agustín de Iturbide (1783–1824), another who had switched sides late in the revolution, installed himself as Emperor Agustín I in July 1822. Santa Anna immediately pledged his loyalty and that of his regiment to Iturbide. The new emperor's subordinate had done well in the twelve years since his commissioning as a cadet. After his rapid rise through the ranks and his remarkable performance during the revolution—in the service of both sides—Santa Anna was rewarded with the rank of brigadier general and the military command of the city of Veracruz.

This latter prize proved a curse for the citizens of that city. Santa Anna's heavy-handedness and predilection for extortion quickly made him an object of popular hatred. He flourished in spite of their enmity and remained ambitious for more power. Only a short time after Iturbide assumed the throne, Santa Anna sought to make a name for himself by treating with the Spanish and pretending to change allegiances again. Ultimately, he set a trap and captured three hundred Spanish soldiers at Veracruz but let the majority escape, managing in the process to cross his immediate commander. Iturbide was furious and relieved Santa Anna of his command.

When the disillusioned revolutionary leader Guadalupe Victoria (1786–1843) subsequently approached Santa Anna with a new scheme, the two joined forces to overthrow Iturbide and his monarchy.[8] This occurred in December 1822, less than seven months after Santa Anna had pledged his loyalty to Iturbide. Santa Anna's troops suffered setbacks in their clashes with Iturbide's forces and retreated to Veracruz to wait until Iturbide resigned under pressure from a number of different factions. In March 1823, reading the writing on the wall, Iturbide abdicated. A mere ten months after taking power, he sailed to Europe and exile.

Still not content, and apparently under no one's control, Santa Anna then took more than five hundred troops to San Luis Potosí. There he raided the treasury and set off on a gambling spree. While he was at it, on June 5, 1823, he unilaterally declared Mexico a federal republic. Coincidentally, Iturbide's usurpers in Mexico City—led by Victoria—simultaneously made the same declaration, thus Santa Anna escaped serious retribution for his brazenness.

Victoria, Santa Anna's fellow conspirator, became Mexico's first president. He would be the only president for the next several decades to serve the entire four-year term allowed under the Constitution of 1824. Ratified on October 4 of that year, this Constitution held that all Mexicans were equal under the law. It also declared the Roman Catholic faith to be the sole religion of the state, and guaranteed freedom of the press. But as virtuous and well-intentioned as the new constitution was, it was made of paper—and Mexico was made of men.

In 1824, Mexico began a bloody charade that made a mockery of the notion of modern and enlightened government. Nonstop political infighting, gory executions, and armed clashes became permanent aspects of Mexican life. During this time, the always-restive Santa Anna plotted to seize Cuba from Spain. A comment by the foreign minister belied the attitude of most Mexican leaders toward the rash and mercurial Santa Anna: "If it succeeds it ought to be a great honor to Mexico; if it fails at least it will rid us of Santa Anna."[9] In due course, Santa Anna was forced to abandon his plans, in part because of pressure from the United States, but in larger part because of the embarrassment he caused to Mexico by his unilateral declaration of war against Spain. Regardless, contrary to the foreign minister's prediction, Mexico was not yet rid of Santa Anna.

Manuel Gómez Pedraza (1789–1851) was elected president in September 1828 and succeeded Victoria. Santa Anna, in collusion with revolutionary hero Vicente Guerrero (1782–1831), capitalized on accusations of election irregularities and immediately rose against Pedraza to seize Fortress Perote near his own birthplace of Jalapa, Veracruz. At that point, events temporarily turned bad for Santa Anna. Harried by a government army of superior numbers, he retreated to the south, seized the city of Oaxaca, and stayed holed up until Pedraza—betrayed on several fronts—gave up his claim to the office in December 1828 only two months after gaining it.

Although the issue had been in doubt, Santa Anna had once again picked the winning side and his treachery was richly rewarded. His coconspirator, Guerrero, assumed the office of president in April 1829 and promoted Santa Anna to the army's penultimate rank: General of Division. As such, Santa Anna marched into Jalapa at the head of more than a thousand men and bullied enough money from the citizenry to support his soldiers. It was an indicator of how he would treat his people for much of the rest of his life.

Despite its defeat in the Mexican Revolution, Spain had by no means given up its claim to Mexico. Indeed, the Spanish crown hoped to capitalize on the sentiments of some of the Mexican elite who hoped for a return to Spanish rule. Believing that years of fractiousness had weakened the resolve of Mexico's people, Spain sent an invasion force of about twenty-five hundred troops from Cuba and landed them near Tampico at the northern tip of the state of Veracruz on July 16, 1829.

This sort of emergency was perfect for a man of Santa Anna's force and energy. As the governor of Veracruz, he quickly marshaled a force of three thousand militia, regulars, and cavalry. After wresting a loan from various businessmen, he sailed north for Tampico. Following several weeks of back and forth skirmishes during which the Spanish force slowly disintegrated, primarily due to tropical diseases, Santa Anna launched an attack with a numerically superior army on September 10, 1829.

The next day, the exhausted and disease-plagued Spanish surrendered on terms that sent them back to Cuba unarmed. Santa Anna became a national hero. Leaders and commoners alike hailed him and rewarded him with gifts and titles. Even the church rewarded him with accolades. His star had never looked so bright. Proclaimed by the Mexican Congress as "Benefactor of the Nation," he went home to his estate of Manga de Clavo, near Jalapa, and waited for the next national emergency to arise.

He did not have to wait long. Before the year was out, the vice president, Anastasio Bustamante (1780–1853), led a coup against President Guerrero. Santa Anna marched to Guerrero's aid, but before he got to Mexico City his troops had deserted him. Disgraced, and having backed the wrong side for once, Santa Anna retired to Manga de Clavo with neither military position nor title.

It was two years before Santa Anna orchestrated another rebellion. In his typically duplicitous fashion, he paid off the gambling debts of Colonel Pedro Telmo de Landero (d. 1832) on condition that Landero initiate a revolt against Bustamante. That revolt began on January 2, 1832, and Santa Anna immediately feigned loyalty to Bustamante. Meanwhile, he stole more than a quarter million pesos from the national treasury and began raising his own army.[10]

Nevertheless, his generalship failed and the government forces defeated him on March 3, 1832. Undaunted, he fled back to Veracruz and prepared the city's defenses for the siege he knew was coming. Yellow fever took its toll on the army sent to batter its way into the city, and Santa Anna simply sat behind his walls and waited. In the meantime, the rebellion that he had fomented gained momentum across Mexico. When the besieging troops withdrew after losing many of their number to disease, Santa Anna marched for Mexico City.

Bustamante's forces never seriously challenged Santa Anna and his men; instead, more and more criollo leaders, as well as common people, joined the rebellion. Santa Anna took Mexico City on January 3, 1833, a year and a day after the rebellion he ordered had begun. He directed Pedraza—the man he had helped depose in 1828—to finish Bustamante's presidency in order to help legitimize the revolt.

Subsequently, campaigning as a candidate for the more liberal Federalist Party, Santa Anna was elected president of Mexico on March 29, 1833, in a landslide. Even so, having achieved the highest office in the nation, he exhibited little desire to actually perform the administrative chores the position demanded. Citing ill health, he declined to attend his own inauguration and delegated his presidential office and responsibilities to his vice president and fellow liberal, Valentín Gómez Farías (1781–1858). For the most part, Santa Anna remained at Manga de Clavo, traveling to Mexico City to take up his office only when it was absolutely necessary that he do so.

In contrast to Santa Anna, Farías had definite ideas for the future of Mexico and embraced the power of the office. Unfortunately for him and his liberal colleagues, his plans clashed dramatically with those of the conservatives, who were his political opponents. Particularly offensive to his enemies were his efforts to shrink the army and change the practice of compulsory tithing to the church. Farías believed that the church should receive only what each individual believed was appropriate according to his personal principles.

The military and the church were Mexico's two most powerful institutions, and Farías and Santa Anna soon had their hands full. A conservative army general, who some suspect was acting at Santa Anna's orders, began another rebellion on June 1, 1833. The subsequent clash included numerous curious twists, among which was the proclamation of Santa Anna—by the conservative rebels—as the supreme dictator of Mexico, a title and role he did not immediately accept. Nevertheless, Santa Anna waited almost a year before stripping Farías of his powers and changing sides once again in April 1834. He had effectively usurped his own government.

The reaction against Santa Anna, who was now acting as a conservative, was strong. Of Mexico's eighteen states, five of them—including the single state of Coahuila y Tejas—rebelled in order to preserve the liberal causes that had led to Santa Anna's election, causes that Farías had implemented. Santa Anna took to the field and easily brought all the defiant states back into line with two exceptions: Zacatecas, and Coahuila y Tejas. During May 1835, he routed the largely untrained militia defending the city of Zacatecas and then emptied the public treasury. He subsequently allowed his men to ransack and abuse the population of Zacatecas however they desired. The resultant plundering, raping, and killing were intended as warnings to those who would contemplate rebellion in the future.

By May 31, 1835, Santa Anna had largely quashed the liberal revolt. On that day, he pronounced himself the dictator of Mexico and abolished the

Constitution of 1824. The only real disturbances remaining were located in faraway Texas where Anglo immigrants treated Mexican authorities with disdain. His contempt for Americans and their ability to challenge him is indicated in what he said to the French ambassador to Mexico: "If the Americans do not behave themselves I will march across their country and plant the Mexican flag in Washington."[11]

Santa Anna and his contemporaries, like the Spanish before them, were wary of their Anglo neighbors to the north and jealously guarded Texas against them. The Americans gave them a lot of very good reasons for such wariness: almost immediately after winning their independence from Great Britain in 1776, Americans began trespassing on Mexican land. The territory of Texas abutted the United States but was more than five hundred miles from Mexico City. It was rich in resources but was also sparsely settled and poorly defended: in short, it was a plum ripe for picking. Americans recognized the opportunities and riches in Texas, and saw it as a worthwhile addition to their union. For all these reasons and more, Americans had fought in Texas against the Spanish, and then against the Mexicans, for a long time before Santa Anna sought to crush the Texas Revolution in 1835.

Most of the earliest Anglo visitors to Texas were hunters, or Indian traders, or horsemen intent on capturing wild mustangs. Others, however, had grander designs, including personality-driven adventures launched for private gain. Posturing and bluster characterized most of these adventures, but individually they had little real impact other than to make the Spanish, and then the Mexicans, increasingly mistrustful of the Anglos. In terms of scale or size, they rarely involved more than a few hundred fortune seekers and usually resulted in little loss of life on either side.

Still, a few of these conspiracies and intrigues included influential Americans among their plotters, even if they did not have official backing from the U.S. government. These were the schemes that most alarmed the Spanish and, later, the Mexicans. Squashing adventurers and brigands was one thing, but taking on the United States, already the most powerful nation in the Western Hemisphere, was quite another.

Irish-born American Philip Nolan (1771–1801) and his men were typical of the sorts of adventurers who sought to exploit Texas for their own personal gain. Nolan was a horse catcher and trader who received passports and permissions of dubious validity to operate in Texas during the 1790s and early 1800s.[12] He had previously lived with, and worked for, the unabashed American traitor, General James Wilkinson (1757–1825), who had grandiose aspirations to take power in Mexico and the Mississippi Valley. Nolan's dealings in the Spanish territory of Texas, however, were almost entirely commercial in nature. Starting in 1791, he made four expeditions of different lengths into Texas. An educated and compelling man whose claims to notoriety included a correspondence with Jefferson, he enjoyed varying levels of success on his adventures. One expedition was disastrous: the Spanish confiscated his goods, and he ended up spending a couple of years with the Indians. Another expedition was more lucrative, and he made his way out of Texas and into Louisiana with more than twelve hundred horses.

Nolan's extensive journeys in Texas made him known to Spanish authorities, who were suspicious of his intentions. On his last expedition, in March 1801, a superior force of Spanish-led troops confronted his party of approximately thirty men near the present-day town of Blum. In the ensuing fight, a musket ball struck Nolan in the head and killed him. His men were captured and subsequently imprisoned. The incident was publicized in the United States, where it inflamed anti-Spanish sentiment.

The most organized attempt to take Texas, and the one that enjoyed the most success, was the Gutiérrez-Magee Expedition of 1812–1813.[13] José Bernardo Gutiérrez de Lara (1774–1841), a ranking officer in the nascent Mexican rebellion against Spain, was sent to the United States in 1811 to secure support for the cause of Mexican independence from Spain. After receiving only uncertain pledges of assistance from the American government, he made his way to New Orleans in 1812, where he managed to enlist a force of approximately one hundred fighters. Many of these men were Americans who wanted to annex Texas to the United States.

Augustus William Magee (1789–1813) was a disgruntled former U.S. Army officer—a graduate of West Point—who had served in the Nacogdoches region before resigning his commission on June 22, 1812.[14] Magee, as the military commander, led the force that Gutiérrez de Lara had raised. This column crossed the Sabine River, brushed aside the disorganized Royalist garrisons along the frontier, and entered Nacogdoches on August 12, 1812. At Nacogdoches, Magee's men were joined by nearly two hundred additional adventurers, predominately Americans and Tejanos. His force thus augmented, Magee marched for San Antonio seeking to engage and defeat the governor of Texas, Manuel María de Salcedo (d. 1813). Salcedo blocked Magee's path with his own force.

Magee shied away both from his objective and from Salcedo and instead led his men into the presidio at Nuestra Señora Santa María de Loreto de la Bahía del Espíritu Santo—known as La Bahía—a site that would later become famous as Goliad. Even though the governor had a smaller army, he gave chase and managed to keep Magee and his invaders holed up until reinforcements swelled his number to more than eight hundred men.

Magee considered that no good could come of his situation and asked for surrender terms that turned out to be absolutely unacceptable to him. Fighting ensued, interspersed with parleys that pleased neither side. Magee died on February 6, 1813, either by his own hand or of some ailment. Shortly thereafter, the mostly American force in La Bahía sallied out to rout Salcedo in two successive fights on February 10 and February 13. The governor retreated to San Antonio, while the invading army attracted more volunteers. Finally, the two forces met outside San Antonio in the Battle of Rosilla. The usurpers dominated again, and San Antonio was theirs.

Subsequently alienated by Gutiérrez de Lara's heavy-handed tactics, which included the execution of a considerable number of the Royalists, many of the Americans abandoned the cause and returned to the United States. A Spanish force sent to punish the adventurers was itself defeated, but intrigue and infighting eventually doomed the invaders. Smaller in number and torn by internal dissent and backbiting, and with Gutiérrez de Lara away on a mission, they were defeated at the Battle of Medina on August 15, 1813, a year after Magee and his men had marched into Texas. The Spanish carried out a series of bloody purges across the region in reprisal for this nearly successful seizure of Texas.

In 1819, as part of the Adams-Onis Treaty that set the border between the United States and Texas at the Sabine River, Spain agreed to sell Florida to the United States for five million dollars. The Treaty also required the United States to give up all claims to Texas, a notion that did not sit well with the increasing numbers of Americans who had business concerns or expansionist hopes related to the region. Financed to the tune of five hundred thousand dollars by various speculators, a group of more than a hundred men crossed the Sabine River on June 8, 1819, and marched into Nacogdoches. After joining the band on June 21, James Long (1793–1822), a Natchez businessman, helped to form a provisional government that declared Texas independent from Mexico on June 23.[15] One of the inducements for those who joined the expedition was the promise of ten square miles of land per man. Of course, the territory belonged to the Spanish rulers of Mexico, and to get the land anyone laying claim would have to fight the Spanish for it.

Not much happened after this declaration of independence. In fact, after failing to receive provisions, Long had no choice but to disperse the group. Some of the men went home, while others seized and occupied sites that might have value in future campaigns. Those efforts were poorly coordinated and ultimately yielded little that was useful. Likewise, negotiations with the Haitian-born pirate Jean Lafitte (ca. 1780–ca. 1826) in his camp at Galveston produced nothing tangible. Within a few months, Mexican Colonel Juan Ignacio Pérez (1761–1823) led a force of five hundred men into the region, and by the end of 1819, Long's men had been pushed out of Texas.

Undaunted, Long gathered more men the following year and established a garrison near Galveston. In September 1821, he led them against La Bahía and overpowered the garrison there in early October. Long's nemesis, Pérez, arrived on the scene a few days later and captured him and his men. The conspirators were sent to Mexico City where Long was killed, allegedly in an accident, several months later.

The most threatening yet ill-defined and least understood threats to Mexico were Aaron Burr's (1756–1836) designs—in league with General James Wilkinson—on huge chunks of the Mississippi Valley and Mexico. Their efforts continued at various levels of intensity through much of the early 1800s. Wilkinson was at different times the senior general of the American army, the governor of the Louisiana Territory, and a paid spy for the Spanish crown. Burr was the vice president of the United States from 1801 to 1804. He made no secret of his desires to seize huge sections of Spain's holdings in Mexico and western North America. He had little success in getting the United States to go after the Spanish territories, but nonetheless was still able to generate private, although illegal, interest.

Burr actually put together an expedition, but Wilkinson, under suspicion of having designs on Mexico himself, betrayed the former vice president.[16] Both men were tried on various charges, but neither was convicted of anything serious. In fact, both of them maintained an intense interest in Mexico through the rest of their lives. Wilkinson was waiting for a Mexican land grant when he died in 1825. Burr was offered a political position in Mexico, but he refused it. However, he closely followed events in Texas until his death in 1836—the same year that Texas achieved its independence.

CHAPTER 2
Americans in Texas

The impetus for the sort of schemes indulged in by James Wilkinson and Aaron Burr began to diminish with the Anglo colonization of Texas that began in 1821.

In the early nineteenth century, Americans were a people who could not stay put. Western migration over the Appalachians into today's Midwest and across the Mississippi River in just a few decades contrasted sharply with the largely unsuccessful Spanish expansion into Texas. The reasons for this contrast were many. First, Americans were relatively healthy and well fed. They had large families and the children that survived to adulthood created pressure for more land; more land was available to the west.

It didn't hurt that the territories adjacent to the newly minted United States were arable and for the most part did not need irrigation, although clearing the forests for a homestead demanded backbreaking labor that often took years. Individual Americans could also easily buy their own land and thus were able to reap what they sowed—that is, they directly benefited from what they put into their own land. In addition, they were fairly well educated: aside from knowing about farming, many also knew how to create, operate, and sustain a business. Finally, they were supported and protected by their national, state, and local governments in a way that encouraged them to develop land.

Certainly they clashed with the Indians, just as the Spanish did. Unlike early Spanish subjects in Texas though, not only were the Americans armed well enough to protect themselves, but they were also organized enough to mount expeditions against the natives—and they were expert at it. For better or for worse, few Indian tribes survived contact with the Americans.

These are only a few of the factors that aided the citizens of the United States as they claimed the wilderness for their own. Certainly, more considerations contributed to their success, but there is no arguing the truth: Americans were good at settling the land. This fact wasn't lost on the Spanish—or, later, on the Mexicans.

An economic contraction in the United States that culminated in the Panic of 1819 brought financial hardship to a broad spectrum of Americans, among them Moses Austin (1761–1821) and his son, Stephen F. Austin (1793–1836). The father was a lead miner and merchant who had left the mountains of southwestern Virginia, where his businesses and mines were floundering, for better opportunities in the territory of Missouri. Missouri had been part of Spanish-owned Louisiana, although it passed from Spain to France in 1800, and subsequently to the United States in 1803. In Missouri, the elder Austin became a Spanish citizen to take advantage of grants and incentives offered by the Spanish crown. After amassing a fortune of $190,000, Austin's mining and mercantile ventures failed as a result of his bad business decisions and economic troubles in the United States, and he looked elsewhere to improve his situation.[1] So it was that, in 1819, he set off for Texas.

The younger Austin spent his early life at school in Connecticut and later attended Transylvania College in Kentucky.[2] On joining his father in Missouri, he helped with the family businesses and served in the militia and the territorial legislature. When his father's enterprises failed in 1819, the younger Austin moved to Arkansas where he speculated in land. His experience in the Missouri legislature no doubt contributed to his appointment as a circuit judge. Still, he wanted a formal education in law, so he traveled to New Orleans where he could find that instruction.

At about this time, which was late in Mexico's War of Independence, the Spanish government began an aggressive colonization campaign to attract more people into east Texas. They recognized that their model of missions and presidios was not working, nor would it likely work, considering the savage nature of the Indians' resistance and the enormous breadth of the territory. Instead, they concluded that settlers needed rewards for the labor that subduing the land would require. Also, they understood that they would realize the best results from settlers who had some experience in bringing a rough country to heel.

Those kinds of settlers were rare in Mexico, yet they were plentiful in the United States, and many Americans were ready to come to Texas. Rather than policing its borders to guard against the Americans who were surging into Texas, Spain decided to use them to generate growth and civilization in the territory. Accordingly, the Spanish created a plan to attract energetic citizens to Texas who would, because of their ties to their own newly acquired property, be legally obligated to the Spanish crown. The Spanish also hoped that these new residents, properly treated, would become morally beholden to Spain. Perhaps over time they would even develop into loyal subjects.

As a direct result of this colonization plan, the elder Austin received permission in 1820 to bring three hundred families into Texas under a special land grant program. Each of those families was to be especially qualified for the rigors of the frontier and was to be of upstanding moral character. Furthermore, family members had to pledge allegiance to Spain, embrace the Catholic faith, and be willing to settle the land at their own expense. In return, each family would receive more than four thousand acres at virtually no cost.

Spain intended to hold Austin accountable as the leader of this new colony, and as such he was responsible for the conduct of the new citizens that he recruited. Spain still had no money, and the new colonists were thus obligated to police themselves. In effect, if the Spanish trial with Austin and his new colony succeeded, it would lend credibility to the notion that Texas could be settled by hardworking, loyal citizens, and at no cost other than land over which Spain had no control anyway. Settlement would create business, and business would generate revenue that the government could tax, potentially creating fresh wealth for Spain.

There was plenty in the deal for Moses Austin. For recruiting colonists and governing the new colony, he would receive more than sixty thousand acres of his own. Still, he recognized the enormity of his task and sent for his son, Stephen. Stephen Austin, newly arrived in New Orleans, had scant desire to help pioneer Texas at the head of three hundred families. He wanted to be a lawyer. Nevertheless, he secured financing for the effort and agreed to meet his father in Natchitoches, in Louisiana, in 1821. Fortune had other plans: Moses Austin died before completing the journey.

Despite the death of his father and his early reluctance to play an active role, Stephen Austin decided to continue with the mission. He made his way to the nearest seat of government at San Antonio to ensure that the new land grant he had inherited from his father was still valid. Satisfied with the promises he received there, he traveled east and scouted the area between San Antonio and the Brazos River for a suitable site for colonization. In late 1821, he led the first of the new settlers into the area around present-day San Felipe.

What this colonization did was legitimize the settlement of Texas by Anglos under very favorable terms, thus obviating much of the motivation to wrest it from Spanish control. Spain stood to profit because the Anglos were going to develop a vast swath of valuable territory that it had never been able to tame on its own—and it would cost next to nothing in terms of hard currency.

By the time that Austin led the first families into the region between the Brazos and Colorado rivers in 1821, however, Mexico had won its war of independence and was in charge of forging its own destiny. This new development panicked Austin: he learned that the new Mexican government did not intend to honor the colonization grants that the Spanish had awarded. He traveled to Mexico City where he, in due course, prevailed on Agustín de Iturbide, who was ruling as Emperor Agustín I, and the Mexican Congress to create new legislation that improved on the original Spanish grants. Signed in January 1823, the new deal offered a league (4,428 acres, if they raised stock) and a labor (177 acres, if they farmed) of land to the head of each family that settled in Texas. For this incredible amount of property, family heads were required to pay the Mexican government thirty dollars after they had established a viable farm or ranch on the property.

The families would be organized under, and administered by, an *empresario*, who was the man who contracted with Mexico to start and manage settlements. If the *empresario* settled two hundred families within six years from the date of the contract, he would receive an award of sixty-seven thousand acres from the Mexican government. Additionally, the *empresarios* could collect fees from the families to help defray the costs of their services, which included surveying and other necessary tasks. Austin eventually charged twelve and one-half cents per acre for his services, although he had mixed success in collecting it.

The new law was scrapped almost as soon as it was signed when Iturbide resigned in March 1823. Nevertheless, in April 1823, Austin convinced the interim Mexican government to allow him to bring three hundred families into Texas under basically the same terms. This exhausting political and administrative effort was only the beginning of the difficulties Austin would encounter in dealing with the constantly changing Mexican government. Government instability, the difficulty in communicating across the huge, nearly trackless territories between Texas and Mexico City, and diverse languages and cultures were just a few of the chronic challenges.

To their credit, the Mexicans recognized the magnitude of the issue. Because, like Spain, they could not afford to put government offices in place as the colonists arrived, they stayed with the precept of making the *empresarios* responsible for law and order within their own colonies. Austin was first among these *empresarios*. This worked reasonably well, especially in Austin's case because he had experience with the law, business, the militia, and Mexico. Within what became known as Austin's Colony, he served as a sort of superior judge using Mexican laws tempered with his own judicial experience, all in the context of what was appropriate for life in the wilderness of Texas.

In 1824, the Mexican government granted responsibility for the administration of public lands to the individual states within the Republic of Mexico. Accordingly, the state of Coahuila y Tejas (newly formed by the Constitution of 1824) passed legislation in 1825 similar to the compact by which Austin had settled his colony. Following the trail blazed by Austin, other *empresarios* began to colonize Texas. The *empresarios* receiving some of the earliest grants included Green DeWitt (1787–1835), Haden Edwards (1771–1849), Robert Leftwich (b. ca. 1777), and Frost Thorn (1793–1854).

Like Austin, these subsequent *empresarios* were responsible for the families they brought into Texas. One key difference between Austin's first contract and the others was that the new families were not required to embrace the Catholic faith, but only to state that they were Christian and beholden to the laws of the nation. In fact, by 1834, people in the Mexican state of Coahuila y Tejas were allowed to practice their own religion and politics as long as they did not disturb the public peace.[3]

Most of the colonists attracted to Texas were from the southern United States, although many Irish immigrants migrated through the northern states and settled in Texas, primarily on the McMullen–McGloin and Power–Hewetson tracts. Although land was essentially free and generally capable of supporting either crops or livestock, the way of life was punishing, dangerous, and primitive. This contrasted greatly with the descriptions of Texas that many of the agents provided to families recruited for colonization. The agents rarely mentioned difficulties with the rulers in Mexico City, the dangers posed by Indians, and the harsh and undeveloped nature of the land. Rather, they emphasized the endless tracts of land, the abundance of game, the richness of the soil, and the mild climate.

Noah Smithwick's memoir, *Evolution of a State, or Recollections of Old Texas Days*, provides colorful and detailed descriptions of life in Texas during the colonization period. He came to Texas in 1827 at the age of nineteen and stayed until moving to California just prior to the Civil War. He recalled arriving at an outpost of the Dewitt Colony along the Lavaca River only a few days after arriving in Texas:

> The colonists, consisting of a dozen families, were living—if such existence could be called living—huddled together for security against the Karankawa, who, though not openly hostile, were not friendly. The rude log cabins [were] windowless and floorless... suffice it to say that save as a partial protection against rain and sun they were absolutely devoid of comfort. Dewitt at first established his headquarters at Gonzales, and the colonists had located their land in that vicinity, but the Indians stole their horses and otherwise annoyed them so much, notwithstanding the [Mexican] soldiers, that they abandoned the colony and moved down on the Lavaca, where they were just simply staying.[4]

Smithwick recounted a woman's quote that Texas "was a heaven for men and dogs but a hell for women and oxen."[5] Some men busily hunted game and chased away Indians, while other men broke the virgin ground with crude plows pulled by oxen. The women were consigned to the dangerous role of bearing children and the drudgery of maintaining rude households without the tools to do it properly.

Nevertheless, the colonists adapted and survived. Much of what needed to get done was done by slaves who, in turn, needed to be fed in order to work. Smithwick describes how one man kept his slaves fed: "Over on the Brazos lived Jared E. Groce, a planter from South Carolina, who had over 100 slaves, with which force he set to work clearing ground and planting cotton and corn. He hired two men to kill game to feed them on, and the mustangs being the largest and easiest to kill the negroes lived on horse meat till corn came in."[6]

Some histories claim that Texas attracted many unsavory characters because Mexico offered so much land for next to nothing, and because its boundaries kept away debt collectors from the United States. These accounts hold that many of the families attracted to Texas were therefore headed by men who could not pay their debts or who had other reasons to flee the law in the United States. In other words, Texas, like its contemporary colonies in Australia, offered a refuge for citizens of less than sterling quality. It was, even more than the traditional American frontier, a place for a new start free of past histories and troubles.

The exact percentage of Texas colonists who were running from the law is unknown, but it seems unlikely that the majority of the new settlers were scofflaws. For one thing, the *empresarios* had to vouch for the character of the citizens they brought into Texas. From the standpoint of the *empresarios*, it would have been foolhardy to bring men that were not likely to function as good citizens. The *empresario's* job was difficult enough without having to deal with criminals.

Some historians have offered this notion of early Texas colonists as less than ideal in order to explain their independent nature, their self-preoccupation, and their contempt of Mexican authority. While this theory might have some truth to it, other reasons likely accounted for those supposed qualities. Settlers needed independent natures to survive in early Texas. Neighbors were far-flung and often not available to lend a hand. If a person couldn't help himself or count on his family, he often simply got no help at all. Likewise, with regard to self-preoccupation, if people didn't watch out for themselves in untamed Texas, who else would?

Finally, resistance to Mexican authority should not have surprised anyone. First, Americans of that period often held any authority, including their own government, in contempt. Mexican authority in Texas was weak to nonexistent, and Mexico had little ability to enforce the law. If Anglos in Texas broke the law, they could generally do so without fear of punishment. Moreover, Anglos tended to be scornful of the dark-skinned Tejanos. Their upbringing in the East had taught them that the Mexicans, like the dark-skinned slaves, were "inferior" and "unworthy of respect." What few Mexican military officers and public officials there were noticed and resented this bigotry and interpreted it as a disregard for the law. The seeds were sown for ongoing enmity between Mexicans and Anglos in Texas.

For the most part, the *empresarios* were able to maintain order within their colonies, but some experienced difficulties that were caused in part by the Mexican government. Chief among these difficulties were disputes relating to the land grants themselves. Although Austin's grants were largely free of prior claims or deeds, those of other *empresarios* were not.

For instance, Martin De León (1765–1833), who was the only Tejano to be an *empresario* in Texas, settled forty-one families on the Guadalupe River in 1824 to create a colony that became the city of present-day Victoria. However, when the Mexican government authorized his settlement, it did not provide boundaries. As it turned out, the grant awarded to Green Dewitt overlapped the claims of De León. Predictably, there ensued years of bitter clashes that were never resolved to anyone's satisfaction. Conversely, because De León's colony was the only predominantly Mexican colony, it received preference from Mexico in the numerous border disputes with Anglo colonies.

Other *empresarios* also had to deal with ill-defined boundaries as well as squatters, legitimate and bogus claims, and encroachment. These difficulties were underscored during late 1826 and early 1827 by an event that became known as the Fredonian Rebellion. Haden Edwards was awarded a huge land grant in April 1825 encompassing the settlement of Nacogdoches and the surrounding area where he could settle eight hundred families.[7] At that time, Nacogdoches had the character of a pirate's den: close to the border with the United States, yet far removed from any real Mexican authority, the town was inhabited by a mix of fugitives from American law, runaway slaves, Tejanos, Indians, Indian traders, adventurers, and a smattering of law-abiding citizens. Unlike Austin's grant, which had no previous claims against it, Edwards' grant was a muddied and confused award that included settled citizens with titles and deeds of various degrees of legitimacy. Edwards took advantage of the authority granted him as an *empresario* in order to untangle the various claims.

His efforts—often heavy-handed—were not very effective. The Mexican authorities believed that he assumed too much power and they overturned several decisions that he made against Tejanos. He also made enemies of a few longtime Anglo residents by contesting their claims. The confusion grew worse as settlers he had recruited from the United States at great personal expense arrived to find the situation in turmoil.

A dispute over the election for the office of alcalde—a position roughly equivalent to a justice of the peace—went badly, and Mexico ultimately stripped Edwards of his land grant in October 1826 and ordered him out of Texas. This revocation also applied to the settlers he had brought into the region. Anarchy ensued, and kangaroo courts further destabilized the situation to the point that the commandant of Texas was dispatched from San Antonio with a force of one hundred infantry supported by dragoons. Edwards and his followers reacted by declaring the independent nation of Fredonia ("freedom lovers") and forming an alliance with the Cherokee, offering to split the land between the whites and the Indians.

The Americans supporting Edwards never numbered more than about two hundred, and the help he anticipated from the Austin colonies and the United States never materialized. In fact, Austin and his followers sided with the Mexican government. The Cherokee further complicated matters by abandoning Edwards' cause.

The only fighting of this short-lived rebellion was a forgettable skirmish between Edwards' group and a mixed band of opposing Anglos and Tejanos that occurred before the Texas commandant arrived. With the Mexican infantry approaching Nacogdoches, Edwards' group disbanded and fled. Ultimately, Edwards' bid to tear that part of eastern Texas from Mexico met with failure. Although he would continue to be a figure in Texas politics, his revolt served no purpose other than to make the Mexican government more wary of American settlers.

Further tainting the colonization efforts were the activities of land speculators who were unsuccessful at attracting colonists into their grants. David G. Burnet (1788–1870)—who would later serve as the ad interim president of the Republic of Texas—was among this group. Burnet was like many of the speculators who invested considerable personal wealth hoping to make even greater fortunes with their grants. Their motivations were varied, with some truly interested in creating viable communities and others simply hoping to enrich themselves. Burnet never attracted a single colonist to his grant and ultimately sold it to the Galveston Bay and Texas Land Company, which also bought other grants. That company operated outside the intent of the *empresario* system and experienced only mixed success.

The Mexican government was growing increasingly concerned with the swelling American population in Texas and sent General Manuel Mier y Terán (1789–1832) through Texas during 1828 and 1829 at the head of a government-sponsored scientific and political commission. His assignment, in part, was to report on Anglo activities in Texas. Terán's impressions were that east Texas, in particular, was almost entirely Anglo. He noted that the colonists refused to learn Spanish, maintained separate schools, and conducted most of their trade with the United States. He warned the government in Mexico City that it should take measures to balance the population in Texas with Mexicans before Americans wholly overwhelmed the region and then absorbed it into the United States. This report, along with the Fredonian Rebellion and the activities of land speculators, caused considerable alarm in Mexico City.

Further fueling Mexican anxieties were overtures by two emissaries from the United States, Joel Poinsett (1779–1851) and Anthony Butler (ca. 1787–ca. 1849), who communicated Washington's desire to purchase Texas.

Taken together, all of these factors induced Mexico to close its borders to American immigration as part of the Law of April 6, 1830.

This law provoked an immediate, negative reaction from Americans with interests in Texas as their trading partners in the United States cancelled contracts: money was lost and dreams were crushed. While Austin was able to arrange exemptions for his and Dewitt's colonies, he was able to do nothing to bring relief for the other *empresarios*. Nevertheless, the hated law did not achieve its objectives. U.S. citizens continued to pour into Texas illegally because Mexico simply did not have the resources to seal the region's expansive borders. In fact, what the law accomplished was to further agitate Anglo concerns as to the motives and attitudes of Mexico City toward Texas, which at that point was almost wholly American. Mexico repealed the law in December 1833 after vigorous efforts by Austin on behalf of all the colonies.

This reaction was typical of Austin. In fewer than fifteen years, his connection to Texas had gone through a dramatic metamorphosis. Whereas in 1820 he had had only a grudging interest in Texas due to his sense of obligation to his father, by the 1830s he had, for all practical purposes, become the leader of Anglo Texas. Although he certainly looked after his own interests and those of his own colonists, he also worked tirelessly to ensure the success of all of Texas as part of Mexico. While he was sometimes criticized for bending too much to accommodate the Mexican government, his philosophy was sound and protected the Anglos from more overt Mexican interference in their lives. His caution against Anglo involvement in the cataclysmic upheavals of Mexican government was, "Play the turtle: head and feet within our own shells."[8] That attitude began to change only after the Mexican government imprisoned him without charges shortly after he had negotiated the repeal of the Law of April 6, 1830.

One of the many Americans who came into Texas illegally was General Samuel Houston (1793–1863). One of the many remarkable men of the period, by the time Houston crossed into Texas he had already lived a kaleidoscopic existence that included long stints living with an adoptive Cherokee tribe and military service in the War of 1812, during which he received three near-fatal wounds. For his fierceness in battle, he came to the attention of then-General Andrew Jackson and became a devoted acolyte of the famous and capable general.[9]

Houston's association with Jackson, in combination with his study and subsequent practice of the law, catalyzed a political career during which he was twice elected as Tennessee's representative to the U.S. House of Representatives. After his congressional service, he became governor of Tennessee. A national figure, Houston's star was rising. He was a passionate, handsome, articulate man. Although his heavy drinking sometimes got him into trouble, he seemed perfectly poised for future greatness.

However, a short-lived marriage crushed the powerful man. Distraught and depressed, Houston resigned his governorship in 1829 and went west to the Indian Territory. He once again lived among his adoptive Cherokee tribe, this time in Oklahoma. There he married a mixed-blood woman, ran a trading post, and mediated between the various Indian tribes.

Even in self-imposed exile, Houston was a spirited man who craved challenge and adventure. He could not stay away from the excitement, the complexity, and the clamor of the "White Man's" world. He corresponded with Jackson and eventually reestablished contact with his political connections in the East. He traveled extensively through Tennessee, the capital city of Washington, and New York. During his time in Washington, he beat up an anti-Jackson Ohio congressman in a dispute over an Indian rations contract. He was subsequently tried before Congress, where the lawyer and poet Francis Scott Key (1779–1843) defended him. Houston's punishment included a fine—which he never paid—and an admonishment.

Texas also caught Houston's attention. Exactly what his particular interest in Texas was may never be known. Perhaps, like so many others, he saw in it an opportunity for a new start. With that new beginning there were also the twin possibilities of adventure and fortune. At any rate, he left his wife and his Indian life and crossed the Red River south into Texas during December 1832. In short order, the fiery Houston threw himself into the thick of the messy Texas political scene. In him, the Texas Revolution would find a real leader.

During the 1830s, tensions in Texas continued to grow. The Anahuac Disturbances of 1832 and 1835 were typical of the strains between the colonists and the Mexican government. Anahuac was located on Galveston Bay near the mouth of the Trinity River. A contingent of Mexican troops garrisoned it, with orders to keep the peace, aid in the collection of customs duties and tariffs, and stop smuggling and illegal immigration into Texas. It was headed by Colonel John Davis Bradburn (1787–1842), an intensely disliked veteran of various armed adventures against the Spanish in Mexico prior to the War of Independence. He was Virginia born but became a citizen of the Republic of Mexico. Once independence from Spain was achieved, he was appointed a lieutenant colonel in the Mexican army.

Bradburn's ham-fisted enforcement of title laws and his uneven collection of customs duties earned him the hatred of the Anglos who had till then conducted their business without paying any tariffs. Frictions escalated into armed clashes in 1832. These clashes included engagements at Velasco and Turtle Bayou—the first armed fights between Mexican forces and Texas colonists. The colonists prevailed; they appealed to Bradburn's superior, who removed him. Shortly thereafter, the Mexican garrison departed.

After a period of relative calm throughout Texas, the Mexican government attempted to reassert its authority in 1835 when it sent troops to support the collection of taxes and duties. Again, there was resistance: William Travis (1809–1836), who had played a key role during the previous disturbance in 1832, gathered a militia that humiliated the Mexican force. This time however, the majority of colonists believed that Travis had gone too far and they forced him to issue an apology. This was done in part so as not to imperil Austin, who was being held captive in Mexico City at the time.

Mexico's inability to maintain order in Texas, as well as resistance by American immigrants to Mexican authorities, created an incendiary state of affairs by the summer of 1835. The Mexican government's growing frustration with Texas is certainly understandable. The mostly foreign population used Mexican land to produce real and marketable goods. However, they largely ignored Mexican markets and traded with the United States, while refusing to pay tariffs or taxes to Mexico City. To add insult to injury, they regularly ignored, disgraced, and even attacked Mexican authorities. Essentially, the foreigners were treating Texas as if it were their own country.

CHAPTER 3

James Walker Fannin
and the Texas Revolution

I f, in the context of the Goliad massacre, Antonio López de Santa Anna would become the chief villain on the Mexican side, James Walker Fannin (ca. 1804–1836) would bear most of the responsibility on the Anglo side. Much less is known of Fannin than of Santa Anna, but the records that can be found suggest an ambitious man without the personal and professional faculties to support his overreaching desires. Although it was clearly a difficult situation that led to his tragic end, it is difficult to find a reason to like him.

James Walker Fannin—as he called himself in adulthood—was born in Twiggs County, Georgia, as the illegitimate son of Isham Fannin and an unnamed mother. His maternal grandfather, James W. Walker, adopted him and named him James Fannin Walker.[1]

The young Walker's family had done well since coming to the New World in the 1600s. During the Revolutionary War, his paternal grandfather, James W. Fanning, fought on the side of the colonies. His great uncle, Edmund Fanning, married the daughter of North Carolina's Tory Governor and sided with the British. Following the war, disgusted at what his brother Edmund had done, which he perceived to be a blight on the family, James W. Fanning changed his name: he dropped the trailing "g."[2] He then traveled with his shortened surname, Fannin, to Georgia. There he established a successful plantation before dying a year or so before his son Isham fathered his grandson.

Although he was hardly the only illegitimate child in frontier Georgia, it is certain that, as a child, Fannin suffered at least some social stigma from his situation. That he was not given his father's name is one indicator of this. Nevertheless, some contact was maintained between his mother's family and his father's.

While James was still a child, his father Isham distinguished himself in the Georgia militia during the War of 1812 but died a few years later in 1817. James was called to his father's deathbed at the age of about thirteen. The experience of watching his father expire had a powerful effect on him and stayed with him all his life. He later remembered it in letters to his younger half-sister, Eliza.

The military service of both his father and grandfather were likely instrumental in gaining James F. Walker admission into the United States Military Academy at West Point. He was still in his early teens when he enrolled in July 1819. Notwithstanding the martial tradition of the Fannin line, however, young James did not perform well, finishing his first year at West Point in the bottom half of his class. Partway through his second year he was put back into the starting class because of his poor academic performance.

Nor did James F. Walker adapt well to military strictures. His teachers often disciplined him and cited him for being absent from class. Finally, after more than two years of poor progress, he submitted his resignation on October 25, 1821. There is no official documentation that records his reason for quitting. Some sources say a dispute over an insult to the southern states, or perhaps an affront to his family, compelled him to participate in a duel. If he were caught dueling, he would have been expelled. Alternatively, he may have left for family reasons, because both of his maternal grandparents were in declining health during this time.[3]

Whatever the case, his military career with the U.S. Army ended before it had begun. While at West Point, he learned little or nothing of the craft of war and hadn't even completed the most basic academic course of study. Still, in future years these facts would not keep him from claiming that he had acquired great military acumen during his abbreviated stint at West Point.

Shortly after leaving West Point, Walker took his paternal grandfather's name. Rather than James Fannin Walker, he took to calling himself James Walker Fannin Jr. He occasionally went so far as to add the "g" back to his last name and was known sometimes as Fanning. Why he did so is not recorded. Perhaps he admired and hoped to capitalize on the military heritage of his paternal grandfather and father. Both were dead and could not rebuke him for the switch. This name change causes speculation about the nature or quality of his upbringing and his relationship with his mother's family. It is difficult to determine whether it was the act of a brash young man honoring his paternity, or whether it was a direct snub to his maternal family.

Still, despite his background as an illegitimate child, or perhaps because of it, Fannin cultivated his social skills and bearing and was able to win minor public offices. In 1830, he was elected judge of the court of Muscogee County, Georgia, but was not installed, perhaps due to an episode of dueling. In 1833, he represented Troup County at the Georgia state convention. He was also appointed as an inspector in the Georgia militia, but his actual duties are unclear.

During this time, Fannin's business pursuits grew beyond those of a simple merchant. He made excursions to Cuba, ostensibly to trade for sugar, but actually to pick up illicit cargoes. In point of fact, he became a trader in African slaves. Slavery itself was still legal in the United States at that time, but the importation of enslaved Africans had been prohibited since the late eighteenth century. Trafficking in these people from Africa was especially unlawful: the penalty if caught on the high seas was hanging.

It was a game that, from a business aspect, Fannin did not play well. As one letter of introduction described him, "I believe he is an enterprising man and from what I can learn he is worth nothing and perhaps as we say [worse] than nothing, and his case is desperate, for he has nothing to lose and all to gain."[4] During 1834, he arranged credit to purchase a schooner, the *Crawford*, and delivered sixteen slaves to Texas but failed to make enough from their sale to pay off the ship. Without any money he was compelled to ask for an extension on his debt.

Sometime during 1834, Fannin and his family settled in Texas. They moved to a house on the Joseph Mims plantation, which was part of the Austin Colony near Brazoria. Fannin's exact reasons for settling in Texas are not known, but one possibility is that he sought to escape creditors in Georgia. A more convincing argument, however, is that he wanted to live where he could best practice his trade. In fact, Fannin and Joseph Mims (d. 1844) entered into a partnership: Fannin's contribution was selling the slaves that he imported, and Mims' contribution was capital, along with the land, infrastructure, and equipment that he had made into an estate since his arrival in Texas as one of Austin's original families.

Slavery was a profitable venture in Texas, even though its legality in that territory was questionable. Some colonists brought their slaves from the United States but called them indentured servents, or obtained special exemptions for them. Mexican officials simply did not have the means or the inclination to enforce their own laws against slavery, some of which, in any case, were in conflict with the agreements made with Texas colonists. An example of such a conflict was the Guerrero Decree of 1829 that abolished slavery in almost all of Mexico. It was not enforced in Texas because it violated the guarantees that immigrants were given with respect to their property. Still, just as in the United States, it was illegal to import enslaved Africans.

One reason why the government in Mexico City looked the other way with regard to slavery in Texas was that the government wanted the region to be tamed and developed in order to increase tax revenues. Among the most marketable commodities of the 1830s was cotton: England's demand for it to support its burgeoning textile industry was nearly insatiable. The newly settled colonists in Texas were already producing cotton and would be able to produce much more if they had sufficient labor. Labor was in short supply in Texas, and the only efficient way to clear and cultivate large stretches of virgin land was with slave labor. A free man had little incentive to work the property of another free man when he could just as easily get his own land. Just as the settlers' ambitions could be met only by labor by slaves, Mexico could increase its income from Texas only by allowing the settlers to have slaves.

Clearly, Fannin stood to make a lot of money. In fact, he sought to do exactly that just as soon as he posted bail in New Orleans after being locked up for a bad debt in April 1835. The following month he purchased 152 Africans in Cuba. (Cuba, a Spanish possession, was one of the intermediate stops for slaves from Africa before they were transported elsewhere in the Western Hemisphere.) Rather than taking these people into the traditionally lawless Sabine River drainage area on the border between Louisiana and Texas where most slave trading was done, he took them up the San Bernard River to African Landing, a mooring point not far from where he made his home on the Mims plantation. That he was able to take them so far into Texas is an illustration of how incapable or unwilling Mexico was to enforce its own laws.

Fannin found a ready market for his human freight in the labor-starved settlers from that part of Texas, although he still owed money when the dealing was done. He again asked for relief from his creditor until the following spring for what he owed on his schooner, *Crawford*. It is almost certain that he owed money to many others. Still, regardless of his debts, Fannin did not neglect his own estate. By the middle of 1835, after less than a year in Texas, he already owned more than three thousand acres, three dozen slaves, cotton interests, and a substantial herd of cattle and draft animals. Although he owed money, he certainly had the means to make and repay it.

In fact, Fannin was quickly becoming a respected citizen in the newly emerging society of Anglo Texas. Perhaps to enhance that respect he started calling himself "Colonel" Fannin. This was remarkably presumptuous for a man whose military experience was limited to two years of failure as a military cadet. In Texas, though, no one particularly objected. That slave trading was illicit doesn't appear to have bothered him any more than it bothered most other Texas settlers. Like Fannin, most Texas settlers were raised in a southern society. For them, slavery was a comfortable, familiar, and economically vital institution. Slaves were critical to their future success, and most other Texas settlers would not even have thought of criticizing Fannin for dealing in that trade.

Indeed, Texas society honored Fannin in August of 1835, when he received a note from the Columbia Committee of Safety and Correspondence. (Committees of safety and correspondence existed all across the colonies and had been recently formalized for the purpose of organizing militias to defend local areas against Indians. As it developed, militias that were useful for fighting Indians were also useful for resisting Mexican authorities.) The note to Fannin addressed him as "Col. J. W. Fannin Jr." and appointed him as a "confidential agent."[5] He was to use what means he could to influence various persons to come together for a Texas-wide consultation.

A consultation was a political gathering through which the various factions in Texas could present a unified political front to the Mexican government. Earlier meetings had been called conventions, but the gathering of 1835 was called a consultation because the other term had revolutionary connotations in Mexico. It was considered key to organizing the colonists in Texas and determining what course the people wanted to follow regarding the relationship of Texas with Mexico. What this affiliation should be was an issue on which the Anglo colonists hardly agreed. Preferences ranged from obedience to the current regime all the way to calls for outright independence. Disharmony in this matter was endemic and had been for years. It was hoped that a consultation would help mitigate some of this dissonance and bring the majority of the colonists to a common position.

Conventions in 1832 and 1833 had addressed many of the same issues, yet the pressures that were building, and the issues at hand, made the upcoming consultation of paramount importance. Organizing such an event was not an easy task. Communications were poor, distances were long, roads were unreliable, and people were often away from home or sick. Additionally, Mexican authorities were suspicious of the Anglos, especially when they gathered for the purpose of questioning Mexican authority.

Fannin's task was made immeasurably easier when Austin made a triumphant return to Texas in August 1835, after having been away for more than two years, much of it as a political prisoner in Mexico City. In that city, he had ensured the repeal of the Law of April 6, 1830. More than a thousand of Texas' most prominent citizens, including Fannin, attended a banquet held in Austin's honor at Brazoria on September 8. The highlight of the event was Austin's speech that included a call for a consultation. The response was passionate and the meeting was guaranteed.

In the meantime, tensions increased across Texas as General Martin Perfecto de Cos (1800–1854), Santa Anna's brother-in-law and the commandant general of the area that encompassed the state of Coahuila y Tejas, sailed from Matamoros on the southern bank of the Rio Grande to Copano, north of present-day Corpus Christi. Santa Anna sent him to assert Mexican authority over the region, especially as it related to tariffs, taxes, and agitation against Mexican law. As Cos prepared to move from Copano to San Antonio, many militants inside Texas—Fannin among them—proposed action against him. Disdain for the Mexican army had grown even more intense since the Anahuac disturbances, when armed citizens had bested Mexican troops. Many Anglos thought taking on Cos wouldn't be much more difficult.

Aside from neutralizing or destroying Cos militarily, attacking him was also an opportunity to capture arms, payroll money, and prisoners. Those prisoners could be used for negotiating capital at a later date. The proposed assault never occurred, however, probably due in part to a lack of resolve and consensus. Such an action would have been a huge and irrevocable step. An unprovoked attack against a ranking Mexican officer would have left no doubt in anyone's mind that the Anglos in Texas were in revolt. Furthermore, other events were afoot that distracted the Anglos from Cos.

Mexican authorities in the presidio San Antonio de Béxar had loaned a bronze, six-pound cannon to the citizens of Gonzales in 1831 so that they could better defend themselves against hostile Indians. With tensions high during the summer of 1835, the military commander at San Antonio, Colonel Domingo de Ugartechea (d. 1839), sent a small five-man detachment to retrieve the gun. The Anglos there not only refused to return the cannon, but also took the detachment prisoner. Word of the confrontation spread, and soon armed volunteers began pouring into Gonzales from the surrounding areas. Among those armed volunteers was Fannin at the head of a small party of men he called the Brazos Guards.

Ugartechea responded on September 27 by sending a detachment of one hundred mounted men, no doubt certain that such an overwhelming force would have little trouble retrieving the gun. That he was aware of the sensitivity of the situation is apparent in the orders he gave to the detachment commander, Francisco de Castañeda: he told Castañeda to do what he could to bring the cannon back to San Antonio, although he was to avoid open conflict if necessary because such a fight might further destabilize the political situation in Texas.[6] Probably mindful of what had happened to the Mexican *soldados* at Anahuac, Ugartechea also warned Castañeda not to undertake any action that might cause embarrassment to the government.

The colonists at Gonzales were under no such orders. When Castañeda approached the high water of the Guadalupe River just short of Gonzales on September 29, he was met by a party of eighteen men. Castañeda asked to speak with the town's alcalde and was informed that he was "out of town." During the ensuing day or so, it became apparent that the detachment would not be able to cross the Guadalupe without a fight. As the number of opposing colonists swelled to more than 150, the Mexican commander moved to a position about seven miles upstream where he made camp.

From his new campsite, Castañeda hoped to cross the river without encountering any resistance, but the Anglos wouldn't leave the Mexican commander and his men alone. On the morning of October 2, 1835, a force of settlers, most of them Anglos, attacked Castañeda's camp and drove him back to a small rise. After a parley and more fighting that caused no casualties

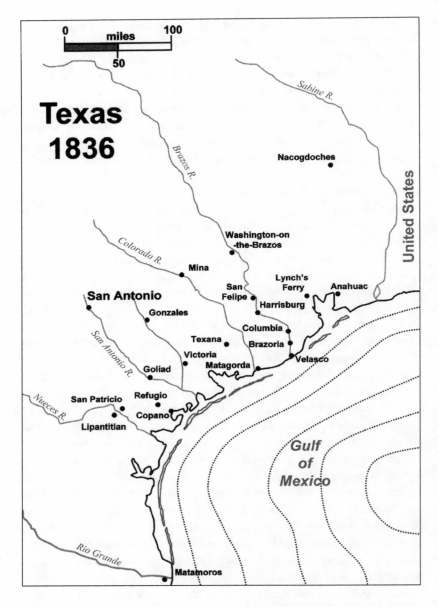

among the Anglos and only a few among the *soldados*, the Mexican force withdrew without the cannon. Although neither side knew it, this small fracas marked the start of the Texas Revolution.

Meanwhile, during the excitement surrounding the events at Gonzales, Cos led his *soldados*, unmolested, from Copano through Goliad and into San Antonio on October 8. He encountered no resistance. In fact, a group of Anglos had traveled from Matagorda to Victoria under the leadership of George M. Collinsworth (1810–1866) with the intent of engaging and capturing Cos at Goliad but failed to arrive in time.

Cos and his column had passed quickly through Goliad but left the presidio thinly defended. On learning this, Collinsworth marched his men south and overpowered the Mexican garrison there on the night of October 9, 1835. Although Collinsworth and his men missed capturing their intended prize, they found themselves the owners of the stoutest fortress in Texas, as well as of a considerable amount of armaments and provisions. Now, almost accidentally, the Mexican army at San Antonio was cut off from the port at Copano.

The coordination of these individual actions among the revolutionary forces was almost nonexistent. There simply was no overarching authority to undertake and ensure any organization and harmony. Certainly, these events did not occur with the full mandate of all the colonists.

A decent start at creating a military leadership for the colonists was made at Gonzales. There, on October 11, only two days after the presidio at Goliad was taken and a week following the scrap with Castañeda, Austin was elected commander-in-chief of the Texas army. By now, and probably because of his long stint in prison in Mexico City, Austin had given up using a conciliatory approach with the Mexican government and instead believed that armed revolt was necessary. The following day, anxious to maintain the initiative, he started for San Antonio with the armed colonists that were gathered at Gonzales, which included Fannin and his Brazos Guards. The Anglos were flush with the excitement of having engaged and thrown back a regular Mexican army unit, and hoped to attack and defeat Cos and the *soldados* that made up the main Mexican force in Texas.

Although the colonists were spoiling for a fight, the Mexicans were in no mood to cooperate. The pitched battle the Anglos hoped for failed to materialize. Instead, Cos and Ugartechea and their men—a mix of about seven hundred infantry, cavalry, and artillery troops—stayed behind their fortifications and were content to make occasional forays for food or other needs while the Anglos established camps in preparation for a siege. The siege began on October 20.

This presented Austin and his commanders with problems. For one, there weren't enough men to completely seal off the Mexican force in San Antonio. This difficulty was exacerbated because many of Austin's men came and went as they pleased. Their attitude was that they were there to fight, and if there was no fighting, there was no reason they shouldn't, or couldn't, go home for a while, or go look after other errands, or simply leave. Consequently, although there were initially about six hundred men, their number fluctuated. This lack of discipline and commitment was an enormous problem with which all the revolutionary commanders struggled throughout the conflict.

Provisions were another critical issue. After the extended foraging excursions of both the Mexicans and the colonists, there was very little left in the area with which to feed and clothe the men, and Austin had scant funds to pay for anything anyway. He directed his men to issue receipts for goods that were procured, but if the owner of the desired commodities refused to trade on credit, the men were authorized to take what they needed by force, which did not help their popularity among the locals.[7]

During this period, Fannin was given command of the First Division of the First Battalion. This is an unusual unit designation. It is unclear how many men he actually commanded, although the assignment does show that he was gaining recognition among the decision makers in the army. Appointed as a colonel above him was the already legendary James Bowie (1796–1836). Fannin's association with Bowie would improve his reputation as a military commander, whether he deserved it or not.

Fannin was assigned with Bowie to reconnoiter a series of missions to the south of San Antonio; he embraced the duty with a rigor that might have caused Austin to regret him and his new position. Over a period of several days, Fannin and Bowie aggressively scouted the area and sent reports that not only gave Austin instructions as to how he ought to run the campaign, but also included repeated demands for more men, more supplies, and more money. Austin already had his hands full, and Fannin's presumptuous counsel and insistent requests for resources that did not exist must have been extremely annoying. This sort of condescension toward his superiors in military matters, in combination with his constant nagging for goods or services that he knew, or should have known, they could not provide, became Fannin's trademark.

Still, Austin relied on Bowie as a competent tactician, and with Bowie he also got Fannin as part of the deal. Anxious to concentrate all his forces at one site, he tasked the pair with finding a position somewhere to the south of where Cos and Ugartechea were holed up at the Alamo. Austin wanted to be close enough so that he could use the site as a headquarters for a siege or as a launch point for an attack.

Austin ordered Bowie and Fannin to secure a position early enough on October 27, 1835, so that there would be time to put the entire force into place before nightfall. That morning, the two men started north along the banks of the San Antonio River at the head of a column of ninety men. After they had inspected some abandoned mission compounds, they were discovered by Mexican scouts, who took their column under fire. The desultory cracking of musket and rifle fire caused no real harm to either side except that Cos was warned of the approaching Anglos.

By this time, it was late in the day and Bowie and Fannin were reluctant to give up the progress the column had made. Although they were closer to the Mexican positions than they were to their own, they decided to stop the men for the night at a point on the river near another mission in the chain that ran south from San Antonio: Mission Concepción. The spot they chose was located in a horseshoe-shaped bend along the river that sat about the height of a man below the surrounding terrain. Situated behind a dry bank, it was protected from any fire that might come from the direction of the Mexicans.

Austin was upset when he learned of the disposition of Bowie and Fannin, but there was little he could do; he certainly could not join his command with Fannin and Bowie by nightfall. Still, with his force split and with part of that force closer to the Mexicans than to him, he spent a worried night, as did Bowie and Fannin. Several cannon shots boomed just barely overhead their position as day turned to night. If there had been any doubt, the rounds from the heavy guns dispelled any hopes that Cos and his men were unaware of their position. The cannon fire also alerted Austin who had his men ready to move toward Mission Concepción at first light.

On October 28, 1835, dawn filtered through a wet blanket of heavy fog that greatly shrouded the position Bowie and Fannin had selected. Nevertheless, the scouts in front of the 275 men that Ugartechea led from San Antonio found them. Scattered gunfire was exchanged for an hour or two until the fog lifted and the Mexicans were able to see sufficiently well to concentrate their fire. Noah Smithwick had been in the country for eight years by this time and was one of the fighters with Bowie and Fannin. He later described the scene:

> When the fog lifted we found ourselves pretty well surrounded; though the bluff and heavy timber on the west side of the river secured us against attack in the rear. In front was a field piece flanked by several companies of infantry; and across the river, to cut off retreat, were two companies of cavalry—but retreat formed no part of our programme. The Mexicans now opened on us with cannon, but we lay low and their grape and canister crashed through the pecan trees overhead, raining a shower of ripe nuts down on us, and I saw men picking them up and eating them with as little apparent concern as if they were being shaken down by a norther. Bowie was a born leader, never needlessly spending a bullet or imperiling a life.[8]

For this type of fight, the position that Bowie and Fannin somewhat fortuitously chose was ideal. The *soldados* put out intense musket, rifle, and cannon fire, but virtually all of it ripped harmlessly over the defending colonists. In contrast, the Mexicans were completely exposed. The colonists scrabbled up to the edge of the bank, then took aim at the silhouetted Mexicans and fired. After discharging their weapons, they slid down behind the safety of the riverbank, reloaded, then climbed back up the bank and repeated the process. Even after several Mexican charges, the Anglos had sustained only one fatality.

The *soldados*, though, were cut to pieces. After their last assault on the Anglo position, the Mexicans turned and fled with the colonists in hot pursuit. The Mexican retreat was so hurried and frantic that they left behind their cannon, more than fifty dead, and a great many wounded. It was an appalling defeat, especially because it was delivered by an untrained band of numerically inferior irregulars. Smithwick's recounting of the fight is colorful:

> "Fire!" rang out the steady voice of our leader, and we responded with a will. Our long rifles—and I thought I never heard rifles crack so keen, after the dull roar of the cannon—mowed down the Mexicans at a rate that might well have made braver hearts than those encased in their shriveled little bodies recoil. Three times they charged, but there was a platoon ready to receive them. Three times we picked off their gunners, the last one with a lighted match in his hand; then a panic seized them, and they broke. They jumped on the mules attached to the cannon, two or three on a mule, without even taking time to cut them loose, and struck out for the fort, leaving the loaded gun on the field. With a ringing cheer we mounted the bank and gave chase. We turned their cannon on them, adding wings to their flight. They dropped their muskets, and, splashing through the shallow water of the river, fled helter skelter as if pursued by all the furies.[9]

Smithwick also recorded his memory of going out on the field among the dead and wounded Mexicans: "Having no knowledge of civilized warfare, the poor wounded wretches thought they were to be summarily dispatched, and it was pitiful to hear them begging for the miserable lives that no one thought of taking. We had no means of relieving them, even if we had had an opportunity. We knew not what turn affairs at the fort might take, and where Austin was we had no idea. The utmost we could do was to give water to those who asked for it, which no one was brute enough to refuse."[10]

Smithwick's recollection that the wounded Mexicans believed they would be put to death is instructive.

Although Bowie had led the Anglos at what came to be known as the Battle of Concepción, Fannin had been at the head of one of the companies that had turned back the Mexican attacks. At the end of that morning, then, "Colonel" James Walker Fannin—the West Point dropout and slave trader—could claim to have successfully led forces in battle. In fact, to that point, no one could declare to have had greater success against Santa Anna's *soldados* than those who had been at that fight: Austin and his men did not arrive until after the shooting was finished.

Fannin would leverage his role at the battle to achieve positions of greater power and responsibility, but he would also take away some bad lessons from the fight, especially the belief that Mexican *soldados* were little better than sheep when confronted with Anglo fighters. In truth, the Mexicans had charged bravely and repeatedly against withering fire. Actually, much of the success the colonists enjoyed that day was due to the location they had defended from: they had enjoyed almost complete protection, whereas the *soldados* had been wholly exposed.

For the next month or so, Fannin used his experience, his education, and especially his ambition to further his standing among the armed men of the revolutionary army in and around San Antonio. Just as important as these qualities was the fact that he was one of the few who actually stayed put— if nothing else, he was there when his commander needed him. Austin was finding it more and more difficult to keep men put. Indeed, after the Battle of Concepción, many men simply went home and the entire campaign was in danger of disintegrating for lack of interest, provisions, discipline, and expertise.

Austin noted his problems in a letter during this period: "In the last few days, more than 150 men have left this camp to return home for winter clothing and other purposes, so that the effective force is only about 450 men after deducting the sick. This force, it is known to all, is but undisciplined militia and in some respects of very discordant materials. The officers from the Commander-in-chief [himself] down are inexperienced in military service."[11]

Another troubling sign was the brief letter of resignation that William H. Wharton (1802–1839) wrote to Austin when he resigned as the judge advocate. Although Wharton and Austin often had been politically opposed, Wharton was a respected and able man and had served with distinction in a number of posts during the previous several years. At any rate, he closed his resignation with a note of disgust saying that "I am compelled to believe that no good will be [achieved] by this army except by the merest accident under heaven."[12] That Fannin was not only available but also willing and able to help in the midst of so much turmoil worked in his favor.

If the colonist fighters lost interest, it was at least partly a result of the indecision and inaction immediately following the Battle of Concepción. Although there were exchanges of gunfire almost daily, the fighting amounted to little more than a few skirmishes. Seeking to reach some sort of consensus as to what sort of action should be taken, Austin called his ranking officers together on November 2 for a council during which two votes were taken. The first vote was against a motion to mount an attack against the Mexicans in San Antonio; most of the men believed that more artillery would be needed for such an attack. The second vote called for uniting the disparate formations at one site north of San Antonio. Fannin's chairing of this council indicated his growing influence.

The practice of voting on major decisions hampered all commanders during much of the revolution. No single, competent commander was empowered to make decisions and act as circumstances and necessity dictated. Rather, the men in charge often were compelled to poll their men and then attempt to execute whatever course of action consensus determined. This system emerged from a number of factors, chief among them that the revolution had no large, traditional standing army and needed all the men it could gather to the cause. The men were volunteers and not conscripts. If they did not feel that they were part of the process they might—and often did—leave. Although threats of court martial and punishment were made, the army seldom acted on those threats: doing so would have caused more dissension and dissuaded others from joining the fight. Still, it slowed matters and forced commanders to follow actions they did not necessarily endorse. Austin, a charismatic and respected figure, made the system work to some degree, but other leaders were less successful.

On Austin's orders Fannin spent a good deal of time chasing after rumored or actual formations of Mexican *soldados*, although he was never able to catch any of them. He also sent correspondences to the provisional government, which had been formed on November 12. In these letters, Fannin offered all manner of suggestions as to what should be done regarding the current military situation.

A reasonable proposal was that a regular army be formed using the U.S. Army as a template. Not so practical was his call for very heavy artillery: simply locating and paying for guns as large as the thirty-two pounder he asked for were daunting tasks. Transporting such a giant and its ammunition across the trackless Texas geography all the way to San Antonio was simply not practical. Fannin also offered to sell all his assets to help fund the fight. If nothing else, he seemed wholly dedicated to the cause, or perhaps he was "feathering his bed" so that when the army was organized and staffed, his name would be remembered for an important post—perhaps even the generalship he wanted so badly.

General Samuel Houston was made head of the regular army on November 12. The next day, he wrote to Fannin and asked him to serve as his inspector general, an administrative post. Fannin's response on November 18 was qualified: he preferred a command in the field, but would do as Houston requested. Still, he made it clear in several passages that he wanted to lead forces into battle: "I would prefer a command in the line, if I could be actively engaged." His very next sentence declared outright his desire for a generalship and for Houston's help in getting it: "Having Elected one Maj Gen. Will they not also make two Brig Genls? If so, would not my claims [be] equal to any other? If I can get either—I would prefer it—and I respectfully request your influence for one."

In case his desire was not obvious to Houston, Fannin took a different tack a line or two later while also underscoring his belief in his worthiness and taking a swipe at those who would plot against him: "My Dr Gen—I can safely affirm to you and my god, that I am regardless of rank in this army, provided we can accomplish our object—But I am well satisfied, that I can fill either of the posts, better than any officer, who has yet been in Command[.]Entertaining this opinion, I will at least tender my services, and others succeed over me by intrigue, in place of either service or merit, the fault will not be mine." Furthermore, he declared that he "shall not quit camp to seek office—but rather prefer the post of danger; where I may seek the enemy & beat him too, when found." Finally, almost as an aside, and with an eye to his future army career, he let Houston know that he would like to take command of San Antonio once it was taken.[13] Houston never answered Fannin's letter.

As it turned out, Fannin left the army at San Antonio without a field command. He was frustrated, tired, and, like nearly all the other volunteers, anxious to return home to see his family. With the military situation in San Antonio still undecided, Fannin requested and received an honorable discharge from Austin on November 22.

On that same day, sixty-four recently arrived volunteers were assigned to the rolls of Austin's command at San Antonio. These men differed from the colonists in that they had come from the United States to aid the Texas cause. They were the New Orleans Greys: they would play a prominent role in Fannin's future. This influx of newcomers was not the only change made during this time. In addition, the provisional government recalled Austin from San Antonio to serve as a commissioner to the United States.

Although Fannin had departed the scene of the fighting, he nevertheless continued to promote himself for a general's billet. What he received instead was an assignment as an agent of the provisional government to recruit volunteers and to contract for the supplies and equipment necessary for them to fight. This assignment was made on December 10, 1835, three weeks after Fannin had left San Antonio.

On that same day, Cos surrendered the Mexican garrison at the Alamo after a bitter five-day battle catalyzed in part by the arrival of the New Orleans Greys. Cos and the defeated Mexicans were paroled on the stipulation that they would leave Texas and never return. Remarkably, in fewer than ten weeks, the relatively disorganized Anglos had driven the Mexican army out of Texas.

Texas forces often paroled captured or defeated Mexican troops throughout the fighting. Paroles were common at the time and were still issued nearly thirty years later in the Civil War. Their use was practical as the Anglo fighters had little interest in, or means for, sheltering and feeding a significant number of prisoners. Possibly they hoped that showing compassion would make them more liable to receive it if the tables were ever turned. In addition, they might have hoped that word of their civilized and generous conduct would generate sympathy and respect in Mexico.

Although the Mexican army had been driven from Texas, Fannin aggressively embraced his new duties. Despite his many faults and his disappointment at not yet receiving a generalship, he did not fail to deliver for the cause. He was empowered by the provisional government and moved energetically about the region east of the Trinity River to drum up men and provisions. As the flow of volunteers from the United States started to grow in December 1835 and January 1836, he was there to meet them.

CHAPTER 4

The Volunteers

I t was recent arrivals from the United States that were causing Mexico
most of its problems in Texas. Most of them, particularly the newest
immigrants, considered themselves to be Americans. In the coming fight,
they would be joined by more of their countrymen coming directly from the
United States. That being the case, it is worthwhile to make a brief study of the
quality and nature of the typical American of the time.

Alexis de Tocqueville described the characteristic American of the 1830s in
his celebrated book, *Democracy in America:*

> In the United States, a man carefully builds a dwelling in which
> to pass his declining years, and he sells it while the roof is being
> laid; he plants a garden and he rents it out just as he was going to
> taste its fruits; he clears a field and he leaves to others the care of
> harvesting its crops. He embraces a profession and quits it. He
> settles in a place from which he departs soon after so as to take
> his changing desires elsewhere. Should his private affairs give
> him some respite, he immediately plunges into the whirlwind of
> politics. And when toward the end of a year filled with work some
> leisure still remains to him, he carries his restive curiosity here
> and there within the vast limits of the United States. He will thus
> go five hundred leagues in a few days in order better to distract
> himself from his happiness.[1]

The Frenchman's observations about Americans were common for a European
touring the New World. De Tocqueville was not alone in noting that Americans in
the first half of the nineteenth century were freewheeling, free traveling, and hardly
constrained by circumstances, class, or borders. In 1835, the typical American was
one of 13 million—a number that included nearly 2 million enslaved blacks. It
was ironic that the American's society and his government allowed him to live his
life more freely than anywhere else in the world, yet he was a citizen of one of the
few developed nations that still permitted slavery.

But not everyone in 1835 America supported slavery. The abolition move-ment was strong and growing, and the 1830s saw the founding of a number of abolitionist societies. Indeed, no other issue in the United States excited emotions as powerfully as did slavery. Mob riots were increasingly frequent, and violence against abolitionists was common. The typical American, if from the southern states (as most emigrants to Texas were), probably supported the South's "peculiar institution," but it is less likely that he or she was an advocate if from the northern part of the nation. Still, black Americans were not considered to be the social or political equals of white Americans, even in the north. Prudence Crandall of Canterbury, Connecticut, was jailed overnight in 1833 for admitting young black women to her school for young ladies. Angry mobs of whites ransacked the school building and forced the institution's closure in 1834.

The typical American was likely born within the nation's borders. The coun-try owed its origins to immigration, but during the 1830s less than 5 percent of the population was foreign born. Of those, most were Irish or German. The great masses of immigrants that would help tame and industrialize the United States wouldn't start arriving for at least another decade.

This characteristic American most likely grew up on a farm, or in a farming town or village. On average, the American man was taller than his European counterpart: he stood about five feet seven inches tall and weighed approximately 140 pounds. European travelers variously described him as pragmatic and unpretentious, yet sallow, stooped, worn, and almost obsessed with the pursuit of wealth and property. The American woman, like her male counterpart, was practical and hardworking. Yet that practicality—along with the rigors and dangers of childbirth—took a physical toll. The English actress Francis Kemble observed that "the women here, like those of most warm climates, ripen very early and decay proportionately soon."[2] Although Kemble no doubt suffered from a sense of superiority that was typical of the British during this period, her observation likely contained a kernel of truth. Conversely, European travelers also recognized in the typical American a pervasive kindness and commitment to democratic principles and justice, regardless of class or social standing.

With regard to health, typical Americans of the 1830s had weathered any number of epidemics. Yellow fever, malaria, whooping cough, smallpox, and especially cholera were threats to their vitality. Their diet, particularly away from the larger cities, was based on cornmeal and meat, usually pork and beef. They also ate vegetables from the garden and whatever game that they could take from the prairies or forests. They drank a lot of liquor—more than at any other time in U.S. history. In fact, the annual per capita consumption of hard spirits such as 90-proof whiskey was nine-and-a-half gallons. Indeed, U.S. Army soldiers were issued four ounces of whiskey first thing each morning.[3]

The Volunteers | **43**

The average American was better educated than the average European, although the type and duration of that education was not consistent nor necessarily equivalent to European courses of study. Instruction was usually organized locally, sometimes at home, especially on the frontier where homesteads were often isolated and far from one another. Still, American society recognized and valued the study of pragmatic pursuits, particularly those related to industry and trade. By 1835, there were more than fifty universities and colleges in the United States.

The average American was used to moving about freely. Land was cheap and there was far more than the population could cultivate. The nation was huge. At more than 2 million square miles, it was already larger in area than any European nation, with the exception of Russia. On the frontiers, he lived with or fought against the Indians who had been cheated out of their land and who would continue to be cheated out of their land, even in the Supreme Court. Fighting with the Indians was near constant at some degree of intensity somewhere within the territory of the United States, from the Black Hawk War in the Illinois Territory in 1832, to the Second Seminole War in Florida (1835–1842).

The president from 1829 to 1837 was Andrew Jackson. Although he would have professed otherwise, Jackson was no friend to the Indian. He had led American troops in many actions against Indians, including the First Seminole War (1817–1818), a war that he had started almost single-handedly. As president, he signed into law the Indian Removal Act of 1830, as a result of which some fifty thousand natives were expelled from their lands east of the Mississippi and forcibly sent west, most infamously along the Trail of Tears. Jackson called this policy—without a trace of irony—the "happy consummation" of the "benevolent policy of the Government," and believed that Indian Removal conferred "obvious advantages" on the Indian tribes.[4]

Jackson's Indian policies were not unpopular with the majority of land-hungry Americans of the southern and western states. Many of them had fought against the Indians and had friends or relatives who had been killed by Indians. They approved Jackson's policies and regarded him as a strong president. Notwithstanding border disputes with England over the northeastern and northwestern boundaries of the United States and minor squabbles with other nations, the country was relatively secure. The fiscally prudent Jackson presided over the only period in U.S. history when the nation had no debt. In fact, in 1835 the nation ran a surplus of $19 million, in addition to which the French authorized payment to the United States of 24 million francs in reparation for French attacks on American shipping during the Napoleonic Wars.

Still, Jackson's fiscal policies were not always popular or sound. After vicious political fighting, Jackson began withdrawing federal funds from the Second

Bank of the United States. This started the central bank on the road to an eventual collapse and helped to usher in what eventually became a particularly unstable free banking era. This, in turn, led to economic uncertainty that made the typically restless average American even more restless. One of the regions that he emigrated to, particularly if he was from one of the southern states, was Texas.

In summary, the typical American in 1835 was generally healthy, reasonably educated, well fed, principled, and—apart from the slaves—free. Americans in the first half of the nineteenth century lived in a nation led by a stable, organized, republican government. Their country was wide open, one of myriad opportunities. Americans could and did travel within and outside its borders, generally as they pleased.

Texas was very much in the American public consciousness in 1835. Newspapers carried stories of the unsettled situation between the colonists and the emergent Mexican Centralist government. In the summer of 1835, the *New York Courier* outlined the perspective of many Americans relative to the difficulties brewing in Texas:

> Each succeeding day is rendering Texas of more importance to the United States from the fact that it is rapidly being settled by our own people, and the very probable supposition that in a few years it will constitute a portion of our Union. In settling the boundary line between Texas and the United States, the Rio Grande should be, and in all probability, will be fixed upon as the dividing line, and thus the thousands of American citizens who are now settling what is yet a foreign country, will once more find themselves enjoying the blessings and protection of our liberal laws.[5]

Eventually, those who shared the viewpoint underscored by the *New York Courier* would be proven correct.

Regardless of popular sentiment, Jackson's policy toward Texas was one of strict neutrality. It was a position he consistently maintained throughout his presidency. In his state of the nation address at the end of 1835, he touched on the topic without mentioning Texas by name:

> Recent events in that country have awakened the liveliest solicitude in the United States. Aware of the strong temptations existing and powerful inducements held out to the citizens of the United States to mingle in the dissensions of our immediate neighbors, instructions have been given to the district attorneys of the United States where indications warranted it to prosecute without respect to persons all who might attempt to violate the obligations of our neutrality,

while at the same time it has been thought necessary to apprise the government of Mexico that we should require the integrity of our territory to be scrupulously respected by both parties.

What Jackson was telling Mexico City was that he realized that there were strong inducements—material and otherwise—for American citizens to rush to Texas and fight on behalf of the revolution. He was also assuring the Mexican government of the neutrality of the United States, even to the extent that his district attorneys had directions to prosecute those who undertook to fight on behalf of the Texas Revolution. But, at the same time, he was reminding them to keep the fight within their own borders and not to let it spill into U.S. territory. Although he did not explicitly articulate it, Jackson was concerned that Mexican forces, in the heat of prosecuting a campaign against the Texas revolutionaries, might cross the Sabine River into Louisiana. Were that to happen, popular sentiment would turn harshly against Mexico, and he would be hard-pressed to keep the United States from entering the fight.

While many of the nation's leaders surely shared the same pro-revolutionary sentiments as the greater populace, once the emotional issues were shelved it probably wasn't difficult for them to realize that a policy of impartiality was the best course to follow. Overt assistance would draw international condemnation that could serve no good purpose and might also heighten the risk of widening the conflict. Although America was quickly growing more powerful, its resources were best put to work along its vast frontiers rather than in war against not only Mexico, but also perhaps against European powers that might come to Mexico's aid.

And, truth be told, Jackson's government probably believed that the revolutionaries in Texas stood a good chance of succeeding without help from the American government. The men, money, and material that the Texans already had, in addition to the greater resources that private individuals from the United States were contributing, were substantial. In addition, geography and the fact that Mexico's government was weak, corrupt, and broke were factors that worked strongly in favor of the Texas Revolution.

Even if Jackson kept the United States neutral, there was a good chance that Texas would succeed in separating itself from Mexico anyway. The immediate result would be a substantial and friendly new nation on America's southwest border that would be linked to the United States by a common citizenry and a similar government. In due course, it would probably be annexed as a new state. All this could be achieved without the United States violating its own neutrality laws or spending any money.

If the Jackson administration did not provide official support to the fight for Texas independence, neither did it prevent the involvement of its private citizens. The Neutrality Act of 1818 primarily focused on preventing the arming and fitting out of private and foreign ships of war in American ports. However, Section 6 of the act prohibited people from organizing, assembling, supporting, or joining private military expeditions on U.S. soil. The maximum penalty was three thousand dollars and three years of imprisonment.[6]

The United States just did not have the means to effectively enforce the Neutrality Act. The nation was huge; it had an expansive, sparsely populated interior; extensive, poorly policed borders; and scores of ports served by a burgeoning commercial fleet. In relation to its geography, the nation's armed forces and judiciary were not up to the task of detaining and prosecuting private citizens who were intent on supporting the revolution in Texas. Further muddying enforcement of the act was the fact that it was nearly impossible to determine intent. There was nothing to prevent a person from exporting weapons or supplies. Likewise anyone could send money abroad for any purpose or go to another country for any reason.

What could legally be prevented or stopped, though, were enlistments organized and held on U.S. soil for the explicit purpose of usurping a foreign government. Usually, organized enlistments were not stopped, though; enforcement was lax. For instance, meetings, many advertised in newspapers, were held all across the country expressly to drum up recruits and funds for service in Texas on the side of the revolution. The U.S. government made no concerted effort to stop these gatherings or to arrest attendees. For their part, sensitive to U.S. laws, the leaders in Texas instructed volunteers to formally organize and declare their intentions only after reaching Texas.

The state that sent the first organized group to fight for Texas independence was Louisiana. Most notably, the New Orleans Greys were mustered at the Banks Arcade at a meeting on October 13, 1835. The arcade was a three-story structure tenanted by a bar, an armory, and an auction house. William Christy (1791–1865) chaired the meeting. Christy, a Kentuckian by birth, was a distinguished veteran of the War of 1812 and had subsequently made and lost a fortune in tobacco and made an armed adventure into Mexico where he was imprisoned and released. He was later admitted to the bar in New Orleans where he practiced law with considerable success. His interest in Texas had been ongoing for fifteen or more years by the time its colonists had turned revolutionary.

The Christy-sponsored gathering netted more than five thousand dollars in donations and more than 115 enlistments. At the time, New Orleans was the primary port of commerce along the Gulf of Mexico, and as such its permanent and transient populations were of mixed origins. This was reflected in the backgrounds of the newly signed volunteers. Of their number, approximately half claimed Louisiana as their home state. Of the 115 enlistees, approximately thirty were not Americans. Of the remaining eighty-five, roughly half hailed from the northern states and half from the southern.

Very few of the New Orleans Greys had any military experience, although their backgrounds and occupations were extraordinarily varied. Their professions included surveying, law, printing, painting, medicine, and architecture, among many others. The wide-ranging avocations of the New Orleans enlistees distinguished them somewhat from the volunteers of other regions, who were generally farmers.

Shortly after the incident at Gonzales in the summer of 1835, Georgians were rallied to the revolutionary cause by statements such as this one promulgated by the Permanent Council of Texas: "You are united to us by all the sacred ties that can bind one people to another. You are, many of you, our fathers and brothers—among you dwell our sisters and mothers—we are aliens to you only in country; our principles, both moral and political, are the same—our interest is one."[7]

The city of Macon, Georgia, hosted a gathering in support of Texas on November 10, 1835. At the time, it was reported to have been the largest meeting ever held in the town. Spirit in support of Texas ran high as speeches were made, resolutions were crafted, and committees were formed to raise funds and encourage the enlistment of men who, like the signers of the Declaration of Independence, were willing "to risk their lives, their fortunes, and their Sacred honor." It was resolved to recruit not only from Macon, but also from the entire state.

The assembly produced twenty-nine enlistments and more than three thousand dollars in donations. Recruiting continued to be successful through the autumn; by the end of November, more than eighty volunteers had left Macon and nearby Milledgeville for Texas. The exodus of so much labor had a real effect on what was still a thinly populated area. The Macon *Telegraph* complained that "the Texas fever has treated us worse than the Cholera! . . . Journeymen and apprentices, men and boys, devils and angels, are all gone to Texas."[8]

The Macon and Milledgeville volunteers joined with another contingent of enlistees at Columbus, Georgia. From there, the group proceeded to Mobile via Montgomery, while picking up additional volunteers. The captain of the *Benjamin Franklin*, the ship that took the volunteers to Mobile, hailed them as "the brave and patriotic band of emigrants from Georgia to Texas in the sacred cause of freedom and the rights of man."[9] That they were described as emigrants is interesting: as emigrants, they were not in violation of the Neutrality Act of 1818. A declaration that they were en route to Texas to fight on behalf of the rebellion would have complicated their legal position. Whether or not the statement was made with this as a consideration is unknown, but the point is moot. Unhindered by any U.S. authority, the Georgia volunteers arrived in Velasco, Texas, on December 20, 1835.

Jack Shackelford (1790–1857) was an articulate, educated, well-spoken, and well-liked medical doctor. Fortunately for the historical record, as well as for him, he survived the slaughter at Goliad. His accounts as the leader of one of the most well-known volunteer contingents in the Texas Revolution are valuable to this story. He is an enduring character in the story of the massacre at Goliad.

Shackelford was born in Richmond, Virginia, but moved to South Carolina as a young man. He served in the War of 1812; by the end of that conflict, he carried a scar on his face that had been put there by a British sword. His wartime service also included time on Jackson's staff. In 1818, he was part of the westward movement that saw settlers from the southern states pour into Alabama to cultivate land from which the Indians had recently been evicted. He was a slave owner: in the newly opened territory, he made a successful living raising cotton and practicing medicine in Shelby County.

Within a few years of moving west, Shackelford sought pursuits beyond his private life. He was popular and was elected to the state's House of Representatives, followed by three one-year terms in the Senate beginning in 1822. He may not have been the best of businessmen, however. Because he was a guarantor of a loan for one of his cousins, he was forced to sell his plantation and much of the rest of his property when the venture went bad.

Shackelford was an intelligent, resourceful, and well-connected man, however. He gave up his medical practice and moved to Courtland, Alabama, where he landed on his feet. In Courtland, he was put in charge of the local U.S. Land Office, where he oversaw the sale of hundreds of thousands of acres intended to facilitate a canal project around Muscle Shoals. He also held office as the treasurer of the Tuscumbia-Courtland-Decatur Railroad. By late 1835, Shackelford had reestablished his medical practice and regained much of his former fortune. His future looked to be a comfortable one.

It was at that time that the pleas coming from Texas took on a particularly strident note. The *Democrat* of Huntsville, Alabama, published the following appeal from General Samuel Houston: "If Volunteers from the U. States will join their brethren in this section, they will receive liberal bounties of land. We have millions of acres of our best land unchosen and unappropriated. Let each man come with a good rifle and 100 rounds of ammunition—and come soon. Our war-cry is 'Liberty or Death.' Our principles are to support the Constitution, and DOWN WITH THE USURPER!"[10]

Shackelford found this plea compelling. Whether his motivation was altruism, boredom, or the promise of property is unknown, but his enthusiasm for the rebellion in Texas stirred the tiny community in and around Courtland to donate generously in men, money, and material. Town assemblies produced more than a thousand dollars in cash and enlisted fifty-five volunteers. Shackelford, as their captain, drilled these men to prepare them for the fight for Texas independence.

The town's women stitched together uniforms—some might have called them costumes—of fringed shirts patterned in red, green, and brown checks. Bright red trousers added to the design's distinctive appearance. Thus attired, the company was appropriately dubbed the Red Rovers; the men adopted a solid red flag as their standard. Equipped with muskets from the Alabama state armory paid for by Shackelford, the Red Rovers left Courtland on December 12, 1835, amid the shouted cheers of the populace. Accompanying Shackelford was his son, Fortunatus (d. 1836), and a nephew, William J. Shackelford (d. 1836). Although they did not know it at the time, they were all on their way to Goliad.

Shackelford's Red Rovers were not the only Alabamans to rally to Texas. Appeals in newspapers provoked a sympathetic response in many of the state's men. Mobile's *Mercantile Advertiser* urged citizens to give more than moral support and asked, "Of what use are paper resolutions if not backed by money or men? Rise then, good men and true, and march to the aid of your brothers in Texas."[11] This call for them to aid their brothers wasn't solely rhetorical: many of the Texas immigrants originated from Alabama, so many were in fact related.

In due course, aside from the Red Rovers, three other groups left Alabama for Texas before the end of 1835. Huntsville was the first town in Alabama to send citizens to Texas. On November 8, 1835, its residents bade farewell to a company of twenty men under the stewardship of Peyton S. Wyatt (1804–1847). It must have been a charismatic group: its number swelled to more than seventy by the time it reached the Texas border. From Montgomery, Isaac Ticknor (d. 1836) mustered a group of approximately forty men known as the Alabama Greys. Ticknor and many of his men were ne'er-do-wells, and as far as Ticknor's neighbors were concerned, his enlistment benefited them as well as Texas. From Mobile, a group of thirty-five men—the Mobile Greys—arrived in Texas at the end of November. In total, the four organized companies of Alabamans amounted to more than 160 men. All of them would come together at Goliad.

The word "grey" and its more modern spelling, "gray," is confusing in the context of the different volunteer groups that made their way to Texas. Six or more units used the name that in all cases referred to the color of their garb. Concise descriptions do not exist of their uniforms, but it is reasonable to assume that the volunteers took advantage of surplus U.S. Army jackets and trousers, which at that time were gray. If they weren't official uniforms, they were copies or facsimiles that closely resembled the uniforms then in use. There is also conjecture that the men may have been outfitted in similar, tough-wearing, gray clothing worn by laborers and readily purchased from stores.[12] The importance of the gray uniforms or clothing diminished with time; the original issue that most of the men started with wore out after hard use and was replaced piecemeal with civilian clothing or whatever other uniform articles were at hand. Clothing was scarce, and it is exceedingly doubtful that the volunteers presented anything resembling a uniform appearance by the time they encountered Mexican forces in the interior of Texas.

Almost at the opposite corner of the United States from where Shackelford and the other Alabamans had started their journey, and at almost the same time, another doctor also departed for Texas. Joseph Henry Barnard (1804–1861) was a thirty-one-year-old former sailor and graduate of Williams College in Massachusetts who shared a medical practice in the small town of Chicago. He walked away from his practice on December 14, 1835, with the objective of joining the Texas citizens in rebellion against Mexico.

Like Shackelford, Barnard would survive the killing at Goliad. And, like Shackelford, his account of his time in Texas is valuable, especially because he kept a daily journal. That journal indicates that he was inspired by principle: "They were in arms for a cause that I had always been taught to consider sacred, viz; Republican principles and popular institutions. They had entered the contest with spirit, and were carrying it on with vigor. . . . I was instantly possessed of a desire to render my personal services, however insignificant they might be, in their behalf. Accordingly, I hastily closed my business and left Chicago on the 14th of December, 1835, in company with two young men bound for Texas."[13]

Barnard started south in fine spirits and with good company. He left Chicago with two other like-minded men on a stage to Peoria. Sharing the coach with them were traveling companions who, "far from giving us any discouragement in our enterprise, on the contrary, they confessed to a secret hankering for a share in the business."[14]

By December 22, Barnard and his Texas-bound party—which by now had grown to five—had slogged their muddy way through winter-wet Peoria, Illinois, to St. Louis in an open wagon. There they waited for transport down the Mississippi River to New Orleans. Barnard recorded that "Christmas came and was a noisy, merry day, and all appeared to enjoy it."[15] St. Louis in the 1830s was still a rough frontier town, but was nevertheless an important stopping point not only for travel up and down the great river, but also for the movement west across the continent.

Shortly after Christmas, Barnard embarked on a steamer for New Orleans.

Manifested on the *Junius*, he and his companions encountered still more men bound for the fight in Texas. After a trip of about ten days and with the weather growing steadily milder, the *Junius* tied up to the wharves at New Orleans. There, the capitulation of General Martin Perfecto de Cos at San Antonio on December 10 was already being celebrated. In fact, his surrender of the Mexican garrison had already been reenacted in a local theater to great fanfare.

While in New Orleans, Barnard called on the Texas commissioners, including Stephen F. Austin. They urged him to waste no time in making for Texas. Accordingly, he outfitted himself with arms, clothing, and supplies, and—after observing a raucous anniversary celebration commemorating the January 8, 1815, Battle of New Orleans—embarked on the schooner *Aurora* on January 10, nearly a month after he had left Chicago.

Just as the leaders of the rebellion in Texas exhorted their former countrymen to come to their aid, Mexican leaders quite understandably sought to rouse their own citizens to put down the revolution. Colonel Gregorio Gómez led the Tres Villas battalion and was commandant of the town of Santa Anna de Tamaulipas. In a letter to the people of his town he denounced the Anglo Texans, "these unnatural guests, in return for the liberty and favors shown them by our country, are attempting now to plunge a murderous poignard in her bosom. . . . They have openly declared the rebellion and attempted no less than dismembering that rich part of our territory, where they have been received with such liberal hospitality."

Gómez correctly pointed out the threat to Mexico's territorial integrity from adventurous foreigners and urged his fellow citizens to "rally round the government; and with the native bravery of Mexicans, let us rush on these gangs of perfidious foreigners." En route to aid their fellow Americans in what they believed was a rightful cause, the volunteers doubtless did not think of themselves as "perfidious."[16]

While it is a fact that most of the volunteers who went to Texas from the United States came from the south, the northern states made contributions as well. New York, in particular, held many events to raise funds—including a meeting at Tammany Hall and a special performance of the opera. In addition, an information office was set up on Front Street to help publicize the plight of Texas. For those who wanted to get their information firsthand—either as a volunteer or a spectator—passage to Texas was advertised at fifteen dollars.

Although support was forthcoming from the northern states, those same states were where most of the American opposition to the Texas revolutionary movement was found. In New York, some newspapers railed against the revolution. The editor of the *New York Evening Post* argued—with some justification—that land speculators and those who stood to profit through slavery were behind the independence movement. That same city's *Courier* and *Enquirer* likewise posited that because earlier overtures by the United States to purchase Texas had failed, land speculators were taking the annexation of Texas into their own hands.

Available records indicate that the chief inspiration for service in Texas was not material gain, however. Rather, the volunteers genuinely wanted to right what they perceived as the great wrongs that the Mexican government had perpetrated against the mostly American colonists. Many of the volunteers were young. Very likely, among those youngsters, the moral impetus was primarily window dressing for what was arguably their greater motivation: to seek adventure.

Still, the material incentives to sign on for military service were not inconsiderable. These inducements were primarily in the form of land bounties, because the revolutionary government would have land aplenty if the revolution succeeded. These bounties gradually increased over time. In December 1835, the government authorized an award of 640 acres for each man who served through the duration of the war; those who signed on for three months were to receive half that amount. Otherwise, the volunteers would receive the same pay, provisions, and clothing that U.S. soldiers had received more than twenty years earlier during the War of 1812—about twenty dollars a month. If the volunteer was killed or died during his service, his heirs were entitled to his land plus an additional award of 640 acres. In March 1836, the land allocations increased to 1,280 acres for a one-year enlistment, 960 acres for nine months, 640 acres for six months, and 320 acres for three months.

Despite these allocations, most of the volunteers were reluctant to sign up for a specific commitment of time. They may have been loath to give up the same liberty that allowed them to so freely leave wherever they had come from. Moreover, as large as the grants were, the land was still raw and wild and dangerous. Many of the men probably had little interest in the sort of toil that would be necessary to make it productive. The notion that many of them were in Texas simply for the thrill of a just fight, or for altruistic reasons, becomes more credible when their lack of interest in the land bounties is considered.

Officers in the revolutionary forces were assigned based on a number of factors: connections, past public service, military experience, reputation, and wealth. Another determinant was how many men they recruited or brought to the fight. William Ward (d. 1836), leading about 130 Georgia volunteers, called himself a major and had several captains serving under him. On a grander scale, Thomas Jefferson Chambers (1802–1865) spent more than twenty-three thousand dollars to recruit approximately a thousand men for a volunteer reserve army. He did so with the promise from the revolutionary government that he would head them as a major general. In the end, though, he and his men never made it into the fight.

Where Texas' regular army was concerned, the revolutionary government was more careful about awarding commissions. If anything, it understaffed the officer ranks to ensure that there would be positions available in the event that particularly worthy or qualified individuals enlisted. The revolutionary leaders eagerly sought regular officers from the United States for the cause. Their hopes were never really realized. Few U.S. Army officers resigned their commissions to serve in Texas. It would have been a risky proposition to abandon a stable career in the service of a secure and growing nation to fight for a rebellion that might not succeed—especially in a nascent army that numbered only a couple hundred men.

In a response to James Walker Fannin who had asked him to consider a position in Texas, one major in the U.S. army replied that leaving the United States would be "clogged with forms and difficulties, and a considerable delay would occur." He also cited his ongoing efforts to prepare his son for a West Point education along with his "many military responsibilities not easily shaken off or settled up."[17]

In trying to convince the revolutionary government to use persuasive means to get U.S. Army officers to come to Texas, Fannin underscored the importance of trained and educated military men. Such officers could not only lead troops in war, but could also prepare harbors, fortifications, and other infrastructure in peacetime. He also pointed out that U.S. officers stood to lose much if they resigned and Texas came to nothing. Officers who considered fighting for Texas must have wondered what their situation would be in the event that they were taken prisoner. Certainly the Mexican government would question Jackson's commitment to the Neutrality Act of 1818 if it captured Americans in Texas who had recently worn the uniform of the U.S. Army. How it would treat those captured officers was an unknown.

It is also likely that senior U.S. Army officers counseled their subordinates against leaving for Texas. After all, the United States possessed expansive frontiers that required protection—particularly against the Indians. There were also minor frictions with various European nations that could potentially explode into something more dangerous. In short, America needed its military officers to help look after its own interests.

The New Orleans Greys were the first organized group of volunteers to take part in the fighting for the revolutionary cause. After sailing from its namesake city aboard the schooner *Columbus*, one contingent of the Greys arrived at Velasco on October 22, 1835. The men, led by their captain, Robert C. Morris

(d. 1836), trekked overland via Goliad and arrived at San Antonio early in November. Morris presented them to Austin, the head of the revolutionary forces there. Led by Thomas Breece (d. ca. 1851), the second half of the New Orleans Greys traveled by riverboat, foot, and horseback, arriving in Velasco on November 21. Assembled as a whole for the first time since leaving New Orleans, the New Orleans Greys—organized, equipped, and motivated as they were—stabilized the deteriorating revolutionary forces. When the Alamo was stormed and captured a few weeks later in early December, it was the New Orleans Greys who formed the core of the fighting forces. Thus it would be for the majority of the Texas Revolution: volunteers from the United States would do most of the fighting.

It was ten days after the capture of the Alamo on December 10, 1835, that the largest group of volunteers to date set foot in Texas. The Georgia companies, with Ward at their head, arrived at Velasco on December 20, 1835. In keeping with the revolutionary leadership's sensitivities to U.S. law, they hadn't formally organized on American soil prior to leaving. Rather, they did so on December 22; the following day, they presented themselves and a letter to Fannin, who was serving as a senior recruiting agent and the inspector general of the Texas army.

An excerpt from their letter recognized Fannin as a brother Georgian, while describing altruistic motives for their sojourn: "As Americans we hail you as the Champion of liberty, as Georgians, we hail you as a brother—Actuated by the inborn love of liberty and detestation of tyranny peculiar to the American character, and recently so eminently developed in you, we paused not to calculate the cost, but with arms in hand at once resolved to unite with our brethren in Texas, and share their destiny."[18] Fannin welcomed his fellow Georgians and acknowledged his affinity for the state in which he had been born and raised, and from which he had so recently departed. He also took the opportunity to caution the newcomers against getting involved in Texas politics. It wasn't bad advice. Indeed, it was counsel he would have done well to follow during his own first year in Texas.

On December 30, 1835, just after Ward and his Georgians arrived in Texas, with many more Americans on their way, the Mexican government, with Antonio López de Santa Anna's sponsorship, passed what came to be called the Tornel Decree, named for Mexican Secretary of Defense and Marine, José María de Tornel y Mendivil. He was one of Santa Anna's most ardent supporters. The document essentially stated that any foreign persons caught armed on Mexican soil with the intent of attacking or challenging Mexico or the Mexican government would be treated as if he were a pirate. Likewise, anyone on Mexican soil who armed such persons would be treated as a pirate. The punishment for piracy in Mexico was death.

This pronouncement was quickly circulated in Texas as well as within the United States. The *New Orleans Bee* published it in February and the *Brazoria Courier* in early March. The *Telegraph and Texas Register* ran the following translation on March 12, 1836:

> WAR AND NAVY DEPARTMENT
> *Circular.* The government has received information that, in the United States of North America, meetings are being called for the avowed purpose of getting up and fitting out expeditions against the Republic of Mexico, in order to send assistance to the rebels, foster the civil war, and inflict upon our country all the calamities, by which it is followed. In the United States, our ancient ally, expeditions are now organized similar to that headed by the traitor José Antonio Mexía and some have even set out for Texas. They have been furnished with every kind of ammunition, by means of which the revolted colonies are enabled to resist and fight the nation from which they received but immense benefits. The government is also positively informed that these acts, condemned by the wisdom of the laws of the United States, are also reported by the general government, with which the best intelligence and greatest harmony still prevail. However, as these adventurers and speculators have succeeded in escaping the penalties inflicted by the laws of their own country, it becomes necessary to adopt measures for their punishment. His excellency the president ad interim, anxious to repress these aggressions which constitute not only an offense to the sovereignty of the Mexican nation, but also to evident violation of international laws as they are generally adopted, has ordered the following decrees to be enforced.
>
> Foreigners landing on the coast of the republic or invading its territory by land, armed with the intention of attacking our country, will be deemed pirates and dealt with as such, being citizens of no nation presently at war with the republic, and fighting under no recognized flag.
>
> All foreigners who will import either by sea or [sic] land, in the places occupied by the rebels, either arms or ammunition of any kind for the use of them, will be deemed pirates and punished as such.

I send to you these decrees, that you may cause them to be fully executed.[19]

Less than three months after it was issued, Santa Anna would use the Tornel Decree to slaughter the revolutionaries.

A thorough discussion of the twisted and tangled politics that characterized revolutionary Texas would take volumes and is beyond the scope of this work. Nevertheless, it is important to understand the major political events that took place during this particular period. Even a brief overview illustrates the difficulties that the proponents for independence faced.

In 1835, Santa Anna threw out the Mexican Constitution of 1824 and forced the states under a centralized national government. The abolished constitution, which had been modeled after the U.S. Constitution and the Spanish Constitution of 1812, had provided for a president, a vice president, two houses of congress, and a judiciary system that included a supreme court. Catholicism, the national religion, was financially supported by the national treasury. Under the Constitution of 1824, the individual states had the mandate to maintain separate executive, legislative, and judicial branches of government, but the national body did not dictate exactly how the state governments should be formed or operated. Their individual constitutions were merely required to be in accord with the national constitution. This meant that the powers and authorities of the states were considerable, although they were still subservient to the national government.

Anglos were too new to Texas to have had much influence on the framing of the national constitution, although Austin did consult with the leaders who crafted it. Nevertheless, immigrants from the United States were familiar with the form of the constitution, and among them there was little dissatisfaction with its contents, although they weren't always satisfied with how it was interpreted or executed. Still, for the most part, they considered it a satisfactory document.

Many of the colonists would have been satisfied if Texas were simply granted status as a separate state within Mexico. As it was, Texas was part of the state of Coahuila y Tejas and was subservient to the capital city of Monclova in Coahuila. Inhabitants of Texas believed that the situation favored Coahuila and that the distances between Texas and the capital made it difficult to conduct administrative and legal transactions. There was also the underlying fact that Coahuila's population was largely Mexican, whereas Texas' population was mostly Anglo.

There were, then, a number of issues to consider in Texas. But in fact, after Santa Anna abolished the Constitution of 1824, perhaps the chief point of contention among the Anglos in Texas was whether to try to force a return to the old document, or whether to break with Mexico altogether. The reality was that most citizens of Texas, both Anglos and Tejanos, did not want to declare an independent nation. They were content with continuing the course that Santa Anna had set, or they merely wanted to reach a compromise with him. The argument that debated separation or moderation continued to be divisive and hotly contested in Texas until independence was finally declared in March 1836.

This argument was a much deeper deliberation than it might seem on the surface. Throughout Mexico—just as in Texas—there were Federalists who wanted a return to the Constitution of 1824, and they were willing to fight for it. Nevertheless, many of the Federalists in Texas, especially the Tejanos, would not fight for independence. Rather, given the choice between what they saw as two evils, they saw the dismemberment of their country as a greater wickedness than Santa Anna's Centralist government. In other words, if a faction in Texas went so far as to declare for independence, there were other considerable factions in Texas that would resist.

This was one of the many difficult issues that were debated when the Consultation that Austin had endorsed in September 1835 finally convened at San Felipe on November 1 of that year. It had been preceded by the ironically named Permanent Council, which actually existed for only a few weeks. The Permanent Council was made up of a variety of representatives from a number of communities. While waiting for the Consultation to convene, it took care of the revolution's most pressing needs. These included sending men and provisions to the volunteer army, organizing a postal system, and soliciting help from the United States.

Only a few days after the Battle of Concepción, the Permanent Council was dissolved, and the representatives making up the Consultation assembled and went to work. One of their first actions was to declare, on November 7, the formation of "a provisional government upon the principles of the Constitution of 1824."[20] However, despite their endorsement of the Constitution of 1824, they noted that Santa Anna had already abused his relationship with Texas to such an extent that its citizens had the right to completely separate from Mexico if they desired to do so. This was intended to appease Federalists who were loyal to Mexico—if not to Santa Anna—while keeping the option for independence open.

The provisional government that was formed at the Consultation elected contentious Henry Smith (1788–1851) as its head. The powers granted him as governor were considerable and included assignment as the chief of the armed forces. James Robinson (1790–1857) was elected lieutenant governor. Both of these men were agitators for independence from Mexico. The General

Council was formed to assist Smith. It was made up of representatives from across Texas but had legislative authority only in emergencies. Unlike Smith and Robinson, most of its members advocated peace or reconciliation. Together, Smith and the General Council were directed to work under the tenets of the Organic Law. The Organic Law was an expedient and temporary framework that was adopted on November 13. It was intended to be a template for governance until a more comprehensive document could be crafted. It was weak and confusing in that it assigned similar duties to both the governor and the General Council. This would cause considerable friction in the future.

The Consultation also called for both a militia organization and a regular army, to be led by Houston. It did nothing to address control over the groups of independent volunteers that were starting to arrive to further its cause. When the Consultation adjourned on November 14, it left a provisional government in place, but that government was weak. It would grow more frail and fractious over the next few months as the Mexican army moved into Texas in numbers never before seen.

During the subsequent fighting, the mood of the people shifted from reconciliation to confrontation. Particularly with Santa Anna at the head of an invading force, the Anglos considered that there was little chance that a satisfactory compromise could be reached. In their view—which turned out to be correct—the Mexican president was there not only to restore order, but also to crush those who defied him.

For their part, the colonists—Americans for the most part, including those who had been in Texas for several years—had legitimate grounds for feeling badly used. Many of them had left secure circumstances in the United States to throw their lot in with Texas. In doing so, they implicitly put their trust in the Mexican government and had sworn to follow that government's rule. By 1835, though, Mexico had changed those rules when Santa Anna abolished the Constitution of 1824.

Admittedly, there was no case for arguing that the Texans were strict adherents to Mexican law because, when it came to business or taxes, they often followed those laws that were most convenient for them. Still, they had learned to live and act and conduct their business relatively peacefully and reasonably within the edicts outlined by the Constitution of 1824. But the strong sense of fairness that the Americans had cultivated in their own country and subsequently brought with them into Texas was considerably agitated by Santa Anna's actions.

Ward's men slipped into the wilderness on March 15 after the fighting at Refugio and stayed on the run without provisions until Urrea captured them on March 22.

Urrea hurried his forces after Fannin's volunteers and surrounded the Anglos on the prairie near Coleto Creek on March 19.

Herman Ehrenberg galloped back to the volunteer position as the Mexican soldados forced the Anglos to halt.

When the volunteers fired their first volley, the effects on the Mexican forces were devastating.

Urrea's formations were generally well ordered and cohesive at the start of the fight.

A volunteer is struck by a Mexican musket ball.

The thundering explosions of the volunteer cannon added to the clamor on the battlefield.

Urrea's soldados *were stymied by the ferocity of the volunteer fire.*

Shackelford's Red Rovers fought under a red banner.

Fifty or more of Fannin's men were wounded, and nine or ten were killed.

As the day wore on, the lack of water hampered the use of the cannon. In addition, Urrea's soldados *especially targeted the men who worked the big guns.*

The British Land Pattern musket, or "Brown Bess," was the standard firearm of the Mexican soldado.

The tightly packed position from which Fannin's men fought made firing and reloading difficult and dangerous.

Urrea formed his men for one final assault in the late afternoon of March 19, 1836.

Although they had held off Urrea's attacks the previous day, the arrival of Mexican cannon sealed the fate of Fannin's men on the morning of March 20, 1836.

Fannin's men are escorted from the battlefield back to Goliad.

Santa Anna's orders to kill Fannin's men weigh heavily on the consciences of the Mexican officers.

A week after the Battle of Coleto Creek, on Palm Sunday, March 27, 1836, the Mexican soldados listen with trepidation as they receive their grisly orders.

Fannin's men are formed into three different groups for a march outside the presidio. Some men are informed they will be repatriated to the United States from Copano; others are told they are marching out to gather wood or to herd cattle.

Within a mile of the presidio, the three different groups are halted and massacred.

The butchery is finished with swords and bayonets.

With the slaughter complete, the bodies of Fannin's men are looted.

Back at the presidio, the wounded from the battle of March 19, 1836, are lined up to be shot.

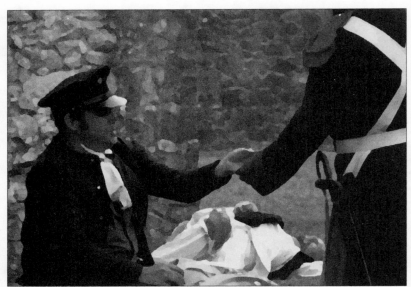

Fannin passed his valuables and personal belongings to a Mexican officer and asked that he not be shot in the face and that he be given a Christian burial. He was shot in the face, and his body was dumped and burned.

CHAPTER 5

The Matamoros Expedition

As volunteers continued to arrive from the United States during late 1835 and early 1836, the presidio at the tiny town of Goliad was far from anyone's mind. Certainly, it was an important strongpoint and way station on the line of communication from Copano to San Antonio, but action was not anticipated there. For a number of reasons, Americans were preparing to clash with Mexicans much farther to the south.

During the previous several years, the political and military situation in Texas had never been less than confused and was, in fact, often chaotic. The interests of too many groups and the absence of any real overarching authority—Mexican, Tejano, or Anglo—made it almost impossible for anyone to rally the people to a common cause. The stillborn Matamoros Expedition perfectly illustrated what could happen when too many different interests collided in a setting of near-anarchy. It also showed quite clearly the inability of any person or governing body in Texas at that time in history to resolve an important issue.

This vacuum of power remained virtually unchanged as 1835 turned into 1836. Although the Mexican army had been defeated and pushed from Texas, the provisional government wielded no real control. In fact, the armed and motivated volunteers arriving from the United States during that time could have, had it occurred to them, organized into a political and military force with just as much influence as anything that then existed in Texas.

But they did not do so. In fact, most of them were caught up in the baffling whirl of activity that sought to capture the Mexican city of Matamoros, in Tamaulipas state. This idea of taking Matamoros had been seriously considered by a number of parties ever since the notion of revolution became more than a farfetched idea bandied about by the more radical Anglos. Matamoros in the hands of rebellious Texans would be a grave concern to the government in Mexico City. Located near the mouth of the Rio Grande, it was an important entry point into Mexico, and the trade tariffs it collected were a valuable source of income. Mexico could not afford to lose the money the city generated, nor could it afford for that money to fall into the hands of the revolutionaries.

Geographically situated as it was, Matamoros was also a vital gateway to the interior of the country. Forces staged from there could strike inland to threaten Mexico City, which made the city important in both offensive and defensive contexts. In addition, many revolutionaries argued that a campaign there would serve to keep the fighting in Mexico rather than in the middle of their own properties farther to the north.

A move by the revolutionaries to take Matamoros was also seen to be important to the cause for another reason: the volunteers coming into Texas from the United States had nothing to do at the end of 1835. General Martin Perfecto de Cos and the Mexican army had been defeated and sent out of Texas. If something was not found to keep the American volunteers busy, many of them would quite simply get bored and go home.

In fact, Anglo leaders made no secret of their designs as they believed— correctly, as it turned out—that just the threat of action against Matamoros would force the Mexican government to commit valuable troops and supplies to defend it. Subsequently, those same resources could not be sent against revolutionary elements inside Texas. Stephen F. Austin even went so far as to suggest publicizing, in the United States, the idea of an attack on Matamoros because "even a rumor of such a thing would keep [Mexican Centralist] troops from being sent to Texas."[1] Indeed, James Walker Fannin's role as an agent for the revolution became a very public recruitment for an assault against the Mexican city.

But it was not just the Texas revolutionaries that had their eye on Matamoros. Mexican Federalists—whose primary objective was a return to the Constitution of 1824—also prized the city. It had been the subject of fighting as recently as 1832, when the American-educated Federalist General José Antonio Mexía (1800–1839) led a successful expedition against the Centralists at Matamoros. The Federalists, aside from the considerations of money and geography, were also hopeful that seizing the city would embolden citizens across northern Mexico to rally to their cause.

This desire for control of Matamoros was not entirely political. Arguably, at least on the Anglo side, a chief impetus for taking the city was pecuniary. From his seat at the capital city of Monclova, the Federalist governor of Coahuila y Tejas had illegally sold approximately fifteen hundred leagues of Texas land— much of it to Anglos—in order to raise money to fight Antonio López de Santa Anna's Centralists. Matamoros was key to the fight against Santa Anna, and so it was a critical first step to legitimizing the Federalist-issued titles these men held. If taking Matamoros would help to secure their claims, these Anglos were ready to embark on an expedition against the city.

Two of the most aggressive of the advocates for seizing Matamoros were James Grant (1793–1836) and Francis W. Johnson (1799–1884). Grant was a Scotsman trained as a physician. He bought a large estate in Coahuila in 1825 after coming to Texas in 1823 and had served in the state legislature of Coahuila y Tejas. During the early 1830s, he had tried his hand at settling families in Texas but was unsuccessful. By late 1835, he had thrown his lot in with the revolutionaries and took part in the siege of San Antonio later that year.

Johnson had partnered with Grant on land deals in Texas. Born in Virginia, he grew to adulthood in various frontier areas before going to Texas in 1826. He quickly rose to prominence and by 1832 was the surveyor general for Austin's colony. A hot-tempered agitator, he was a staunch advocate of independence from Mexico. As the fervor against the Mexican government increased during 1835, so did his responsibilities: he was named as the revolutionary adjutant and inspector general. By the end of that year he had acted on his belligerent sentiments and was, in fact, in command of the Anglo forces when the Mexicans surrendered at San Antonio.

By January 1836, Johnson and Grant had teamed and were marshalling men, provisions, and equipment to march on Matamoros. They were not the only ones who had designs on the city, however. Philip Dimmit (1801–1841) was born in Kentucky and had gone to Texas in 1823. He married into an influential Mexican family and quickly prospered as a successful merchant. Among his operations was a wharf and warehouse that made up Dimmit's Landing on Lavaca Bay. He was liked and respected by both the Mexicans and the Anglos, and his extensive contacts within Mexico—connections that he enjoyed because of his wife's family—provided him valuable intelligence that he shared with revolutionary elements in Texas.

Dimmit became a strident supporter of independence. By mid-October 1835, he had taken over command at Goliad with a force of men he had raised on his own. It is an indicator of the confusion of this time that these men were not part of any organized group and owed no allegiance to anyone other than Dimmit. Dimmit was anxious to take action, and agitated for a move against Matamoros, but suggested that a Mexican Federalist lead it, rather than an Anglo. He argued that this would help to legitimize the action and would also serve to reduce criticism that the fight was one of Anglos against Mexicans. His plan, which he believed "would be approved and sustained by a majority of [Mexican] people in that section of the country," gained the support of the General Council, as well as of Austin. Like Dimmit, Austin strongly believed that a Mexican should lead the effort.[2]

To help pave the way for such an action, Dimmit dispatched Captain Ira Westover (1795–1836) from the garrison at Goliad at the head of about forty men. The force marched south and increased in size to about sixty as it picked up adventurers. After crossing the Nueces River, the group took the Centralist position at Fort Lipantitlán—which was really little more than a crudely fortified camp—on November 3. The Mexicans at the fort made up a small rear party left in place while the bulk of their number was afield looking for—and not finding—Westover and his men. At any rate, the outnumbered Mexicans gave up without a shot being fired. The Anglos looted the stores there before razing the position's crude earthen battlements as best they could.

The following afternoon, Westover's force ambushed the bulk of the Mexican garrison as it approached the Nueces River. The Mexicans were roundly defeated, and suffered twenty-eight casualties, while only one American was injured when a musket ball carried away three of his fingers. Later, the Mexican commander parleyed to allow his wounded into nearby San Patricio where they could be treated. Westover consented, and the stricken *soldados* were brought out of the field. At the same time, the Anglos challenged the Mexican commander to another engagement, but the latter demurred, citing the effectiveness of the American long rifles. In the end, he left the battlefield and led the rest of his men to safety at Matamoros.

The modest success at Fort Lipantitlán aside, certain events made Dimmit more cautious about taking Matamoros. During October 1835, Mexía assembled a group of 150 men, most of whom were Anglos, to seize the eastern Mexican port of Tampico, more than three hundred miles south of Matamoros. He hoped that his force, raised primarily from New Orleans, would quickly take control of the city and subsequently catalyze a groundswell of popular support in eastern Mexico against Santa Anna's Centralist government. Texas revolutionary leaders knew of this plan and generally endorsed it. Any distraction that focused Mexico City's attention away from Texas was welcome. Still, Austin thought that Mexía's efforts would be better spent against Matamoros.

Regardless, Mexía and his men attacked Tampico on November 15, 1835, but it did not work well. Coordination with supporters inside Tampico was poor, and the Centralist forces had been reinforced. Mexía and his forces were defeated and forced to retreat, and thirty-one of their number remained behind as prisoners. Of these, three died of wounds. As an indicator of the Mexican government's attitude toward actions of this type, the remaining twenty-eight men were tried by court martial, found guilty, and shot a month later. There was little official response from the U.S. government: Santa Anna took note.

Mexía's raid had not produced an uprising in support of the Federalists. This did not bode well for an Anglo attack on Matamoros; Dimmit began to believe that an attempt to seize the city would receive little support among the citizens of northern Mexico. He relayed his concern to Austin that such an effort "would be as likely to be opposed as to be approved."[3]

Houston and Austin also grew more circumspect. Particularly after Mexía's failure, an expedition against Matamoros began to appear more as an adventure than as a critical move for the future of the revolution. Likewise, it would divert too many resources from central and eastern Texas. Importantly, too, it might result in the alienation of Mexican citizens who might otherwise have been at least ambivalent to the revolutionary cause in Texas.

Still, Dimmit believed in the strategic and financial advantages that taking Matamoros would provide. Also, despite his reservations, his contacts in Mexico assured him that a successful campaign there would rally more Mexican Federalists against Santa Anna. His communications to the provisional government were so persuasive—despite his own misgivings about popular support from the Mexican people—that on December 17 Governor Henry Smith ordered a less-than-enthusiastic Houston to undertake the project. Lieutenant Governor James Robinson and the Military Council chairman, Wyatt Hanks (1795–1862), confused matters when they ordered a separate expedition against Matamoros, to be headed by Edward Burleson (1798–1851).

Nevertheless, the growing wariness of Dimmit, Houston, and Austin and the fact that two separate expeditions against Matamoros had already been ordered did nothing to dissuade Johnson and Grant from their own plans. They spent much of January 1836 marshalling men and resources. Johnson raised the ire of many when he won over volunteers at San Antonio—chief among them being the New Orleans Greys—to his cause.

Johnson sought to legitimize his and Grant's efforts when he brought their proposal in front of the provisional government at San Felipe. Additionally, he was looking for whatever funds, provisions, arms, and men he could get. He insolently assured the assembly there that "the moment is appropriate and should not be lost. . . . You may rely on all going well . . . if we are not interfered with by officers of the regular army."[4] Smith disliked the idea, because he did not trust their motives. Many believed that Johnson and Grant were seeking to create a new nation separate from both Mexico *and* Texas.

While Johnson was working the provisional government in San Felipe, Grant declared himself the Acting Commander-in-Chief of the Federal Volunteer Army and commandeered nearly all the provisions, arms, and medical equipment in San Antonio. He did so over the protestations of the commander there, James C. Neill (1790–1845). Word of this got back to Houston, whose misgivings about a Matamoros expedition were increasing daily. He shared the information with Smith before starting for Goliad, where Grant was also headed.

Smith was furious and tried to dismiss the General Council for their advocacy of the entire Matamoros business. The Council members responded by impeaching him—an act he did not recognize—and promoting Robinson from lieutenant governor to governor. The Council still wanted Matamoros; they authorized Johnson's plan on January 14, 1836. So, by mid-January 1836, various components of the Texas revolutionary government had authorized or ordered at least three separate expeditions to take Matamoros: expeditions to be led by Houston, Burleson, and Johnson. From this point, with Smith refusing to acknowledge his impeachment and Robinson asserting his authority as the new Council-appointed governor, the provisional government, such as it was, unraveled nearly completely. It was particularly confusing because both Smith and Robinson continued to claim the governorship.

By this time, Grant had made his way to Goliad, where he tried to assert authority over Dimmit and his garrison. In fact, the two parties came very near an armed clash because Dimmit would not yield to Grant's demands for provisions. One of the men recorded that both groups "were kept in readiness for a fight."[5] Grant remained insistent and championed his advocacy of the Constitution of 1824 while reasserting his claim to the entirely self-fabricated title as Acting Commander-in-Chief of the Federal Volunteer Army. Disgusted, Dimmit gave up his command and left Peyton S. Wyatt (1804–1847) in charge. It is ironic that many—perhaps most—of the men from both parties would find themselves back at Goliad a month or so later, united under a single authority.

Houston, en route to the scene, was concerned that the situation was out of control and that the cause for Texas would degenerate into armed infighting. Even if cooler heads prevailed and disaster was averted, he was worried that any action taken against Matamoros might result in a military disaster that Texas could not afford. Rumors were rampant that Santa Anna was coming to Texas with a large army. Furthermore, the Centralists were indeed reinforcing Matamoros against an attack.

The situation was still tense when Houston approached Goliad on January 14, the day that the General Council—in his absence—authorized Johnson and Grant to execute their expedition. He ran into Dimmit who was leaving and who gave him further details of Grant's actions. When Houston finally arrived at the presidio, he found the situation between Grant's men and Dimmit's former command extremely tense. He quickly asserted his authority as the commander-in-chief and ordered supplies distributed between the two parties, and called a parade formation.

Then, anxious to discourage any action against Matamoros, he argued that technicalities invalidated any authority from the provisional government to attack the Mexican city. His argument was evidently unpersuasive: Grant and his men stuck with their plan to meet Johnson at Refugio. From there they proposed to move to San Patricio, which would serve as their final staging point before marching on Matamoros.

While Houston worked to stymie Grant's expedition, he also frantically tried to reinforce Neill at the Alamo. Although there was yet no threat, it was likely that the old mission would become contested if the Mexican army came back into Texas. Houston dispatched James Bowie to San Antonio with about twenty men, and likewise hurried a messenger to overtake Dimmit and divert him to buttress Neill with whatever men and supplies he could muster.

Houston also decided to travel with Grant's men to Refugio in order to meet William Ward and the Georgians and dissuade them from joining Johnson and Grant. He wrote to Smith that he would have proceeded to San Antonio himself except that "the Matamoras rage is up so high that I must see Colonel Ward's men." Houston believed that meeting Ward in person was the only means by which he could be sure of making his point. His stress was evident when he noted to Smith, "You have no idea of the difficulties I have encountered."[6]

When Grant left Goliad with two hundred men and ample provisions, Houston was with him. At Refugio, Houston found several smaller groups of volunteers ready and waiting, but Ward's men were nowhere to be found. Johnson arrived on January 20, 1836, with the authorization from the General Council to press on with Grant in an expedition against Matamoros.

Houston was exceedingly agitated by the Council's action. Their authorization ignored his own advice as the commander-in-chief and, in his eyes, was issued illegally. He was also worried because volunteers recruited to the campaign were being promised "the first spoils taken from the enemy."[7] This essentially authorized them to seize what they wanted from the civilians of Matamoros—in other words, to plunder and loot. Such actions were hardly a recipe for creating support among the Mexican population.

Houston was also concerned about the military aspects of such a venture. At best, a force from Texas would number only a few hundred. Matamoros was a city of twelve thousand. The notion that these few hundred men would be able to march 150 miles from San Patricio to take the city—even if it were only lightly defended—seemed, at best, overly optimistic. He noted that "a city containing twelve thousand souls will not be taken by a handful of men who have marched twenty-two days without bread-stuffs, or necessary supplies for an army. If there ever was a time when Matamoras [sic] could have been taken by a few men, that time has passed by."[8]

Houston ordered all the men gathered for another formation. He would try again, as he had at Goliad, to warn them off the expedition. His task was not an easy one: Grant and Johnson had all along beguiled the volunteers with stories of the riches that awaited them in Matamoros. An easy fight against the Mexicans would bring them glory, while Mexican booty would bring them wealth. Houston took a different tack. He praised them for their spirit and their courage, but reminded them of the grave dangers that threatened Texas.

It would be best, he said, to wait in central Texas and engage Santa Anna and his *soldados* when they were worn, hungry, and exhausted by the hardships of their invasion from the interior of Mexico. In addition, he outlined the difficulties that awaited them at Matamoros. Federalist aid had not developed as expected, and Mexía and his men had been defeated at Tampico attempting a similar assault.

For the most part, Houston's approach worked. Despite some resistance and debate, most of the men saw the sense in Houston's argument. The majority of them agreed to wait at Refugio for Ward's men and other reinforcements. From there, they would marshal as necessary to protect the interior of Texas. Nevertheless, Houston's entreaties had no effect on either Johnson or Grant, or on about seventy of their men.

That group, in direct defiance of Houston, marched for San Patricio. Houston, having forestalled a potential tragedy—despite the intransigence of Grant and Johnson—made his way back to Smith and took a month's furlough from the army. From his perspective, he needed the separation. As the commander-in-chief, he knew he would be rebuked by the General Council, and likewise by his enemies, and he did not want to be around for it. As the military situation developed and as the revolutionary government evolved into its next iteration, Houston headed north and east to negotiate with the Cherokee in order to keep them out of the fight.

Houston's mission was important; fighting the Mexicans would be difficult enough, but fighting both the Mexicans and the Indians would be nearly impossible. If Santa Anna's army pinned down the revolutionary forces, the Indians would be able to maraud the settlements unchecked. With their farms and families ruined or killed, there would be little incentive for the revolutionaries to fight.

In fact, clashes with the Indians were a part of life for the early Texas settlers because neither the Spanish nor the Mexicans had been able to subjugate or destroy them. When Austin brought the first settlers into the Brazos River region, relationships with the Karankawa quickly deteriorated from a tentative beginning that was marked by mostly petty affronts. In 1824, after a series of increasingly serious clashes, he sent punitive expeditions against them. Eventually, hostilities diminished when he made treaties that pushed the Karankawa west of the San Antonio and Guadalupe rivers.

The colonists found it difficult to deal with the natives; it was often impossible for them to determine the intentions of the individual Indians or small groups of Indians that moved across the land that the settlers claimed. Some were friendly, but others were not. The distances between farms and ranches were large, and families were essentially on their own. This made them especially wary of any native groups that approached their homesteads, regardless of what their intentions might actually have been.

Treaties were concluded with a number of tribes during the 1820s and 1830s, but as the difficulties with the government in Mexico intensified, and as the political situation became more unsettled, the Indians took advantage of the discord. The Comanche, who had never really come to any lasting agreements with anyone, were among the most vicious, and encounters with them were often fatal.

Noah Smithwick recorded an example of this. In January 1836, he joined Captain John Tumlinson (1804–1853) whose father and brother had been killed by Indians soon after they had arrived in Texas. When Smithwick joined Tumlinson, he was encamped at the head of about sixty men on the Colorado River about thirty miles north of present-day Austin. Their mission was to chase off rampaging natives. In the evening after he had joined them, Smithwick recorded that "as we were preparing for our supper, a young white woman, an entire stranger, her clothes hanging in shreds about her torn and bleeding body, dragged herself into camp and sank exhausted on the ground."

She told the men that she had been traveling with her husband and brother and two small children the previous morning when Comanches ambushed their party, killing the men and taking her and the children captive. The youngest child wailed so much through the rest of the day that "at length one of the Indians snatched it from her and dashed its brains out against a tree." That night, during a cold rainstorm, the unbound woman left her remaining child, an infant boy, and sneaked out of the camp. When she found Tumlinson and his band the following evening she begged them to rescue her remaining child.

Hearing her story the men immediately gave chase and traveled through the night. They found the Comanches by mid-morning the next day and immediately attacked. During the ensuing melee one Indian was killed and the rest fled, leaving the kidnapped boy behind. In the confusion of the fight, one of the would-be rescuers tried twice to shoot the boy, but his gun misfired each time. When it finally discharged on the third try, the child was saved only because one of the other men saw what was about to happen and shoved the barrel away at the last instant. On returning the infant boy to his mother, Smithwick wrote, "There was a suspicious moisture in many an eye long since a stranger to tears, when the overjoyed mother clasped her only remaining treasure to her heart."[9]

The Indians that Houston went to treat with were the same ones he had already spent so much time with: the Cherokee. They were different from the Comanche: they were a settled, agricultural people living in villages. They had been pushed west from their native lands in the southeastern United States. By the mid-1830s, after years of the U.S. government moving them from one location to the next, they were eager to have a permanent home. Treating with the Mexicans against the Anglos in Texas was one possible means of achieving that goal. Allied with Santa Anna, the Cherokee would be a real menace. Rather than marauding in small bands as the Comanche normally did, the Cherokee were capable of mobilizing a small army against the colonists.

It was a means to forestall just such an attack that Houston sought when he left Refugio after dissuading most of Johnson and Grant's men from attacking Matamoros. No matter what the odds were against the Mexicans, they would become much worse if the Cherokee entered the contest against the revolution. Ultimately, Houston successfully drew on his deep relationships with his adoptive tribe to keep them out of the fight.

After Houston left, Fannin arrived at Refugio on February 4, 1836, with William Ward's Georgians and a collection of other volunteers. He had led them to Refugio via Velasco and Copano, adding to the group's numbers along the way. That they were bound for Matamoros appears to be understood. A letter home from one of the men while the group was in Velasco described how they were next going to proceed to Copano to join with a group of several hundred other fighters before "taking up the line of march for the invasion of Mexico."[10] If the government in Mexico City was worried about adventures by armed American mercenaries, it was for good reason.

Fannin, having recruited men for the expedition against Matamoros, was now ready to lead them himself, although that had not been the original intent when he was made an agent of the revolutionary government late the previous year. He believed that he could do it, though, because Houston's absence essentially left him in charge: as a colonel, he was the ranking revolutionary officer in the field. On the same day he arrived in Refugio, he noted in a letter to Robinson and the General Council that he was prepared to march south to San Patricio, where Johnson and Grant were waiting for him. From there, he would lead the combined forces to Matamoros.

Suddenly, Fannin, the illegitimate son and West Point failure, found himself in the position he had always dreamed of: in charge of an army. His first action as head of that army was set to undo Houston's earlier work. It is certain that, following his arrival at Refugio, he was told of Houston's previous passionate admonitions against a Matamoros expedition. And he was certainly aware, even before he arrived at Refugio, that the proposed campaign was an incendiary issue that Houston strongly opposed. In fact, he wrote Robinson on January 31, "You will all allow that we already have too much division; and one cause of complaint is this very expedition, and that it is intended to displace general Houston."[11] But then, Houston was out of the country and Fannin wasn't. This attitude of Fannin's was consistent with his inclination to choose what orders he wanted to follow. It was a proclivity that was made easier by the ridiculous state of the revolutionary government.

All the same, Fannin's designs on Matamoros changed almost instantly with the arrival of a dispatch from Captain Robert C. Morris, a New Orleans Grey and a veteran of the fighting at San Antonio two months earlier. Morris wrote to Fannin from San Patricio; he had been unimpressed by Houston's arguments against an attack on Matamoros. This was due in part to plans by Johnson and Grant to link with elements of the Mexican army that were purported to be ready to rally to the Federalist cause. In addition, Morris had been promised command of a regiment, once this combined force was formed. Still, events had unfolded that alarmed him enough that he was compelled to send a warning to Fannin.

Morris had received a visit from Plácido Benavides (d. 1837), a rancher and the alcalde of Victoria. Benavides was a respected and well-liked supporter of the Texas cause. His information had always been reliable—as it would prove to be in this instance. He relayed word from the alcalde at Matamoros that more than a thousand Mexican *soldados* and cavalrymen had recently arrived to reinforce the city. Furthermore, he stated that Santa Anna was massing thousands of *soldados* along the Rio Grande in preparation for an immense invasion of Texas. Morris reported that "Santa Anna has sworn to take Texas or lose Mexico."[12]

Where Matamoros was concerned, Santa Anna hoped to lure the Anglos south to the city, then sweep their rear and exterminate them. At the same time, he intended to launch an offensive into the interior of Texas; San Antonio and Goliad were obvious objectives. With those strong points taken—and with most of the revolutionary fighters trapped or annihilated at Matamoros—he would be able to range across Texas at will.

Morris' letter finished with a postscript noting that Santa Anna was motivating his soldiers with the prospect of plunder. This description presumably came from Benavides via the alcalde in Matamoros. He had heard that the *soldados* were being given nearly free rein in their own country in order to keep their morale high. Morris wrote, "[Santa Anna's] soldiers have assassinated many of the most influential citizens, and the wives and daughters are prostituted—the whole country is given up to the troops to induce them forward."[13]

Fannin's response to this news bordered on panic. Taking a newly fortified and forewarned Matamoros was out of the question. This was particularly so because, if Benavides' information was correct, Santa Anna's plans hinged on such a move. Fannin would be a fool to march into such a trap.

He wasted no time in drafting a message to the General Council. Aside from forwarding Morris' correspondence that outlined Santa Anna's plans, Fannin's letter included rants against the Mexicans and alluded to the dangers that the *soldados* posed to the wives and daughters of the settlers: "What can be expected for the *Fair daughters* of chaste white women, when their own [Mexican] country-women are prostituted by a licensed soldiery, as a inducement to push forward into the Colonies, where they may find *fairer game?*" [emphasis in original].[14] It is worth noting that in the following quote he—and likely most Anglos in Texas—considered himself an American: "Can it be possible that they—that any American—can so far forget the honour of their mothers wives, and daughters, as not to fly to their rifles, and march to meet the Tyrant?"[15]

While he was at it, he also complained that his volunteers were poorly provisioned, armed, and clothed, and that they had not been paid. The fact that his force was made up almost entirely of newly arrived volunteers from the United States additionally provoked his ire: "But when I tell you, that out of more than four hundred men at and near this post, I doubt if twenty-five citizens of Texas can be mustered in the ranks—nay, I am informed, whilst writing the above, that there is not half that number; does not this fact bespeak an indifference and criminal apathy, truly alarming?" Additionally, he chastised the established colonists: "Will the freemen of Texas calmly fold their arms and await until the approach of their deadly enemy compels them to protect their own firesides?"[16]

Flush with his authority as the ranking member of the army in the field, Fannin also penned a number of disjointed recommendations that included calling out all the militias, and readying boats along major rivers to facilitate a retreat "should it be our unfortunate lot to be compelled to make one."[17] He also suggested forming a reserve on the Colorado River and using the tiny Texas navy to guard the coast. He additionally cautioned against investing too much in cavalry as it tended to be expensive, and the horsemen often made fraudulent claims for lost or stolen mounts and tack.

As to his disposition, he advised he was no longer striking out for Matamoros. Rather, he was taking his men to Goliad.

The rumors that Santa Anna was preparing an invasion of Texas were true. Although the Mexican treasury was bankrupt, Santa Anna arranged for a loan from a prominent banking concern for four hundred thousand pesos at 48 percent interest.[18] Aside from the usurious interest rate, the loan included other benefits for the lender that were no doubt related to the fact that Santa Anna received a significant number of bonds as part of the arrangement. Santa Anna stood to make a tidy sum of money just by arranging financing for the campaign in Texas.

At San Luis Potosí, more than five hundred miles south of San Antonio, Santa Anna assembled more than six thousand troops to invade Texas. After resting at Saltillo, he started across the desert for Texas. The winter weather was brutal. Rain, snow, and ice storms cost him a hundred or more of his poorly clad and poorly provisioned men.

After regrouping and resting at the Rio Grande, Santa Anna led his men across the river and into Texas on February 16, 1836. With him was Cos, whom the colonists had paroled the previous December. To gain that parole, he had sworn never again to bear arms against the people of Texas. Lying, the flexible interpretation of honor, and the constant changing of allegiances were so woven into his fabric that this violation of his word probably did not trouble his conscience. In addition, after having lost San Antonio, he was probably too frightened of Santa Anna to defy his orders to go back into Texas.

As Santa Anna was crossing into Texas, General José Urrea (1797–1849) advanced to Matamoros, just as Morris had warned Fannin. On February 18, he pushed north into Texas at the head of 650 cavalry and infantry. He had received word of the Johnson and Grant expedition, and he was determined to destroy it. By mid-February 1836, after an ignominious defeat and expulsion from Texas two months earlier, the Mexican army returned to Texas in greater numbers than ever.

CHAPTER 6

Fannin at Goliad

At Refugio, James Walker Fannin had taken charge of William Ward's Georgia volunteers and Isaac Ticknor's Alabama Greys, as well as various other smaller groups and unassociated individuals. He left Refugio on February 12, 1836, at the head of a column of approximately 250 men, and marched twenty-five miles north to Goliad. On arriving, he assimilated the small cadre of men who garrisoned it, as well as the subsequent groups of fighters who rallied to his command—often without prior notice— over the next few weeks. These included Captain Jack Shackelford's Red Rovers from Alabama, the Kentucky Mustangs, parts of the New Orleans Greys, and other smaller groups of volunteers from various parts of the United States.

Dr. Joseph Barnard's experience was fairly typical for volunteers who came into Texas in the first month or so of 1836. Barnard, the Chicago physician who closed his practice and traveled south to join what he believed to be a glorious rebellion against a tyrannical government, arrived at Matagorda in early January on the same day as Shackelford's Red Rovers. Barnard tried to determine his next step. While doing so, he familiarized himself with the state of the rebellion.

He was less than impressed with Texas politics. His contempt at the fallout between Governor Henry Smith and the General Council was obvious: "The disgraceful row between Gov-Smith and the Council was now known, in which the former made a great display of billingsgate, and the latter suspended him and threatened an impeachment."

He also despaired at finding an official entity to which he could offer his services. He had planned to tender his talents to the revolutionary army, but "now, there seemed to be no army, at least regular troops." In New Orleans, Austin had advised him to contact Houston, but again, "no one could inform me where he was or where his head-quarters were established." He considered setting up a private medical practice but did not have the resources to do so.

After a while, he made his way to Dimmit's Landing on Lavaca Bay. There was not much to do, and Barnard and a few companions "amused [themselves] by hunting and fishing."[1]

Shackelford and the Red Rovers had traveled to Texana on the Lavaca River, and Barnard joined them there in early February. He liked the Alabama doctor, and resolved to attach himself to the Red Rovers. In early February, a courier brought a dispatch from Goliad calling for all volunteers to rally at the presidio there. The men from Alabama wasted no time in responding to the appeal. Barnard's recollection of the camp after the first afternoon's march illustrates the less-than-perfect discipline typical of volunteer groups in Texas:

> We numbered about seventy men; of these sixty or more being Shackelford's Company of Red Rovers, and eight or ten others who went on with us to join other companies. We had started in high spirits, for the opening of new scenes of adventure, the excitement of the enterprise, and the novelty of the scenery through which we passed, combined to cheer our minds into a very complacent mood. But alas! the truth must be told, other kinds of spirits were at work in our midst; some of the men had become tipsy and pugnacious, and no sooner had we struck camp than a violent quarrel and a row seemed on the point of commencing; knives were drawn, pistols presented, and I fully expected to witness a scene of tumult and death. Captain Shackelford, however, interfered and such was the power of his influence and the great esteem in which he was held, that he soon succeeded in allaying the excitement and soothing the angry feelings.[2]

The company camped after the next day's march and Shackelford set up a secret drill to test the mettle and training of his men. In the small hours of the night, a musket report boomed the men awake. While some of the men responded in adequate fashion—fully dressed with loaded and ready weapons—others did not. Barnard wrote, "One was heard making lamentation he could not get on his boots; another could not find his bayonet and a third bawled loudly for his ramrod. Some turned out barefooted and got their feet badly lacerated with the thorns and [briars]." After charging through the brush and firing after imagined Indians, Barnard noted that the men were satisfied with "our martial display," and turned back to sleep.[3]

The next day, the company marched in the face of a cold, wet wind that scattered the men across the prairie. Exhausted, frozen, and soaked, they straggled into the town of Victoria in small groups. They spent the succeeding two days there recovering before setting out for Goliad once more.

It was mid-February, probably February 14, when Barnard and the rest of the company crossed Manahuilla Creek and caught their first sight of the presidio at Goliad. After marching the last few miles and wading across the three-foot-deep San Antonio River, they were met by a contingent that escorted them inside the walls of the old presidio. There they were given an enthusiastic welcome; Fannin's garrison was growing.

The presidio, or fort, at Goliad was the third and last of a series of mission and presidio combinations to bear variations of the same name. The Spanish built the original presidio in 1721 to protect a mission built at the same time on Garcitas Creek near Lavaca Bay. They named the presidio Nuestra Señora Santa María de Loreto de la Bahía del Espíritu Santo, whereas the mission was called Nuestra Señora del Espíritu Santo de Zúñiga. In popular use, the name of the presidio was shortened to Presidio La Bahía, loosely translated as the Fort by the Bay.

Indians, disease, and the needs of the missionaries caused the first complex to be abandoned in 1726 and moved about twenty-five miles inland to a site along the Guadalupe River near present-day Mission Valley. Here, the mission and fort prospered. For a number of political and strategic factors, however, it was deserted in 1749 in favor of the present location at Goliad.

The Spanish, perhaps out of habit or perhaps for sentimental reasons, continued to call the presidio La Bahía, although it was at least thirty miles from the closest coastline. Unlike many of the old Spanish missions in Texas, the site at Goliad was intended from the beginning as not just a mission, but also as a stronghold. Constructed on high ground, the presidio was the most imposing structure within a hundred miles or more. Its chapel on the north wall featured a tall bell tower that served as an excellent lookout post. Bastions for artillery marked the corners of its eight-foot-high walls that enclosed an area of about three acres. Inside were barracks and other structures, including blockhouses for storing ammunition and other provisions.

By early 1836, the fortress had seen considerable service, including Indian campaigns—particularly against the Lipan Apache and Comanche—actions against French, English, and Dutch forays, and fighting during the Mexican revolt against Spain. It also was the site of several brief fights against American interlopers.

As formidable as it was, time and the elements—as well as fighting from previous campaigns—had crumbled the old presidio's structure. Now, in February 1836, Fannin immediately set the men to work in order to make it more defensible. The stone walls were already three feet thick, but they were further reinforced with additional dirt, stone, and pilings. Where required, the walls were repaired. Soil from a ditch excavated around the interior perimeter was used to further shore the walls. Fighting positions, or bastions, for artillery were reinforced and new ones built. Outside the walls, shacks and other structures were burned or pulled down so that they couldn't be used for cover by an attacking force. Importantly, the men built a covered trench to the nearby San Antonio River, thus ensuring that the presidio would have access to water in the event of a siege.

Joseph M. Chadwick (1812–1836), Fannin's adjutant general, supervised the strengthening of the fort. Chadwick was a young topographical engineer who had grown up in New Hampshire and who had, like Fannin, left West Point after two years. After spending time in Illinois, he joined Ward's Georgia volunteers, who elected him sergeant major. Still, he had been in Texas for less than two months by the middle of February. He was evidently a likeable man; one contemporary source states that he possessed "a native suavity of temper and urbanity of manner, which at once made him the *Pride of the battalion*" [emphasis in original].[4]

John Sowers Brooks (1814–1836) assisted Chadwick. Fannin had made the young, red-haired Virginian his aide. Brooks also took on duties as chief engineer in charge of artillery and ammunition. His military experience—just less than a year with the U.S. Marine Corps—was negligible. He had served a short time on the frigate *Constitution* and was quickly promoted to corporal, but was dissatisfied with his prospects. Citing ill health and other difficulties, he petitioned the commandant of the Marine Corps for an early release from his four-year enlistment obligation. In reality, as a letter he wrote to his brother the previous year reveals, he was anxious to journey to Texas where he hoped to receive an officer's commission in service against Mexico:

> The Mexicans have embodied troops, which are now marching upon the colonists. Col. Austin is a prisoner in the City of Mexico; and I can [perceive] nothing in the aspect of their affairs to prevent the contest, which this state of things predicts. There is then some hope, of my finding active employment in a military capacity there; and from my knowledge of the American system of tactics, and the necessarily disorganized condition of any forces which the Province can embody, it will not be difficult, I think, to attain a more elevated station than that I now occupy. My services as a drill master would be valuable; and in the event of a war, I am sanguine enough to believe that I will soon entitle myself to a commission.[5]

Brooks was duly discharged from the Marine Corps in August 1835, after eleven months of service. Nevertheless, his short service still exceeded that of most of the volunteers. Brooks had no illusions about his own talents when he recognized this pitiable lack of military experience among the men at Goliad. In another of his letters home, he wrote about being placed in charge of the ordnance and ammunition magazine: "From this circumstance, you will readily and rationally infer, that there are but few professional soldiers here, when one of my age with but few months experience has so many important trusts confided to him."[6]

The men disliked the work. They could have done the same sort of backbreaking labor on the farms that many of them had left behind. Most of them had left their homes to liberate Texas from Mexico, and grubbing around in the dirt was not the same as scrapping with *soldados*. Unlike their situation at Goliad, they could have stayed clothed and fed had they stayed home. Sadly, the fledgling Texas government had for the most part neglected the men that had come to fight for it. Many of the men were barefoot: their boots and shoes had fallen away in tatters in the months since they had left their homes. Many of their clothes were what they had taken with them to Texas and were likewise little more than rags.

The clothes that most of the men wore were a combination of work clothing, surplus military garb, and such odds and ends that the men acquired as they could. All of their clothing had been sewn by hand. The shirts were typically made of linen or cotton, and were loose fitting, with full sleeves and long tails. Shirts were topped with heavier overshirts of either the same material, or wool, or linsey-woolsey—a combination of linen and wool. Belts and sashes kept clothing in place and also served to hold pistols and other gear. The trousers were made of the same material as the shirts and were commonly held up with suspenders. They usually had a flap in front that buttoned to the waistband.

Hats of different types were also worn, usually made of straw, felt, or animal skins. Their wide brims provided vital protection from the sun. Boots and shoes were made of leather. Other clothing included vests—which were very common in either single or double-breast styles—and cloaks or capes. One volunteer noted how he was quite fond of a strikingly beautiful Mexican serape that he acquired after arriving in Texas.

In addition to scarce clothing, there were other shortages. Food grew scarce, particularly flour and meal. Furthermore, ammunition was in short supply. The stores that had been taken when the presidio was captured had been depleted—James Grant and his men had made off with much of it—and although there were a dozen or more cannon at his disposal, Fannin did not have the gunpowder and shot required for an extended siege. Similarly, the men lacked adequate powder and ball for their muskets and rifles. When recruited, the volunteers were supposed to provide their own weapons and one hundred rounds of ammunition. Since arriving in Texas, these individual supplies were at least partially used up in hunting, or lost or destroyed by the elements and hard travel.

Most of the men had not been paid since arriving in Texas. The revolutionary government was essentially broke and was financing the fight with promises of land after independence was won. Still, some remuneration was expected. The volunteers came to Texas anticipating salaries equivalent to what the U.S. Army would have paid, or about twenty dollars a month for a private. Nevertheless, there was little cash money dispersed among the men. In short, then, the volunteers at Goliad were underfed, poorly dressed, unshod, inadequately provisioned with ammunition, and not paid. And rather than fighting Mexicans—the chief motivation for many of them—they were engaged in hard manual labor to fortify an old Spanish presidio.

Perhaps worst of all, they were being led by a man to whom they were not completely loyal. Accounts suggest that feelings among the volunteers for and about Fannin ranged from mild respect to bilious hatred. Burr H. Duval (1809–1836), the leader of the Kentucky Mustangs, wrote in a letter to his father, "As I anticipated, much dissention prevails among the Volunteers, Col. Fannin, now in command (Genl. Houston being absent), is unpopular— and nothing but the certainty of hard fighting, and *that shortly* [emphasis in original], could have kept us together so long."[7] Here, Duval reinforces the notion that, most of all, the men that made up Fannin's garrison were spoiling for a fight.

Likewise, A. J. Ferguson (d. 1836) of the Alabama Red Rovers wrote to his brother, "Our commander is Col. Fannin, and I am sorry to say, the majority of the soldiers do not like him, for what cause I do not know, without it is because they think he has not the interest of the country at heart, or that he wishes to become great without taking the proper steps to attain greatness."[8] This perspective from the ranks supports the notion of Fannin as an opportunist, a pretender to prominence, who could not perform at the level of command he had attained. A military adage holds that an officer cannot hide his incompetence from the troops, and thus Fannin's failure to impress his men is telling.

To be fair, Fannin was in a difficult position regardless of his talent or lack thereof. Few of the men he was charged with leading had more than a rudimentary understanding of martial discipline or the hierarchy of a military chain of command. The majority of them—including those of the Georgia Battalion, the Alabama Red Rovers, and the Kentucky Mustangs—were mustered along with men they had known for years, if not all their lives. The men who led them into Texas were men they had elected. Fannin was an outsider and they didn't know or necessarily even trust him.

Even if their elected leaders were accountable to Fannin to some degree, the rank-and-file fighters felt little loyalty to him. That he was not able to feed, clothe, or pay them only exacerbated their lack of respect. Finally, there was no fighting on which to fix their attention and energy. Some of the men even blamed Fannin for this. They believed that he was reluctant, or even afraid, to fight the Mexicans. In fact, the New Orleans Greys wanted to join the rest of their number at the Alamo, but Fannin refused to provision them. In effect, he had them hostage and they bristled at their inability to do anything about it.

Most of the men at Goliad grumbled at the lack of Texas settlers among their ranks. Many of them had come to Texas with the romantic notion that they would be fighting shoulder-to-shoulder with their wronged brothers against a cruel and despotic Mexican government. More than once, they invoked the spirit of the American Revolution. Instead, they found themselves fighting alongside other idealists from the United States, or perhaps just as often, among rough adventurers, opportunists, and land speculators.

Fannin also complained that there was scarcely a colonist to be found among his men. Like his men, he felt betrayed and believed that the volunteers were doing the settlers' duties for them. In a note to Robinson he carped against the reluctance of those who actually lived in Texas to rally to his ranks. If a fight came and he and his men failed to carry the day, then the blame, he argued, should not fall on him and the volunteers, but rather "on those whose all is in Texas & who notwithstanding the repeated calls have remained at home without raising a finger to keep the Enemy from their thresholds."[9]

There were various reasons for the low participation rate among the settlers. A primary factor may have been that they simply did not care enough about the cause to risk their lives and their property: the grievances against Antonio López de Santa Anna and the Mexican government did not affect many of them in any important way. If they joined the rebellion and it was defeated, their lives and property would be in jeopardy. If, on the other hand, they simply stayed out of the fight, they would be no worse off regardless of which side won.

Many of the settlers saw no need to join the army. After all, there was no one or nothing to defend against. Following their successful eviction of General Martin Perfecto de Cos from San Antonio—a fight that the colonists had largely fought themselves—the Mexican army had left Texas. Some of them believed that, for all intents and purposes, the cause was already won.

From a practical standpoint, the settlers were farmers and ranchers. Raising crops and tending livestock took more manpower than was generally available—hence the ready market for Fannin's imported slaves the previous year. If the able-bodied men who muscled a life from the soil abandoned their farms, there would be no harvest or income to sustain their families into the next year. In fact, this consideration applied generally across the United States as well, as indicated by the occupations and stations in life of the American volunteers who had come to fight in Texas. There were few who left family and farms behind unless they left as young sons of established homesteads. Many of them were young men who had no wives, children, property, or even prospects.

The settlers also feared Indian attacks. The assorted tribes were a constant threat even when there were armed men to defend the farms. Undefended, the newly settled homesteads were at even greater risk. Indeed, Indians would continue to fight the settlement of Texas for several more decades beyond the revolution.

As has been mentioned before, many of the volunteers were rough men who acted in rough ways. They sometimes damaged or stole property, especially when drunk and especially when drunk around Mexicans—and being drunk was an all-day event for some of these men. The Georgia men alone were billed for seventy gallons of brandy during their time at the presidio. Duval described how that particular contingent of men gained their moniker:

> Not long after our arrival at Goliad the sobriquet of Mustangs or Wild Horses was acquired by our company from the following incident; M-, our second lieutenant, was a man of great physical powers, but withal one of the most peaceful and most genial men when not under the influence of liquor. But occasionally he would "get on a spree," and then he was as wild as a "March hare" and perfectly uncontrollable. The Mexicans seemed to know him and to fear him, also, and when he was on one of his "benders" they would retreat into their houses as soon as they saw him and shut their doors. This proceeding, of course, was calculated to irritate M-, and he would forthwith kick the door from its hinges. On a certain occasion he battered down the doors of half a dozen houses in one street; and from that time the Mexicans called him the Mustang, and finally the name was applied to the company.[10]

Obviously the behavior of some volunteers caused hard feelings among a number of the established settlers in Texas, particularly the Tejanos. This made the Tejanos less inclined—if they had ever been so inclined—to support the fight against Mexico.

Ever since George M. Collinsworth's company had taken it the previous October, the presidio had been referred to as Fort Goliad. Perhaps in an effort to boost the garrison's morale, Fannin undertook to rename it. Three names were considered: Fort Independence, Fort Defiance, and Fort Milam, a name suggested in honor of Benjamin Rush Milam, a veteran colonist and agitator who had escaped from Mexico City and was just making his way back into Texas when he fell in with Collinsworth's band as they seized the presidio. A sniper killed him just two months later as he helped lead the seige at San Antonio. The name Fort Defiance was chosen in a lottery, but it was not particularly popular and many of the men continued to call the presidio Fort Goliad either out of habit or as a purposeful show of disrespect to Fannin.

In this discussion of names it should be pointed out that the town of Goliad had not been known as such for very long. Since being founded in 1749—with the accompanying mission and presidio—it had been popularly known as La Bahía, the same name as the presidio. However, in 1829, the Mexican commander of the garrison at the presidio petitioned the government to change its name to Goliad, which was a near-anagram of Hidalgo, after Father Hidalgo, the priest who sparked Mexico's rebellion against Spain. Although the name was officially changed, the town continued to be known as La Bahía for many years afterward.

While the men at Goliad labored to fortify the old presidio under the direction of Chadwick and Brooks, William Travis and James Bowie and their nearly two hundred men who were under siege at the Alamo, the fortified mission in San Antonio, were becoming desperate. Santa Anna's army had been spotted outside San Antonio on February 23 and, realizing they were badly outnumbered, the volunteers sent a dispatch to Fannin at Goliad asking for help.

The plea arrived on February 25 and Fannin wasted little time. He gave orders for the garrison to start the next day to march the ninety miles to San Antonio in order to reinforce and resupply Travis and Bowie. His decision is questionable. He had to know that if the Mexicans had reached the Alamo on February 23, there was no reason to suppose that they would not have the mission invested in a viselike siege well before he could arrive. Also, realistically he would not be able to reach Travis and Bowie until February 29, at the earliest.

Fannin's judgment is even more curious because he surely was not foolish enough to believe that he could move his men into the Alamo without Santa Anna engaging him first, nor could he expect to surprise the Mexicans with an attack on their rear or flanks. The country between Goliad and San Antonio was settled with Tejanos, many of whom were sympathetic to Santa Anna. Their reports would give the Mexican forces plenty of time to prepare for Fannin's foray. Of course, Santa Anna also had his own cavalry for reconnaissance.

Regardless, Fannin left Captain Ira Westover and a small contingent at Goliad and started for San Antonio with nearly four hundred men on February 26, 1836. For their part, the New Orleans Greys were excited because their entire cadre would be reunited for the first time in months. The rest of the men, too, were keyed up because they were finally going to fight—most of them for the first time. Within an hour of starting, and essentially within sight of Goliad, they forded the San Antonio River, the same watercourse that ran past the presidio. The crossing presented no real problems for the volunteers, but one or more of the wagons were damaged and the men made camp until they could be mended. Things came undone from there.

Rather than an urgent mission to rescue comrades under siege, the expedition issuing from Goliad started to resemble a picnic gone bad. After spending the night in the wet and cold, the men woke to discover that the oxen had wandered off because no one had bothered to picket them, so there were no animals to pull the wagons that had presumably been repaired. It was then discovered that there was not enough food to feed the men during the journey. That being the case, the notion of resupplying the garrison at the Alamo was out of the question.

Fannin recorded that he was approached by the men and asked to convene a Council of War. In this meeting it was decided that, under the circumstances, the best course of action was to abandon Travis and Bowie and return the short distance to the presidio. It is not known for certain whether or not the New Orleans Greys were included in the Council of War. Accounts suggest that they would have clamored strongly for the march to continue, had they been included. On the other hand, it can hardly be imagined that they would have stood by while the others consulted.

Regardless of the Greys, this grotesquely pitiable effort underscores Fannin's lack of leadership and the absolute paucity of discipline exercised by his men. Aside from whether or not the decision to attempt to aid Travis and Bowie was a good one, the conduct of the relief march was deplorable. The rescuers essentially gave up before they even began.

The blame can hardly rest with anyone other than Fannin. Despite the need to hurry to San Antonio, a military leader with any sort of training, or even commonsense, would have inspected the men, their equipment, and their provisions before setting out. A good commander would have outlined his intentions for the march as well as his expectations on reaching the beleaguered defenders at the Alamo. In addition, an experienced commander would have picketed the livestock and posted guards during the overnight halt. Doing so was just basic frontier craft if nothing else. It is not recorded that Fannin ordered any of these actions.

And what of the broken wagon or wagons? Repairing them or getting replacements, especially so close to Goliad, should not have been an issue. And food? If there were enough rations for the volunteers to return and subsist at the presidio—only a mile or two away—surely they could have made a quick sortie to retrieve as much as necessary for the trek north.

One conclusion that comes to mind is that the wet, the wind, and the cold rain that fell overnight sucked the spirit of camaraderie and solidarity out of the men and their leader. It is likely that the bitter weather punched home the reality of the upcoming ninety-mile slog promised. That reality would have been misery for the poorly dressed, poorly fed, and poorly led volunteers. It is hard to imagine that they believed they would have been ready to take on Santa Anna's *soldados* when they reached San Antonio.

It could be supposed that Fannin knew that the rescue attempt was folly and simply went through the motions so that the men would discover for themselves that doing so was unrealistic. This supposition attributes more cleverness to Fannin than he probably was capable of exercising. Regardless, a good leader would not have needed to let the men discover such a thing themselves. In all likelihood, Fannin was lazy, ignorant, and afraid of his men, and simply let himself be swept along.

In fact, he no longer wanted to be their leader. None of the volunteers that trudged dispiritedly back into the presidio on February 27 knew that Fannin had already written to Robinson stating that he no longer desired the command at Goliad. In the first letter, written on February 21, he buried a single sentence in the body of his writing, but included no explanation. He wrote, "I hope you will soon release me from the army, at least as an officer."[11]

This was a peculiar statement, particularly because Fannin chose not to elaborate. Perhaps he was preparing Robinson for the letter he penned the following day. In it, among other matters, he reviewed his own difficult leadership position and complained about the volunteer army that he presumed to command. In mentioning the army, he meant the entire force of men that was fighting against the Mexican government, and not just the several hundred volunteers under his authority at Goliad.

One of his chief difficulties was that Grant and Johnson separately claimed the title of commander-in-chief for themselves. In addition, Houston—to whose authority and experience Fannin probably would have submitted—was keen to be at the fore again even if he had gone on furlough soon after Smith had been fired. The government, such as it was, did absolutely nothing to clear the matter.

Robinson, whose position as the acting governor was tenuous at best, considered Fannin his primary commander, perhaps because he had the most men in the field. Nevertheless, he never officially declared Fannin as the commander-in-chief of the revolutionary forces. No one during this time—not Fannin, not Grant, and not Johnson—was ever formally designated as such. Fannin rightfully bemoaned the absurdity of the entire situation in the second letter: "I am critically situated. General Houston is absent on furlough, and neither myself nor army have received any orders as to who should assume the command."[12]

In the same letter, he further complained about the nature of the force he headed: "I did not seek in any manner, the one I hold, and if I am qualified to command an army, I have not found it out." The implication here seems to be that the men under him hardly qualified as a real army. Fannin, who failed after more than two years to complete even the first year's curriculum at West Point, had the audacity to further declare, "I well know I am a better company officer than most men now in Texas, and might do with regulars, &c., for a regiment."[13] In other words, he believed that he might get better results if he had a regularly trained regiment under his command—as might any commander.

Fannin knew as well as anyone in Texas that trained regular regiments did not exist, nor would they in the immediate future, yet he consistently ignored this reality in dispatches to Robinson. Rather than working to transform the force he had, which was the only force he was going to get, he seemed to expect a trained regiment—shiny buttons and all—to arrive out of nowhere expressly for his command.

As February of 1836 drew to a close, Fannin had already acknowledged, at least to himself, his shortcomings as a leader in the face of adversity. He was ready to go home, but his timing could not have been worse. Santa Anna was outside the gates of the Alamo with an army that dwarfed anything that Texas could field, and General José Urrea was likewise sweeping up from the south with a considerable force of infantry and cavalry. The small successes the Anglos had enjoyed the previous several months would seem piddling compared to the setbacks about to come.

CHAPTER 7

Urrea's Invasion

The first of the Anglos' setbacks came in the very early morning of February 27, 1836, while James Walker Fannin and his miserable relief expedition was huddled against the cold and wet only a mile or so from Goliad. The defeat took place more than fifty miles to the south of Goliad at the predominantly Irish settlement of San Patricio. Francis W. Johnson and James Grant had made the tiny and largely deserted town the headquarters for their increasingly unlikely Matamoros expedition—and General José Urrea knew it.

The two men had been far afield with their small force raiding horses from ranches to the south. Johnson returned with a herd on February 26, while Grant, with about twenty men, stayed out and continued chasing up new mounts. At San Patricio, Johnson split his party of about thirty men, leaving a dozen of them to guard the horses that were corralled at the ranch of Julián de la Garza, about four miles south of town. While most of the rest of the men billeted themselves in homes on the main square, he chose to lodge in a house set farther back from the center of town.

Urrea commanded the army marching north out of Matamoros. Well informed by Mexican locals, he approached San Patricio from the south at the head of his column of cavalry and infantry. He dispatched Captain Rafael Pretalia with thirty men to deal with the group at the Garza ranch while he took the rest of his force to town. Pretalia surprised and attacked the Anglos at the Garza ranch, killing four of them and capturing the other eight.

Johnson's men that were bivouacked in the houses around the town square put up a fight as Urrea's men took them under fire. They were hopelessly outnumbered, and Urrea offered them their lives if they would lay down their arms. They refused, and fought until they were overwhelmed later that morning. In the meantime, Johnson, alerted by the sound of the fighting, escaped with five other men even though a contingent of *soldados* had his place surrounded.

Urrea recorded that sixteen men were killed and twenty-four taken prisoner, although this does not correlate with Anglo accounts, which place the numbers far lower. It is possible that noncombatants from the town were caught up in the fight, but nonetheless it was the first of several claims by Urrea that did not agree with other records.

Urrea was born in present-day Tucson, Arizona, and was a contemporary of Antonio López de Santa Anna's, but lacked all the conniving characteristics of his commander-in-chief. Despite this, or perhaps because of it, he had advanced through the ranks at a more moderate pace. He was respected as a capable commander and as a veteran of fighting dating back to the Mexican War of Independence of 1810–1821. He had spent the previous year helping Santa Anna put down the revolution in Zacatecas before campaigning against the Comanche in Durango, where he also served as the acting commandant general.

While Fannin and his men continued to make the presidio ready for a fight, the Convention of 1836 came together at Washington-on-the-Brazos on March 1, 1836, in response to a call by the General Council made the previous December. The provisional government that had been put in place in November 1835 following the Consultation was essentially paralyzed by the General Council's impeachment of Governor Henry Smith, and by Smith's subsequent refusal to recognize that impeachment, or Lieutenant Governor James Robinson's promotion to governor. The revolution badly needed a functioning government, and the gathering at Washington-on-the-Brazos would be a first step in providing it.

Convened in a cold, drafty building that local merchants provided in hopes of gaining a little extra business, the Convention eventually attracted fifty-nine representatives; most of those came from the districts not under immediate threat from the Mexican army. Whereas previous conventions and consultations skirted the issue of independence, that question had become largely moot by this time. After only one day, the delegates drafted and approved a declaration of independence on March 2, 1836, and began signing it the following day.

In the declaration, the representatives underscored the iniquitous nature of the government in Mexico City, and then highlighted what they perceived as their entitlement to protect themselves: "In such a crisis, the first law of nature, the right of self-preservation, the inherent and inalienable rights of the people to appeal to first principles, and take their political affairs into their own hands in extreme cases, enjoins it as a right towards themselves, and a sacred obligation to their posterity, to abolish such government, and create another in its stead, calculated to rescue them from impending dangers, and to secure their future welfare and happiness."[1]

The delegates further outlined their reasons for seeking independence. Their statements clearly show that they believed Mexico had misused them, and that the Mexican government had gone back on its promises. Santa Anna's abolishment of the Constitution of 1824 figured prominently in the discourse. Their ties to the United States as Americans were also made obvious:

> The Mexican government, by its colonization laws, invited and induced the Anglo-American population of Texas to colonize its wilderness under the pledged faith of a written constitution, that they should continue to enjoy that constitutional liberty and republican government to which they had been habituated in the land of their birth, the United States of America. In this expectation they have been cruelly disappointed, inasmuch as the Mexican nation has acquiesced in the late changes made in the government by General Antonio López de Santa Anna, who having overturned the constitution of his country, now offers us the cruel alternative, either to abandon our homes, acquired by so many privations, or submit to the most intolerable of all tyranny, the combined despotism of the sword and the priesthood.[2]

Although not especially elegantly composed or written, the declaration, with all its detail, makes a good case for the separation of Texas from Mexico. Toward that end, it implicitly asserts the superiority of the Texas Anglos over the Mexicans in the rest of the nation because "the Mexican people have acquiesced in the destruction of their liberty, and the substitution ther[e]for[e] of a military government; that they are unfit to be free, and incapable of self government."[3] Less than two months later, Santa Anna would declare essentially the same thing: "A hundred years to come my people will not be fit for liberty."[4]

The Convention stayed busy. On March 3, it passed resolutions for closing the land offices and made provisions for organizing ranger regiments. On March 4, the Convention elected General Samuel Houston commander-in-chief of both the regular army and the volunteers. This was significant because the provisional government had not tried to assert its authority—at least not with any vigor—over the volunteer fighters that were coming into Texas. Houston's temperament, ability, experience, and reputation made him the right man for this job. The appointment also meant that Fannin and his men at Goliad now fell indisputably under Houston's command.

On March 7, the Convention passed resolutions for organization of the army, to include the conscription of all males between seventeen and fifty years old; Finally, Fannin's pleas that all of Texas be mobilized had been heeded. Then, March 14 produced decisions that allowed land bounties of 1,280 acres for volunteer fighters who served the duration of the conflict, with lesser parcel sizes allotted for those who served less time.

The constitution—after having undergone numerous drafts and amendments—was completed on March 17. It declared Texas a republic and outlined a government very much like that of the United States with executive, legislative, and judicial branches. A president was to head its executive branch, a house of representatives and a senate would make up its legislative branch, and a supreme court would be included in its judicial branch. The constitution also included a declaration of rights similar to the U.S. Bill of Rights. The transition from Mexican law to that of the new republic was handled in a very practical manner: "That no inconvenience may arise from the adoption of this constitution, it is declared by this convention that all laws now in force in Texas, and not inconsistent with this constitution, shall remain in full force until declared void, repealed, altered, or expire by their own limitation."[5]

It was a real constitution based on a familiar and proven predecessor, but there was no time to ratify it. With Santa Anna's army loose in Texas and with much of the population either in flight or preparing for flight, the Convention elected an ad interim government comprising an executive branch only, with David G. Burnet (1788–1870)—the failed *empresario*—as its president. It would function as the government of Texas until such time as valid elections could be held and the constitution could be properly debated and ratified. On March 17, 1836, with Santa Anna's army a growing threat, the Convention dissolved, and its members dashed away to their respective duties. In the coming months, the ad interim government would oversee the revolution as best it could as it withdrew time and again, sometimes only hours ahead of the Mexican army.

Urrea and his men were busy killing Grant and the remainder of the stillborn Matamoros expedition on March 2, 1836—the same day that Houston and the members of the Convention were approving their declaration of independence. The Mexicans ambushed Grant's party of twenty men at Agua Dulce Creek, about twenty-five miles south of San Patricio. Of their number, twelve were killed, four were captured, and six managed to get away. Ironically, Captain Robert C. Morris, who had so urgently warned Fannin against the Matamoros expedition, was among the slain. Grant himself was also killed. Accounts vary as to how he actually met his end. The most gruesome story states that he was tethered to the legs of a wild mustang that, upon being released, trampled him into a pink bag of mush. Other records declare that he was simply shot. Ruben R. Brown paints a heroic picture of his leader:

> After [Grant and I] had run six or seven miles, they succeeded
> in surrounding us, when, seeing no further chance of escape, we
> dismounted, determined to make them pay dearly for our lives. As
> I reached the ground a Mexican lanced me in the arm and Grant
> immediately shot him dead, when I seized the lance to defend

myself. Just as he shot the Mexican I saw Grant fall, pierced with several lances, and a moment later I found myself fast in a lasso that [had] been thrown over me, and by which I was dragged to the ground. I could do no more. After Grant fell, I saw ten or a dozen officers go up and run their swords through his body.[6]

Although Santa Anna ordered Urrea to slay the men he captured at both San Patricio and Agua Dulce, Urrea did not do so. One account says that the Irish priest at San Patricio, Father Thomas Molloy, learned of Santa Anna's orders and protested to Urrea against the barbarity of such action. (Another person also protested this barbarism, who we will discuss in chapter 16: Francisca Alavéz, or the "Angel of Goliad.") Urrea backed down, and the men were not killed. For this, Santa Anna later upbraided him. Ironically, the only men of the Matamoros expedition ever to reach Matamoros arrived not as conquerors, but as Urrea's prisoners.

Many white settlers fled their ranches and properties as Santa Anna's forces advanced into Texas. Their fears were largely of the unknown: they simply had no idea what the *soldados* might do as they swarmed into the heart of the settled land. Abuses did occur, although the Mexican soldiers normally did not molest civilians, particularly when they were being closely watched by their officers. Indeed, many of the pioneers—particularly the Catholic Irish—fled south, deeper into Mexico, because they believed the chances of being caught up in the fighting would be less there.

On the other hand, in many cases the colonists' property was plundered. This was partly due to the fact that the Mexican supply situation was so spotty that the army had to rely in large part on what it could buy, borrow, or steal. It is also quite likely that the settlers' homesteads were sometimes ransacked out of spite or as a form of retribution for offenses real or imagined. Urrea wrote that after killing and capturing Johnson's men at San Patricio he received permission from Santa Anna to take whatever he needed or wanted: "His Excellency [Santa Anna] thanked me and praised me highly for my services, authorizing me to provide for my troops by taking cattle and supplies from the colonists as well as all their belongings."[7]

As a result of the already sparsely inhabited land becoming still less populated, the remaining settlers were even more vulnerable to marauding Indians, disaffected Tejanos, bands of Mexican soldiers, and Anglo thieves and renegades. Noah Smithwick remembered the villainy of Anglos against their own people: "There were men—or devils, rather—bent on plunder, galloping up behind the fugitives, telling them the Mexicans were just behind, thus causing the hapless victims to abandon what few valuables they had tried to save."[8]

The remaining families—particularly if they supported the revolution—often needed protection or help evacuating. The head of one of these families was Lewis T. Ayers (1798–1866). Ayers, who was thirty-seven years old, was a husband, father, and merchant. He was a native of New Jersey but had actively supported Texas rights after his arrival in 1834. Ayers recorded how, as Santa Anna's forces advanced into the region, Tejanos and Indians ransacked the homes and outbuildings that the Anglos had left: "There has been a good deal o[f] plundering during the day by the Mexicans and Indians, Feather beds opened and feathers scattered to the winds, for the purpose of ascertaining if there was any money secreted in them[.] In the morning [of February 28, 1836,] a party of 7 Rancheros came armed to my house for the purpose of plunder, but seeing Mrs. Foley my brother-in-law A. Osborne and myself all well armed they did not think it best to attempt it and were quite civil."[9]

A survivor from Grant's party, David Moses, wandered onto Ayers' ranch on March 3. Ayers wasted little time in starting for Goliad with Moses. His motivation was attributable in part to his wife's insistence. He had received numerous threats from Tejanos, and she feared for his safety until such time as the situation was stabilized. On arriving at Goliad, Ayers dined with Fannin and some of his staff and asked for help in getting his family and others escorted from where they were hunkered down at Refugio to someplace more secure. Fannin assented to help when he could, but at that time his wagons and oxen were bringing back much-needed supplies from Port Lavaca.

Ayers stayed on at Goliad, "seemingly in the greatest mental agony," while the garrison continued to fortify the presidio.[10] Meanwhile, Fannin nervously awaited the stores his men so desperately required. In fact, many uncertainties tormented him during this period. He knew nothing of the situation at the Alamo, ninety miles to the northwest, except that the circumstances there were desperate. The garrison's commander, William Travis, had directly asked him for help on at least two separate occasions, but Fannin had not replied to the first request and his response to the second on February 25 had been worse than feeble.

Fannin also, no doubt, realized that regardless of the outcome at San Antonio, his reputation would suffer. If Travis and James Bowie held out, they would be the heroes who managed to fend off Santa Anna's army even though Fannin refused to help. On the other hand, if Travis and Bowie were defeated, their loss would largely be blamed on Fannin and his failure to relieve them. The beleaguered commander was also lonesome for his family. He lamented his separation from them as one of the principal reasons he wished to be freed from his post: "After near eighteen months absence, nothing but dire necessity can keep me from my wife and children."[11]

His apprehension was understandable. Life in Texas was hard: sickness, accidents, and Indian raids took a heavy toll on families. Keeping in touch with loved ones was difficult, as well. Letters passed across the interior via foot or horseback, but not everyone was literate and much news was conveyed by word of mouth. In addition, letters were often lost, destroyed, or simply not delivered. Mexican patrols or spies or even rival factions often intercepted official correspondence. This made administering the dysfunctional revolutionary government even more difficult.

John Sowers Brooks was among the most prolific letter writers among the men at Goliad. His correspondences, written from the perspective of a young, homesick adventurer, provide a unique outlook of the goings-on within Fannin's command. He sent many messages home but received no replies. In the last few of his letters, he chastised his family for what he perceived as their lack of regard for his want of their news. He was especially harsh with his sister, Mary Ann Brooks:

> My dear Sister: Another opportunity of writing to you occurs, and I embrace it because they are infrequent, and becoming hourly more so. The precarious channel, through which all letters must arrive at, or go from this place, affords, indeed, the only satisfactory explication of your mysterious silence; and the belief that yours have been intercepted or miscarried, is consoling indeed, for it renders doubtful what, in my moments of desperation, I have often feared is certain that you had forgotten your poor, wayward brother. Why is it so? Why have you not written? War, it is true, "opens a vein that bleeds Nations to death," but why should it invade the sanctity of social connection? Why should it dissolve fraternal bonds or sunder domestic ties? Is it necessary that we should be morally, as well as physically separated? That the associations of infancy, the remembrances of child hood, the anticipations of youth, and the common pleasures, hopes, and fears of better and happier days, should be forgotten and we pursue our weary and desolate track through life, as if neither had existed? Is it necessary because we are separated, because the billows of the Atlantic, or the Pillars of the Alleghany [*sic*] are between us, that all the ties which bound us, in other days should be severed? I trust not. Why then do you not avail yourself of that medium of communion, which language proffers? Have I rendered myself unworthy of your affection?[12]

Brooks' desperation for word from loved ones was probably shared by the rest of the men who made up the garrison at Goliad. Mail service from the States, usually via New Orleans, was unreliable at best. In combination with the other shortages, the dearth of news from home did much to hurt their morale. Pay for the volunteers—or its lack—was another constant source of complaint. Brooks wrote in one letter, "Do not fail to write me immediately, and send me some money if possible. I am very much in want of it, I assure you. The Government has obtained a loan and will soon pay us off—when I can pay you." In another later note he wrote: "I have neither clothes nor money to buy them. The Government furnishes us with nothing, not even ammunition."[13] At this later date, Brooks seemed to hold little hope that anything good would come from the revolutionary government.

The acute shortages of nearly everything were remedied somewhat on March 10 and 11 when fresh supplies were brought in from Port Lavaca. Foodstuffs, clothes, and ammunition were now more readily available. The supply trains included more cattle and several wagonloads of corn.

A party of eighteen men made up largely of Captain Jack Shackelford's Red Rovers, under the command of William Francis, met this supply train en route. Fannin had sent them from the presidio on March 10 to investigate reports of spies from Santa Anna's army hiding among the Tejano populace. After meeting the supply wagons, the party continued south to scout for the locals, most of whom had left the town at this point. The bellicose attitudes of the volunteers as well as the danger of a fight at the presidio had caused them to move to ranches about fifteen miles south of the town. There they hoped to wait out the coming fight in relative safety.

There was no doubt that some among the displaced Tejanos were sympathetic to the government in Mexico City and that they provided intelligence about Fannin's disposition to Santa Anna's army. Fannin knew this, but there was little he could do except attempt to gather his own intelligence where he could, or to make an effort to intimidate those who might be predisposed to work against the revolutionary cause. At the same time, it was important for him to try to inculcate goodwill toward the rebellion, or at the very least endeavor not to alienate those who were indifferent to the cause. Nevertheless, these were difficult tasks, particularly considering that most of the volunteers were newcomers to the region and understood little of the local language or customs.

Francis' foray produced no significant results during the next couple of days. The party came on a group of displaced townspeople on March 11 and was welcomed and fed by them. Dr. Joseph Barnard recorded their generosity and the fact that the Tejanos candidly communicated to them that they had left Goliad at least in part because of the disruptive behavior of the volunteers: "They received us kindly, and treated us with hospitality, professed the warmest hospitality to our cause, and denied having any communication with the Mexican army. They gave us a reason for leaving town and coming here, that many of the volunteers were unruly and turbulent, disposed to impose on them and their families, and that to avoid any quarrels with them they had removed."[14]

Just as he had promised Ayers, Fannin dispatched a mission to Refugio on March 11—the same day that Francis and his men stumbled on the refugee townspeople. That sortie, under the leadership of Captain Amon B. King (1807–1836), was charged with bringing back the Ayers family and any other Anglos that wished to evacuate the Refugio area. King had spent time there with his men during January and presumably was familiar with the area. In order to carry out his orders, Fannin had given King thirty men and all of the garrison's oxen, wagons, and carts.

After setting out from Goliad at about nine in the morning, King's men marched hard and reached Refugio that same evening. There they found most of the Anglo families from the area taking sanctuary at Mission Nuestra Señora del Refugio. Sabina Brown Fox, one of the colonists, remembered the braggadocio of the volunteers and that "they said to one another 'Jolly, now for a fight, maybe they will come tonight.'"[15]

King's men bedded down for the evening at the mission. To their disappointment, the Mexican fighters did not show that night. The next morning, they set out for the nearby Esteban López ranch where Ayers' family, among others, was taking refuge. While recovering this group, King—who had been the town marshal of Paducah, Kentucky, for several years—arrested a small band of six Mexicans, "including Judge Incarnation Basques of Goliad," that had been plundering nearby homes.[16] From them he learned that there was yet another group of marauders approximately eight miles to the south. Ignoring his primary mission of evacuating the Anglo families, King took more than half of his men in pursuit of the other group.

King's insubordination headed him straight into trouble. Rather than arresting and punishing the second band, he and his men were ambushed themselves by a group of rancheros and Karankawa Indians led by Captain Carlos de la Garza (1807–1882). Escaping without loss, he and his men gathered the Anglo families and fled back to Mission Nuestra Señora del Refugio where they were taken under siege. The siege was strengthened when Garza and his men were joined by lead elements of Urrea's cavalry.

The volunteers inflicted significant casualties and even captured some prisoners during the clashes through the rest of the day and into the night, but they were trapped. They were going nowhere, and neither were the animals and carts that Fannin needed so badly back at Goliad.

Francis led his group back into the presidio on March 12 to find the garrison in somewhat of a tumult. There was excitement and anxiety over King's mission about which there had been no news. On the same day, an express dispatch arrived from Houston. The message directed both Fannin and James C. Neill—who was at Gonzales at the head of about four hundred men—to march immediately for the Alamo. Fannin straightaway began preparations to set out with three hundred men for Cibolo Creek, where he planned to meet

Houston. Still, the garrison could move no cannon or supplies until King and his men returned from Refugio with the oxen and wagons.

Later—probably on the same day—the news they all feared arrived: the Alamo had fallen and the entire garrison had been slain. Those few men who had survived the fall of the fort had subsequently been killed on Santa Anna's orders. Fannin no doubt considered himself to be substantially responsible for the catastrophe.

Discouraging reports continued to arrive. Late the night of March 12, an Irishman from Refugio arrived with a dispatch describing how King and his men were trapped at the Refugio mission; they were low on ammunition and had little hope of holding their position or escaping without help.

Fannin had put his command and, by extension, the revolution at risk by sending his entire transport on a mission to evacuate a scattering of families that may or may not have been in immediate danger. Doing so with such a small group as King's, especially with the knowledge that Mexican units were in the area, had been foolhardy.

He now had several options. First, he could leave King and his men to their own devices and continue to consolidate his position at the presidio while awaiting an attack from one or more of Santa Anna's armies. This course of action left open the possibility that, in the aftermath of the catastrophe at the Alamo, the colonists might be energized to rally to his flag. With his ranks thus augmented by fresh and fervent fighters, Fannin and his men stood a much better chance of resisting an onslaught by the Mexican army.

But abandoning King would have been unpopular with his men and would have definitely engendered more hate toward him from the volunteers. They may even have mutinied. Still, militarily, King's men made up only a small percentage of his forces. Emotions aside, rescuing them was a proposition that presented more risk than value.

A second option was to raze the presidio, spike the cannon, and make a fast march to link up with Houston and Neill. (To "spike" a cannon meant smashing a hot metal spike down the touchhole of the barrel where the fuse was ignited, and then breaking it off. With the touchhole thus blocked, the gun was rendered into a big, heavy, useless, metal tube.) This alternative of linking up with Neill and Houston—without the heavy guns—had a reasonable chance of success and would have had the effect of creating the largest revolutionary force in the field to that point. A formation of a thousand or more fighters might stand a chance against Santa Anna's armies.

But again, this course of action presented thorny problems for Fannin. Aside from deserting King and his men, Fannin's fighters would be forced to abandon a formidable bastion that they had fortified with their own hands. The men were still spoiling for a fight and were confident that behind their newly reinforced redoubt—notwithstanding the disaster at the Alamo—they could withstand any siege.

Another downside to a withdrawal would be the requirement to destroy newly received and much-needed supplies; these were supplies that were necessary all across the revolution. They had been procured and delivered at great expense, and the decision to burn them could not be taken lightly. The cannon were also valuable and not easily replaced, and the fledgling revolutionary army needed the firepower that they provided. Defeating Santa Anna and his army on the contemporary battlefield without artillery would be a long shot. Fannin knew that spiking the big guns and leaving them behind would draw condemnation and censure.

In the end, Fannin took an enormous risk. He decided to split his already diminished force in order to save King and retrieve his transport. Fannin directed William Ward, his second-in-command and also the commander of the Georgia Battalion, to head up a formation of about 120 men to march to King's relief.

Ayers, especially anxious for his family now that King had run into trouble, was invited by Fannin to help guide Ward and his men to Refugio. Nevertheless, Ayers had trouble procuring a mount. Fannin's behavior, as described by Ayers, provides a glimpse of Fannin as a leader. It shows his reluctance to cause offense and his inability to make an unpopular decision: "Having been detained here for want of a Horse [until] this time I have volunteered my services and Col Fannin has consented—I ought to have stated that I had been told by Col. F. to take any Horse I could find, in censequence [sic] I had got up several one at a time when some volunteer officer or private would claim them and be permitted by Col. F. to take them away for sake of union and peace while at the same tim[e] he thought it important that I should m[ake] all possible haste."[17]

Ward started his column for Refugio several hours before daylight on March 13. The prairie was sloppy wet and the going was difficult, yet the men covered the twenty or so miles by late that afternoon. Details are scant, but it appears that Ward's formation was much larger than the group of Mexicans that had King holed up at the mission at Refugio. Nothing more than a "single salute from their rifles served to drive off the enemy, who had invested King in his position."[18] The ensuing mayhem caught the besieging Mexicans completely by surprise. Indeed, a fully saddled, panic-stricken horse nearly ran into the church where the huddled families were cooking their evening meals.

Ward asked after King and was met by an unnamed "redhead with a white palmetto hat" who answered that he was "not the keeper of Capt. King."[19] There were more verbal exchanges before the redhead—obviously not a supporter of the rebellion—stalked out of the mission. The volunteers would see more of him during the next day or so.

This incident is indicative of the friction generated by the revolution. Colonists—Tejanos and Anglos alike—often shared different political views but otherwise coexisted reasonably well. It was only when forced to choose a side that those political differences ruptured into hostility. As this episode shows, race did not always delineate the two sides—not every Anglo supported the revolution.

Once he arrived at the mission at Refugio, Ward disobeyed Fannin's orders. Rather than collecting the various families and immediately returning to Goliad with King, he delayed. He did this even knowing that Urrea's army was somewhere nearby. Certainly his men were tired, and unquestionably it would have taken time to get the families ready for the march, but the need to get to safety was urgent. Returning the wagons and oxen to Goliad was even more critical than resting, and time was running out.

Ward and King wasted time arguing. Their clash was another manifestation of the discord and contentiousness often typical of the volunteer army. Without so much as a nod to the chain of command, King declared that he was familiar with the area and that he knew the military situation best. He then asserted that Ward should give up command of his men to him. Of course, Ward, who was second-in-command to Fannin and therefore senior to King, disagreed. In the meantime, Urrea's army continued to close in on Refugio.

That the volunteer contingent did not start immediately for Goliad was no doubt attributable in part to the fact that the men were simply spoiling for a fight. References to this passion appear repeatedly in various accounts dealing with the revolution. If nothing else, it appears that the men who came to Texas for a scrap were determined in their pursuit. Of course, one of the duties of an officer is to ensure that enthusiastic troops fight not where and when they want to, but at the best place and time to defeat the enemy. Both Ward and King failed in this duty.

Ward let the volunteers off the leash on the evening he arrived. He gave Isaac Ticknor permission to mount a quick foray against one of the nearby Mexican camps. What practical purpose this was intended to achieve is unknown. At any rate, Ticknor led fourteen men beyond the mission's walls toward the Mexican positions. He and his party, as related by Joseph W. Andrews, "crept up [slyly] upon the enemy; and firing on them & keeping it up for a few rounds retired in safety to the mission without the loss of a man or having one wounded."[20]

Regardless of the raid's purpose, its execution was a success. Ward went out to the scene the next morning and counted twenty-two dead Mexicans. He returned to the Refugio mission with several horses that the Mexicans had abandoned; they were still in full tack with bridles and saddles.

Among the dead was one of a group of Mexican artillerymen to whom, just a few days earlier on March 11, Fannin had granted an honorable discharge. These men had been led by Captain Luis Guerra with whom they had earlier fought as Federalists as part of General José Antonio Mexía's force against Santa Anna's Centralist government. After the Centralist victory at Tampico, they joined Fannin to continue the fight against Santa Anna. However, the recent declaration of independence put them in an awkward situation, and they declined to fight against their own people.

Lewis M. H. Washington's account held that a Mexican spy had approached them with a message from Urrea. He paraphrased Urrea's offer, "a full pardon for their former 'traitorous and libelous conduct at Tampico,' if they would 'forsake the ignoble and criminal cause of the *pirates*,' as the volunteers were termed, 'and return, like *honorable Mexicans*, to the glorious and triumphant standard of their *blessed* country.' But in the event of their obstinately refusing to accept the magnanimous offer extended to them, they would, just as certain as the *Blessed Virgin* was then looking down from Paradise upon them, be captured and executed as traitors, *without the benefit of clergy*" [emphasis in original].[21]

Fannin sympathized with Guerra and his men and recognized the difficult situation they were in. In truth, except for Guerra himself, Fannin had never thought much of the Mexican artillerists. Washington recorded that Fannin "had never viewed them as being efficient or reliable." In fact the chief reason he accepted them into his command two months earlier was that they brought with them two good artillery pieces: "double-fortified long sixes."[22] When he granted them discharges—with the understanding that Guerra and his men would proceed to New Orleans and take no more part in the war—he probably believed that he was not losing an effective fighting component, but rather getting rid of dead weight and a potential source of perfidy. It is believed that Guerra ultimately made his way to New Orleans while the rest of his artillerymen rejoined the Mexican army.

Later in the morning of March 14, Ward and King had still not agreed how to join or lead their forces. A withdrawal to Goliad was not the priority. King, apparently responding to Ayers' pleading, took Ayers and a group of his own men to a ranch approximately six miles to the south. There he hoped to capture and punish more marauders as well as recover some of Ayers' property. At the same time, Ward sent Warren J. Mitchell (d. 1836) with a small party to reconnoiter the area immediately beyond the mission. After torching some deserted ranches, the small group was taken under fire while refilling a pair of barrels from the Mission River that ran nearby. Mitchell and his men raced back to the mission and suffered no harm.

Urrea and his army had finally arrived.

CHAPTER 8

Clash at Refugio

O n March 14, at the same time that Warren J. Mitchell and his reconnoitering party rushed back into the Mission Nuestra Señora del Refugio, the Mexicans prepared their attack. General José Urrea knew that a difficult fight was in store, later writing, "I reconnoitered their position to my satisfaction; and, convinced that it afforded means for a good defense, I realized that in order to take it I would be obliged to suffer heavy losses."[1] The Mexican commander had nearly a thousand men in place that morning; as stragglers and scouts rejoined his army, that number increased by several more hundred. Urrea would not be timid about committing them to the coming clash.

William Ward readied the volunteers for the assault. Although the mission was not a fort, and was not intended to garrison troops or serve as a strongpoint, it was still the stoutest structure in the area and afforded Ward and the rest of his men decent protection. Also, on three sides of the church the Mexicans would have little cover to use during their attack; the approaches to the mission were well guarded by the Anglo fighters. To the rear of the compound was a walled yard that extended perhaps fifty yards. Behind the yard, the ground sloped steeply and could not be covered with fire from the mission. Ward posted men at the rear wall of the yard to protect this approach.[2]

The Mexicans mounted their first attack with cavalry and infantry from all four quarters simultaneously; they were supported by a single cannon. On three sides they charged hard and loud, in lines abreast, while up the slope behind the walled yard they came silently in column, hoping to surprise the defenders. Ward ordered his men to hold their fire until the enemy was close: they had no ammunition to spare, having marched from Goliad with only thirty-six rounds of ammunition apiece.

The volunteers fired their first volley, and "as many Mexicans [as rounds fired] bit the dust."[3] Ward's volunteers made good use of their ammunition. The Mexican ranks faltered in places and a few groups retreated, but generally the advance continued. A second volley decimated the attacking formation, and the Mexicans retreated on three sides.

The *soldados* coming up the slope behind the churchyard were surprised as the volunteers rose up behind the wall almost as one and fired their first rounds. An excerpt from Urrea's *Diario* recalls this particular scene: "Our advance was so successful that the infantry arrived within ten paces of the cemetery without a single man being wounded. The enemy, coming out of its lethargy, opened up a lively fire upon our men. The troops, being mostly recruits from Yucatán, stopped spellbound the moment their first impetus was spent, and all efforts to force them to advance were unavailing."[4]

The forward lines of the attackers were felled and it seemed as if the whole of the force advancing on the churchyard would pull back. Nevertheless, the officers rallied their wavering *soldados*, and the Mexicans moved forward once again. This attack was bolstered by simultaneous charges against the flanks of the churchyard. At almost the same time, a renewed assault on the front of the church was mounted.

Ward maintained his post at the churchyard wall where he could best urge on his men. Most of the men fighting there were Georgians and few of them were older than eighteen. The defenders on each side of the church added their fire to the defense at the rear as the revolutionaries beat back attacks from the flanks. It was not long before the *soldados* "fled like frightened deer" under the accurate and intensive fire of the volunteers.[5] To his credit, an excerpt from Urrea's *Diario* corroborates this observation: "I, therefore, ordered a retreat. This operation was not carried out with the order that might have been expected from better disciplined troops."[6]

At the front of the church, however, the Mexican officers held their fighters to task. Several attempts to close the distance to the wall nearly succeeded. The ground near the church was littered with bodies. The numbers of Mexicans mounting each successive attempt dwindled until finally the remaining *soldados* gave up and fled to the river. As the attack abated, Ward and his men hoped that Urrea would decide that the value of their position was not worth the cost he was incurring.

The morning of that same day, March 14, Captain Amon B. King and his men were still far afield when Mitchell and his group raced back into the mission just ahead of Urrea's army. Oblivious to the situation at Refugio, King and his party ambushed and killed eight Mexicans sitting at a campfire. The circumstances surrounding this attack are not well recorded, but among the decimated group was another of Captain Luis Guerra's artillerymen. On this *soldado's* body were found letters from Urrea that dated from the period when Guerra and his cohort were still serving under James Walker Fannin. The rest of the slain men were local rancheros, and their part in the fighting is unknown. That they were combatants is not a certainty: it is possible they were bystanders caught in the crossfire.

After passing through several deserted ranches, King led his group back toward Refugio in the late morning. When the men heard gunfire from the direction of the town reverberating over the scrubby, tree-dotted prairie, they knew that Ward was under attack. Less than a mile from the mission, they stumbled into the rear of Urrea's army, which numbered more than a thousand. With flight the only option, King and his men raced for a wooded area near the river, less than half a mile distant. Reacting quickly, Mexican horsemen gave chase but were unable to catch the volunteers before they reached the woods. During this rush, six of the volunteers were separated from the rest of the group. Whether they deserted, were wounded or killed, or just could not keep up is unknown.

Under cover of the trees, the rest of the volunteers hastily went to ground, took up defensive positions, and prepared for the Mexican attack. It came soon enough. After months of waiting for a real fight, King and his men now fought for their lives.

Ward's group—itself under siege—heard the shots as King and his men were taken under fire. A hurried relief force was organized and the would-be rescuers sallied toward the fight. Almost immediately, the main body of Urrea's formation intercepted them while a unit of cavalry began a maneuver to cut them off from the safety of the mission. With nearly a thousand troops between them and King, and with their escape route back to the mission in jeopardy, they recognized the rescue attempt was foolhardy. Accordingly, Ward withdrew them back to the mission. King and his men were on their own.

Ward's hope that Urrea would give up his assault on the mission was not realized. Another attack came a few hours after the first. The second assault lacked the ferocity of the first, but whereas the volunteers had survived the initial assault without suffering any casualties whatsoever, the second resulted in the death of Thomas Weeks from Mississippi, who caught a musket ball in his chest.[7]

The second attack also saw the reappearance of the "red-head that wore a white palmetto hat" who had exchanged harsh words with Ward the previous afternoon. The orange-haired Anglo helped to lead the *soldados* in their assault on the mission. The volunteers readily recognized him and singled him out, but failed to hit him. Sabina Brown Fox, one of the colonists taking protection within the church, remembered how "sulphur smoke rose high in the air and rifles of the Georgians rattled like shot in a gourd, and they whooped for joy when they saw the Mexicans fall, but they did not get that redheaded fellow they wanted so bad."[8]

The Mexicans did not lack resolve. A third attack followed the second, but this attempt to breach the walls was likewise unsuccessful. Sometime during the afternoon the Mexicans brought up another small cannon. The volunteers feared that the attackers would load the gun with "hot shot" to start the roof of the church blazing. To counter this threat, the call went up to concentrate fire on the *soldados* tending the cannon. From the church's belfry, Ward's sharpshooters shot and killed the Mexican gunners. Next, the men stormed the Mexican lines and brought back the cannon: "Out they went over heaps of dead Mexicans while their comrades in the belfry were dropping Mexicans thick and fast around the cannon. They reached it and took it without losing a single man and rolled it into the church and a yell went up that seemed to shake the rafters of the house."[9]

Through the day, the defenders continued to kill Mexican *soldados* with their rifle and musket fire. Contemporary accounts describe piles of Mexican *soldados*, both dead and wounded. Volunteer losses were light; after Weeks was killed during the second assault, only a few more men were hit. One Georgian named Hall was struck in the leg after racing out to cut the saddle from an abandoned Mexican horse. Abraham Osborne—Lewis T. Ayers' brother-in-law—was hit in the breast, while Ward himself was lightly creased in the head by a musket ball.[10]

Mexican casualties incurred at Refugio are difficult to confirm. Anglo eyewitness accounts range from approximately sixty to more than four hundred killed, but the higher number is likely much overstated. Mexican records are confusing. Urrea's second-in-command, Colonel Francisco Garay, admitted thirteen dead and forty-three wounded, but it is difficult to determine whether this was in just one of the day's assaults or all of them. Garay's description opens with criticism of Urrea for pressing the attack beyond what Garay believed was reasonable:

> He allowed them to advance farther and to remain where they were after exhausting the ammunition of their cartridge belts, the only ones they were carrying, at about thirty yards distance. For a good period of time they were exposed to the accurate fire of the enemy, suffering considerable damage and unable on their part to return the fire. Those in charge of the cannon found themselves obliged to abandon it since it was located so close to the building that they could not maintain possession of it. An extraordinary effort was necessary to pull it back, and this was finally done with considerable losses. Although at the beginning only three detachments were sent to attack the enemy, as soon as the latter took refuge in the church, the rest of our foot soldiers got into the fight, and even part of the Cuautla cavalry advanced also on foot.

However, it was all in vain. Strong in their position because of our lack of caution, they mocked us with impunity, causing us to pay dearly for our rashness. We had on our part thirteen dead and forty-three wounded, among them four officers, and they had had only one man wounded.[11]

For his part, Urrea explicitly stated in his *Diario* that he lost only six infantry and five dragoons, all of whom were killed by the volunteers on March 14.[12] Despite this claim, the likelihood that the number of *soldados* killed was very high can be inferred from the note that Urrea put into his *Diario* for the next day, March 15. The entry makes it obvious that he was sensitive to criticisms of his leadership. Those criticisms very probably centered on the excessive losses that his men sustained: "Envy and calumny have united in trying to denounce me for the engagement of the 14th. Those who have criticize [*sic*] my conduct were ignorant of my position and of the intentions of the enemy."[13] Regardless of the casualty count, Ward and his volunteers still held the church at Refugio at the end of the afternoon on March 14.

King and his men defended themselves as stoutly as Ward and his group did. On the ground and among the cover of the trees, they had an advantage over the attacking Mexican cavalry and infantry. Ayers recorded that the Mexicans attacked almost immediately after King's men hastily set up their defensive position. The fighting lasted about half an hour until the Mexicans fell back, leaving about twenty of their dead and wounded on the ground. King's group sustained no casualties.[14]

An hour later, King's group was attacked again, this time from two sides. After an hour of fighting, the Mexicans withdrew again, and again left behind a large number of killed and wounded. Whereas the volunteers had sustained no casualties in the first short engagement, this time a man immediately next to Ayers was killed. A musket ball shattered King's arm, and four other men were wounded. Ayers himself barely escaped injury when a musket ball struck one of a pair of pistols that he had fastened to his waist.

Ayers recorded that the Mexicans undertook a third attack on King's men from the opposite side of the river as dusk turned to dark, but that they inflicted no harm. "Capt. King then directed us to lie close, protecting ourselves as much as possible by the woods, and not to fire again, holding ourselves in readiness for an expected attack on our side of the river, which however did not take place, the enemy after wasting as I suppose all their powder and ball and without doing us any personal injury, retired."[15]

Urrea claimed his men killed eleven of King's party and captured seven, which illustrates again the disparity between the claims on both sides: both sides exaggerated. Ayers' account suggests that the Mexicans must have suffered more than twenty killed during the attacks, but neither Urrea nor Garay admitted any casualties as a result of the assaults against King's group.

When it came, the night was dark and rainy. King led his group, now numbering about twenty, under cover of the dark across the Mission River. He took them across without regard to the water's depth, as he believed, probably rightly, that the fords would be guarded. As it developed, the water was more than chest deep and the men were unable to keep their powder dry. Upon reaching the other side, the bank was so steep that the men scrabbled in the dirt and mud and were able to climb to level ground only by boosting and pulling each other up. The wounded men suffered greatly in these exertions.

Once across the river, King started his men toward Goliad.

At the mission, as late afternoon turned to dusk, the main force of Mexicans withdrew out of rifle range to their encampment approximately a quarter of a mile away. There they set up pickets about a hundred yards apart in order to keep Ward and his volunteers from escaping.

Ward needed to do something. His men were exhausted, hungry, thirsty, and nearly out of ammunition. Worse, Urrea had them surrounded with a force numbering more than a thousand men and was presumably planning to renew his attack in the morning. The situation looked like another Alamo in the making. Ward dispatched two men to Goliad with requests for help.[16]

At about this time, a message for Ward arrived from Fannin. In the message, Fannin directed Ward to leave Refugio and meet the remainder of the Goliad garrison at Victoria. Ward asked the messenger, an elderly man, to guide his column to Goliad. The man reminded Ward of the fable of old dog Tray. In this tale, a good dog is caught among a pack of sheep killers and subsequently slaughtered alongside the culpable dogs. In short, Ward would not have the man's services that night.[17]

Fannin's new orders created a dilemma for Ward. Ward's original mission had been to rescue King and several families. Now, surrounded by a large army, he had no idea what had happened to King and had no good way to escort the settlers out of harm's way. In addition, a quick retreat to Victoria would require him to leave his few wounded men behind. They would be left to the mercy of the same men that the volunteers had been engaged in bloody combat with earlier that day.

All these concerns aside, actually slipping out of the church, through the Mexican lines, and across thirty-five miles of countryside to Victoria would be no easy task. On foot, even without the settlers they had been sent to rescue, his men would be easy prey for the Mexican cavalrymen on the open prairie. He would have to lead them via river bottoms and wooded areas as much as possible, so that they would more easily be able to evade the enemy cavalry.

Another message came to the volunteers very late that night from Garay, commander of the Mexican infantry. He sent Edward Perry, an Irish colonist who had been captured that same evening. Perry had been carrying Fannin's reply to Ward when he was caught. Garay, presumably to make certain that the volunteers knew that the Mexicans were now aware of Fannin's plans, forwarded the message to Ward. In the dispatch Fannin related that he had orders from General Samuel Houston directing him to destroy the fortifications at Goliad and retreat to Victoria. Ward knew that he could expect no help from Fannin.

Perry also relayed Urrea's demand that the volunteers surrender. Urrea warned that heavier artillery would arrive on the following day and that he planned to batter down the church. If Ward and his men did not surrender immediately, Urrea would show them no quarter the next day. Ward directed the Irishman to return and defy Urrea's surrender demand. The volunteers would not give up the fight and preferred to sell their lives dearly. Accordingly, Ward's answer was delivered by Perry, who survived the day and even the revolution.

Despite his bravado, Ward did not want to continue to fight against impossible odds; he gave orders to abandon the mission. The men prepared to leave, but there was no water for the few wounded men who they were going to leave behind. In the dark, a sortie was launched to a spring located within the Mexican lines. They ambushed several *soldados* guarding the rivulet and killed four of them while several others escaped into the night. Water gourds were filled and taken to the wounded, who the men had wrapped in blankets taken from slain Mexicans. Having done as much as they could for their wounded comrades, Ward and his men departed them "with tears and sobs," and slipped away from the mission into what had become a rainy night.[18]

An episode in the church accentuates the lack of military training among the volunteers. As the men made ready to escape, they tried to wake up Henry Wood who was—like all of them—no doubt exhausted after the day's fight. Wood refused to rise: he believed he was being rousted for guard duty. Unable to get him to his feet, the volunteers left him behind. They also left behind William Simpson to help protect the dozen or so colonist women and children who were sheltered in the church.

Ward's men slipped through the Mexican pickets without being attacked. No doubt they were aided by the dark, rainy night. On the one hand, moving more than a hundred men through the lines of a force made up of more than a thousand *soldados* was certainly no easy task. On the other hand, perhaps the volunteers were simply allowed to pass through. A cold, lonely, and frightened sentry, or even a small group of sentries, may have chosen survival over valor. Sounding the alarm could have been fatal: the volunteers had been lethal all through the previous day. Or, the sentries could simply have been asleep.

Urrea remarked on the escape of the volunteers: "In order to prevent their escape, I placed several lookouts at the points through which they might effect it, but the necessary vigilance was not exercised by all of them and the enemy escaped, favored by the darkness of the night which a strong norther and the rain made more impenetrable and unbearable. On the other hand, our troops were very much fatigued as a result of having marched all the day and the night before and of having spent the 14th in constant fighting without taking food."[19]

Regardless of how or why they were able to escape, Ward and his men initially traveled southeast toward Copano rather than north toward Victoria as Urrea expected. Whether this was by design or by mistake is not known, but it probably accounted for the fact that, although they nearly stumbled back into the Mexican lines several times, they were not detected. By the morning of the next day, having regained their bearings and gotten clear of the Mexicans, they started for Victoria.

That morning, Urrea's men entered the church at Refugio. Two of the wounded volunteers were bayoneted to death. Accounts conflict on whether Wood and Simpson escaped or also were killed. Osborne survived: the women hid him between two mattresses.

With the help and collusion of one of the newly released Mexican prisoners that King's men had rounded up only a few days earlier, the women managed to carry Osborne and the mattresses to a nearby house. Mrs. Osborne was successful in gaining an audience with Urrea, who came to the house at her request. Falling at the general's feet, she begged for mercy for her husband. Unaware until that point that Osborne even existed, Urrea asked to see his wounds. After a quick inspection, he departed and sent his surgeon to tend the stricken man. Osborne ultimately survived.[20]

Out on the prairie that same morning, March 15, after having spent most of the night wandering about hopelessly lost, King and his men were discovered and attacked by a group of rancheros. With their gunpowder wet or spent, the volunteers were essentially defenseless and had little choice but surrender. The men were tied two-by-two with a single rope and marched approximately eight miles back to Refugio. Along the way, other parties of Mexican rancheros joined them with additional prisoners. The number of captives swelled to thirty-three by the time they reached Refugio.

At the mission, preparations were made to shoot the captured volunteers. But before the killings could be carried out, Colonel Juan José Holzinger (d. 1864), Urrea's artillery commander, intervened. Holzinger, whose actual name was Johann Josef Holzinger, was a German who had arrived in Mexico in 1825 as an employee of a British mining firm. Trained as an engineer, he was hired by Antonio López de Santa Anna to build a residence

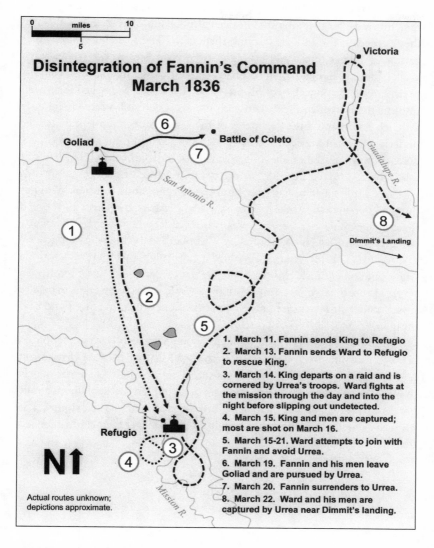

Disintegration of Fannin's Command
March 1836

0 miles 10
5

Victoria

Goliad

Battle of Coleto

Guadalupe R.

San Antonio R.

Dimmit's Landing

Refugio

N↑

Mission R.

Actual routes unknown; depictions approximate.

1. March 11. Fannin sends King to Refugio
2. March 13. Fannin sends Ward to Refugio to rescue King.
3. March 14. King departs on a raid and is cornered by Urrea's troops. Ward fights at the mission through the day and into the night before slipping out undetected.
4. March 15. King and men are captured; most are shot on March 16.
5. March 15-21. Ward attempts to join with Fannin and avoid Urrea.
6. March 19. Fannin and his men leave Goliad and are pursued by Urrea.
7. March 20. Fannin surrenders to Urrea.
8. March 22. Ward and his men are captured by Urrea near Dimmit's landing.

on the general's estate. This early association led to his later assignment as a captain of engineers in Santa Anna's army during the overthrow of the Mexican Centralist government.

Holzinger noted that there were several Germans among the thirty-three captives. Anxious to save some of his own countrymen, he used his rank to postpone the slayings until the following day. No specifics were recorded of their disposition during the rest of that day and into the next, but Ayers noted that "Our treatment during the next 24 hours was most brutal and barbarous."[21]

Meanwhile the *soldados*, after taking their revenge on the wounded volunteers lying helpless in the church, turned their attention to plunder. Fox remembered later that after the Mexicans "robbed us of everything of value," they turned to the task of burying their dead. The *soldados* stacked their comrades' bodies into a pile "as big as twenty cords of wood."[22] They then availed themselves of a trench that had been dug earlier by a Refugio colonist to demarcate the boundary of his property. The Mexicans dragged their dead into the ditch then covered them with the excavated soil. Where previously a trench had marked the perimeter of the man's property, a running ridge underlain by dead Mexican *soldados* now served as the boundary line.

Ayers was released the next day, March 16. He recorded that he "had not asked for neither did I expect any mercy at the hands of the enemy." Yet, his wife was not inclined to hang her future on her husband's bravado. With her four children in tow she, like Osborne's wife, threw herself at Urrea and begged for clemency on Ayers' behalf. Urrea was a gentleman, as well as apparently being powerless when confronted by a woman's tears; the Mexican general granted Ayers his life. Ayers maintained a curiously flippant attitude for one who came so perilously close to death. He remembered that "after receiving a severe lecture on account of my hostility to Mexico and charging me to behave myself better in the future and let politics alone, I merely bowed and said nothing."[23]

Meanwhile, Holzinger had obtained clemency for two German prisoners. Six colonists were freed for various reasons, at least one because Urrea again relented in the face of a woman's tears. The remainder—approximately twenty—were not saved. The Mexicans marched them to a spot about a mile north of the mission, shot them dead, and stripped them of their clothes. The Mexicans did not bury them, but stripped their bodies of their clothes and left them for the animals to devour.[24]

CHAPTER 9

Flight from Goliad

Geneneral Samuel Houston arrived at Gonzales to take charge of the army on March 11, 1836. On that same day, two Tejanos brought news into town of the fall of the Alamo. Houston wasted no time: that very night he wrote a message to James Walker Fannin in which he included details of the disaster, enclosing separate orders directing the abandonment of the presidio at Goliad. Captain Francis J. Dusanque (d. 1836) was tasked with carrying the dispatch through the one hundred miles of prairie and scrub woodland that separated Gonzales from Goliad; it was country that was filled with hostile Indians.

Dusanque arrived at the presidio and delivered the message to Fannin on March 14 after both Amon B. King's and William Ward's parties had left for Refugio. One can only guess at what went through Fannin's mind as he read Houston's orders:

> ARMY ORDER Headquarters, Gonzales, March 11, 1836. To Col. J. W. Fannin, Commanding at Goliad, Sir: You will as soon as practicable on receipt of this order, fall back upon Guadalupe Victoria with your command and such artillery as can be brought with expedition. The remainder will be sunk in the river. You will take the necessary measures for the defense of Victoria, and forward one-third of your effective men to this point, and remain in command until further orders. Every facility is to be afforded to women and children who may be desirous of leaving that place. Previous to abandoning Goliad, you will take the necessary measures to blow up that fortress, and do so before leaving its vicinity. The immediated [sic] advance of the enemy may be constantly expected as well as a rise of water. Prompt movements are therefore highly important. SAM HOUSTON, Commander of the Army.[1]

Fannin now had unequivocal orders from the duly appointed commander of the army. But Fannin was arrogant and had little problem flouting those commands: by his way of thinking, Houston was not on the scene and he was. He considered that only he understood the situation at Goliad and only he had the information needed to make the right decision. Nevertheless, he was still having difficulty making any decision at all.

When Houston's orders to bring three hundred men and join him at the Alamo had arrived two days earlier, on March 12, Fannin had had no oxen and wagons to evacuate his cannon and supplies—King and his men had taken them all to Refugio, and Fannin had no idea what was happening there. Those same concerns still applied on March 14: Fannin had no transport and still had no news of what was going on at Refugio. Barring a catastrophe, both Ward and King should have returned already. He worried that Ward's force, as large as it was, might have encountered an even larger Mexican contingent. With his garrison at Goliad now smaller by more than a third, and with the Mexican army loose in the vicinity, Fannin had orders in hand that directed him to retreat as soon as he could.

But making the decision to do so was not a simple matter, even if his choices had not changed since he had sent Ward out to rescue King. The easiest and most expedient option was for him to order the men to pack only what they could carry and to lead them on a fast march to Victoria to join with Houston and James C. Neill. Doing so would require him to leave the cannon and a great deal of ammunition and supplies. He no doubt was sensitive to the fact that—as obvious and correct as this choice might turn out to be—his detractors would criticize him for abandoning resources that were so dear and necessary to the fight. Having just gone several weeks without good provisions, Fannin understood as well as anyone exactly how valuable they were.

A quick retreat to Victoria unburdened by cannon or supplies was an attractive idea, but its actual execution would not be without danger. On foot, Fannin's men ran the risk of being chased down by Mexican horsemen or by mounted rancheros loyal to Antonio López de Santa Anna. If the enemy pursued them and forced them to fight, they would not have any heavy guns, and the only ammunition available to them would be what they were carrying.

The heavy guns, especially now that the Alamo was lost, were more precious than ever. Fannin did not like the idea of spiking them. They had been entrusted to him and were the single greatest collection of firepower in the revolutionary cause. Leaving them behind would weaken that cause considerably. Again, Fannin was sensitive to the censure he was sure to receive if he abandoned the cannon and mortars. And Houston had told him to retreat with whatever guns he could move expeditiously.

In truth, he could forgo the idea of rapid flight and try to take the guns and munitions and stores with him, but doing so would require draft animals and wagons. At that moment, there were none at Goliad: they were still somewhere with King, assuming he was still alive. Getting reliable replacements, and on short notice, would be difficult. Fannin's men had already taken or bought all the animals from the surrounding farms and ranches, and there were not many remaining. What draft animals did remain the settlers jealously guarded from the needy volunteers. They still needed to make a living, regardless of what happened with the revolution. The settlers needed their tools and provisions, as well as their livestock. Further disinclining them to help the revolutionaries was the fact that Fannin and his men had nothing much with which to pay them.

Another factor that Fannin had to consider was the disposition of his men. For more than a month, he had browbeaten them into fortifying the presidio. They had resisted at first, but as a fight with the Mexicans became more and more likely, they threw themselves into the effort with increasing vigor. By the beginning of March, they had transformed the once-decrepit fortress into a reasonably defensible position. Now, more than two weeks later, it was downright formidable. The volunteers were still itching for a fight and were eager to test their handiwork against the invading armies. A letter from Burr H. Duval, the leader of the Kentucky Mustangs, captured the mood of the men. He wrote to his father that "I have never seen such men as this army is composed of—no man ever thinks of retreat, or surrender, they must be exterminated to be whipped—Nothing can depress their ardour."[2] Duval could not know then that his words would turn out to be prophetic.

But now, Fannin, who had never been very popular with the men, had to consider issuing an unpopular order to retreat. He knew that at the very least there would be rumblings and complaints, and that the men would question his nerve, and that some would outright call him a coward. The volunteers might even mutiny and refuse to leave the defenses they had labored so hard to build. Perhaps they would even elect a new leader, although, as a regular officer rather than a volunteer, Fannin would still command the much smaller group of regular soldiers.

Finally, following the arrival of Houston's orders on March 14, Fannin made a commitment to at least prepare to leave Goliad, but he wanted to wait until Ward and King returned from Refugio, if they were still living. Still, he lacked reliable news as to their disposition. The couriers he had sent to Refugio had all been killed or captured, and the paucity of information made further decisions difficult.

By the end of March 16, General José Urrea had massacred most of King's men at Refugio and forced Ward and his group to flee. Urrea left a contingent of men there and dispatched a party to occupy Copano, then he took his main force and started for Goliad. Mexican efforts to put down the rebellion were going well, from their point of view: San Antonio and Refugio had fallen, and the next big prize was sure to be Goliad.

Unlike Fannin, Urrea had excellent intelligence about his adversary's intentions: his horsemen and the local rancheros kept him well apprised of rebel activities. Moreover, Urrea received even better information from captured couriers. Most of Fannin's communications were in Urrea's hands within hours of them being written. Urrea wrote in his *Diario*:

> A messenger of Fannin was intercepted and we learned beyond all doubt that the enemy intended to abandon the fort at Goliad and concentrate its force at Victoria; that they only waited [for] the 200 [actually, Ward's force was approximately 120] men that had been sent to Refugio to execute this operation. On the 14th and 15th I had fought and dispersed the latter force. In order to observe the enemy and cut off its communication with Victoria, I ordered Capt. Mariano Iraeta and sixty men to take a position on the road between this place and Goliad to watch it.[3]

It is worth noting that although Urrea had easily swept aside Francis Johnson and James Grant at San Patricio and Agua Dulce, had captured or killed King's men at Refugio, and had sent Ward running, he nonetheless had his own very real difficulties. First, many of his troops were from the southern Yucatán Peninsula and suffered miserably in the comparably frigid Texas climate. This suffering was exacerbated by his tenuous supply situation. His men were living largely off what they carried and what they scrounged, and were only occasionally provisioned via the army.

He also recorded that his officers and men grumbled about the prisoners that he compelled them to feed and guard: "I constantly heard complaints, and I perceived the vexation of my troops. I received petitions from the officers asking me to comply with the orders of the general-in-chief and those of the supreme government regarding prisoners. These complaints were more loud on this day [March 16], because, as our position was not improved, I found myself threatened."[4]

The orders of the "general-in-chief" and the "supreme government" were those delineated in the Tornel Decree that, essentially, directed the slaying of armed foreign rebels. Santa Anna was the general-in-chief; as the dictator of Mexico, he was also the supreme government. In this instance, most of the prisoners that Urrea's men wanted to shoot were from King's group. At length, Urrea acquiesced: "I authorized the execution, after my departure from camp, of thirty adventurers taken prisoner during the previous engagements, setting free those who were colonists or Mexicans."[5]

General Vicente Filisola (1789–1850), a fellow Mexican officer in the Texas campaign, took pains to defend Urrea's orders to kill the Anglo prisoners:

This action has been hurled in the face of General Urrea, as well as some others. . . . without keeping in mind that a circular letter from the government [the Tornel Decree] decreed these provisions against infamous bandits who were taken under arms and who were profaning the territory by shedding Mexican blood. He had no powers to set aside these orders under the circumstances that made necessary the shooting of some men who were fighting without a banner, murdering Mexican detachments, burning houses, attacking the property of legitimate owners and peaceful citizens, and were trying in addition to steal a great part of the national territory. The war in Texas was exceptional; it was not a civil war; nor was it a war of one nation against another. In it, the thief was fighting against the owner, the murderer against his benefactor, and nothing was more natural than that these hordes of assassins and thieves should be done away with.[6]

Urrea's comment that he found himself "threatened" also merits discussion. That he felt at peril was not totally unreasonable. He knew that Fannin had several hundred men that could conceivably sally out of Goliad to engage him rather than make a run for Victoria. In addition, Ward and his men had escaped and were somewhere nearby. They had bloodied his men badly at Refugio, and they might be able to do it again. Additionally, there was supposedly another large group of fighters assembling at Victoria. It was not irrational for Urrea to worry that these three disparate forces might join and move against him. He was also probably concerned that there were other revolutionary forces in the area that he was not even aware of.

It is a commander's duty to worry, regardless of his situation, yet Urrea's circumstances were good and improving. The total forces under his command exceeded one thousand, and Santa Anna had already sent to join him more than five hundred additional veteran troops from the San Luis Potosí and Jiménez battalions, both of them under Colonel Juan Morales (1802–1847). On Urrea's orders, Morales and his men were to take up a position just a few miles north of Goliad. By the evening of March 16, they were within a day's march of Goliad. Likewise, Urrea bivouacked that night halfway between Refugio and Goliad, only about a dozen miles from where Fannin's men were making ready to leave the presidio.

In reaction to Houston's orders of March 14, Fannin sent a series of dispatches, intercepted by the Mexicans, that showed that he intended to prepare to withdraw. One message ordered Ward to return to Goliad or meet Fannin and the rest of the contingent at Victoria. Another, sent to Victoria, directed the quartermaster at Victoria to send carts and wagons to the presidio at Goliad. Fannin also wrote to Colonel Albert C. Horton (1798–1865) and urged him to hurry to Goliad with his cavalry in order to scout Fannin's retreat.

As discussed earlier, Ward knew from colonist Edward Perry, who had couriered a message from Fannin, that he would have to attempt to join Fannin en route to Victoria, after the volunteers had destroyed the fortifications at Goliad. Horton was already on his way to Goliad and arrived there with approximately thirty riders and twenty yoke of badly needed oxen on March 16. Wagons and other provisions likewise arrived from Victoria due largely to the superlative efforts of the quartermaster who, although he was ignorant of current events at Goliad, knew that Fannin needed whatever he could get his hands on.

Fannin selected nine cannon that he wanted to take from Goliad and ordered the others buried. He had finally made his decision: he had decided against a light march on foot and instead prepared to take as many guns and provisions with him as he could. The men knew by now that the plan was to leave the fort. Fannin's earlier guesses at the reaction of the volunteers were only partly correct: there was some grousing and bitterness, but there was no spontaneous election undertaken to replace him, nor was there any outright insubordination. Perhaps the fate of their brothers-in-arms at the Alamo tempered their ardor for a fight. The similarities between their situation and that of the Alamo were marked, although Goliad was undoubtedly a far superior fortress.

In fact, the Alamo had been very much on their minds. Two weeks after the attempt to relieve the Alamo that had failed just outside Goliad, Jack Shackelford wrote to his wife about the dire situation at San Antonio. He called to her attention the "powerful Army of four or five thousand men, said to be commanded by Santa Anna in person. The [garrison] does not contain more than two hundred men."[7] It is almost certain that every man in Fannin's command wondered at the possibility of another disastrous siege, this one at Goliad.

During the next day there was still no reliable information from Refugio. Captain Hugh M. Frazer (d. 1836), an immigrant from Nova Scotia and leader of the Refugio militia, bravely volunteered to travel the road south to discover what he could of the fates of King and Ward. He left on March 16 and returned the following day with the news that King and his men were dead and that Ward had been chased into the wilderness and was still on the run. That same day, Horton scouted toward San Antonio and did not get far before discovering that Morales and his force of more than five hundred men were only a short distance away.

Fannin wasted no time in bringing his staff together. All agreed that the evacuation would begin the following day, March 18. Almost immediately, the leader of Fannin's own network of spies and scouts brought new reports that additional Mexican forces were quickly closing on Goliad from several directions. These were probably advance guards for Urrea, who was by now approaching from the east.

Quite understandably alarmed, Fannin worried that the Mexicans would attack that very night before the garrison could make its escape. He ordered that the cannon that had just been buried be pulled out of the dirt and remounted. At the same time, he directed that the men burn and raze the last buildings still standing around the presidio to provide clear defensive fields of fire in the event of an attack.

The men labored through the night making ready for both a hurried departure and a possible attack. Early on March 18, the draft animals, mostly oxen, were hitched to the carts and wagons. With that task complete, there was little left to do other than to fire the provisions that could not be taken. They did not follow Houston's orders to "blow up" the fort, however. The garrison needed it for protection, and there likely were not enough explosives in all of Texas to actually demolish the presidio. In addition, Fannin hoped to leave as discretely as possible, because his men were unprepared to fight a running battle all the way to Victoria. A booming detonation or series of explosions would eliminate the already slim chances that the volunteers would get away unnoticed.

Any hope of a surreptitious escape on the morning of March 18 evaporated when Horton and his small band of horsemen gave chase to a group of Mexican cavalry that they discovered scouting around the presidio. Shackelford recorded that "Horton behaved in a very gallant manner, and made a furious charge upon the enemy."[8] The Mexicans fled, but when Horton reined his group back toward the fort, the Mexicans were joined by a large number of infantry and turned the chase around: Horton and his men became the hunted. This back-and-forth continued for several hours with neither side inflicting casualties on the other. The remainder of the volunteers cheered Horton's men from the roofs and walls of the presidio. Contemporary accounts suggest an almost festive atmosphere.

Finally, Horton's men were cornered in an old church across the San Antonio River from Goliad, and Shackelford and his Red Rovers set off to rescue them. The Alabamans waded across the river in freezing water nearly up to their chins, then worked their way into position for a flanking attack on the Mexicans. However, just as they were about to charge, cannon from the presidio opened fire and put the Mexicans to flight. Shackelford was disappointed at the timing because "we had every advantage of position, and could we have met even that [much larger] force on such terms, I should not have feared the result."[9]

Urrea himself had made a reconnaissance of Goliad on that same day, while sending scouts to Victoria and also meeting with Morales just west of Goliad.

In fact, it was Urrea who directed Morales to send men to help rout Horton. He recorded that "this action was sufficient to make the enemy retreat." But Urrea's biggest concern was that Fannin would get away from him at Goliad, much as Ward had escaped him at Refugio: "I had plenty of warnings that made me fear the flight of the enemy, so I reinforced the advanced cavalry pickets which I had placed along the river to keep watch. Our troops were obliged to bivouac all night, exposed to a continuous rain and a strong north wind which made the cold unbearable. No rest was possible during the entire night."[10]

The senseless skirmishing of March 18 cost Fannin and his men an entire day. The action had unnecessarily tired Horton's mounts and given the Mexicans an opportunity to test the garrison. And incomprehensibly, the oxen had been left in harness all day, unfed and unwatered. This maltreatment of the animals that would be, in large part, responsible for their lives during the retreat was absolutely indefensible. Certainly, these men knew better.

While Urrea and his men shivered in the evening chill, Fannin still dithered over his options. He finally decided to evacuate the fortress that very night under the cover of darkness. Horton was sent out again to reconnoiter an escape route. Charles B. Shain, a Kentuckian and member of Duval's company, was one of the men sent out on foot with Horton. Less than four months later, in its issue of June 30, 1836, the *Louisville Kentucky Journal* published his recollections of that evening:

> That night we intended starting after dark, but some of our horsemen came up from the river, and said that there was a picket guard of the Mexicans at each ford. Col. Fannin then ordered Col. Horton to take his horse company and cross over the river with one of our company behind each of them, and to watch until we could have the artillery and baggage carried over. We thought it a very singular order, but we obeyed. The horsemen went forward, and, in a short time, one of them came galloping back, and told us that there were at least 200 horsemen in the act of crossing. In a few minutes we heard horses coming and were ordered to form and receive a charge. They came within fifty yards of us before we could see them on account of the darkness. Captain Duval hailed them, when we found them to be our own men that we had sent to see if there was any chance of crossing that night. We were very near shooting at them. One of our guns snapped; and if it had gone off, we should certainly have killed nearly every man, for we all had our triggers sprung and our rifles cocked. It was so dark that the Mexicans did not pursue us. We then returned to the fort.[11]

Horton reported to Fannin that the crossings were guarded and that even if they were not, finding and keeping to the road in the darkness would be impossible. Fannin was obviously still torn by indecision when he inspected the presidio's redoubled defenses later that evening in the company of Captain Ira Westover. They came to where Abel Morgan (ca. 1792–1873) manned his post. Morgan was a forty-four-year-old native North Carolinian and former legislator of that state who came to Texas through Kentucky. He left for Texas at least partly because his wife Zilpha possessed a "very turbulent disposition," and "always led her husband a disagreeable life." Perhaps for that reason, Morgan had enlisted under the name Thomas Smith, and that was how his comrades knew him.

Morgan normally served as a medical orderly, but this particular evening he was assigned to guard duty. He recorded his encounter with Fannin and Westover:

> I suppose in about half an hour [after taking his post] Col. Fanning and Capt. Westover came to me, Col. Fanning asked me what I thought about retreating and leaving the fort; I told him that my opinion was that [it] was too late; for I made no doubt from what we had seen that we were entirely surrounded by the enemy, and that we had something like six weeks' provisions and men enough to keep the enemy from breaking in for some time, as we had then about 360 men. Col. Fanning seemed to have his mind unsettled about it. Capt. Westover agreed with me, and said if we had left some three or four days before, he thought we might have escaped; but he made no doubt that we were surrounded now.[12]

In the end, Fannin stuck with his decision to abandon Goliad. That decision was also in compliance with Houston's orders, albeit up to five days after those orders had been delivered to him.

The morning of March 19 dawned gray and foggy, with visibility severely limited. It was God-given weather for Fannin and his men—perfect for them to slip undetected from the old presidio. Inexplicably, though, Fannin took far too long to organize his men and get moving. Almost every account agrees that it was not until about nine in the morning before the garrison passed out of the old fort. Although many of them acknowledge the late departure, none of the accounts gives any reason for it, nor do any of them recall that there was any sense of urgency. There is no mention of last-minute staff meetings or arguments, or shouting and disorder.

Rather, the late departure reflected poor organization. Herman Ehrenberg (ca. 1818–1866) was a young Prussian who had been in the United States for only a short time before coming to Texas with the New Orleans Greys. Some sources declare that he was the son of a Prussian prince, although this claim is not substantiated. His account noted that the volunteers were slow to leave, essentially, because they had packed poorly: "The number and size of the provisions and ammunition wagons that we took with us were too large."[13]

Fannin also let his men eat breakfast and then insisted that they put fire to everything that they were not taking with them. Stacks of provisions were brought into the chapel and incinerated. Ehrenberg reported that meat from nearly seven hundred head of cattle had been dried in anticipation of a long siege and that all of it was reduced to ashes, along with much of the meal that had been brought in from Port Lavaca during the previous couple of weeks. The whole act of firing so much stuff seems distinctly odd, especially because the volunteers were anxious to leave undetected. It would seem that the smoke from so much burning material would have definitely alerted the Mexicans. Certainly this "smoke signal" would have been weighed against the fact that the Mexican forces would have made good use of the meat and other provisions if they were left behind.

Nevertheless, the notion that some of the men might have been trying to attract attention, or might have been deliberately sluggish in an effort to provoke the Mexicans into attacking is one that canot be discounted. There were undoubtedly some among them who still wanted to try the presidio's defenses against the Mexicans. Finally though, Fannin shooed his men out of Goliad and started toward Victoria. Incredibly, he got them out of the fort undetected.

This was even more remarkable when the wagon teams are considered. The oxen were poorly broken, and even that was done to Mexican methods rather than American. While there were a few Mexican drovers among Fannin's column, most of the men at the reins were Americans who had little or no experience with Mexican draft animals. Exacerbating all of this was the fact that the oxen had been badly treated the day prior during the inconclusive skirmishes and were already tired and unruly. More than one account mentions the balkiness of the animals. Morgan recalled that they were "wild and contrary," while Dr. Joseph Field (d. 1882) recorded that "many of them as they issued from the fort, ran furiously into the prairie, and were unmanageable. Others would go no way but backwards."[14]

With nine cannon, an ammunition cart, and at least two baggage carts, Fannin and approximately three hundred men were finally on their way to Victoria through the persistent fog that cloaked their departure from the Mexicans. Shackelford's Red Rovers led the march, while Duval's company covered the road to the rear.

The going was slow: the oxen were miserable, the carts were overloaded, and the cannon were heavy. The road crossed the San Antonio River almost immediately and the column's progress was held up for almost an hour getting the heavy guns up the steep banks. The oxen were not up to the task of doing the work by themselves, and the men had to help muscle the cannon out of the water and back onto the road. Shackelford wrote that he "waded into the river myself, with several of my company, assisting the artillerists by putting our shoulders to the wheels, and force the guns forward."[15] The largest gun, a howitzer, fell into the river and had to be manhandled out.

The men quickly realized that their transport was not up to the task of moving everything that had been loaded. It was not long before the heaviest, balkiest and least needed items were jettisoned. Ehrenberg recounted that "the way was strewn with objects of all kinds and here and there a wagon that was left standing or knocked to pieces. The rest of the baggage remained standing a mile from Goliad on the romantic banks of the San Antonio, or was dropped in haste into the clear water to the river. Chests filled with musket provisions or the belongings of the soldiers disappeared in the waves."[16]

Fog aside, it seems incredible that Fannin was able to get his big guns, his stores and provisions, dozens of oxen, and his men out of Goliad undetected. Urrea's *Diario* corroborates that Fannin's departure was unobserved: "Our advance guards turned in a report of no news." He busied himself that morning, which was his thirty-ninth birthday, with reconnoitering the area and positioning an artillery piece "within a rifleshot" of the fort. That work finished, he made ready to cross the river with a contingent of cavalry in order to more closely inspect various avenues of approach for an attack against the old presidio "when I received notice that they had abandoned their position and were on the way to Guadalupe, Victoria [the formal Mexican name for the town of Victoria]."[17]

Some have suggested that Urrea purposely allowed Fannin's men to escape so that he would be able to overtake and annihilate them on open ground. This certainly would have been much less costly and time consuming than conducting a protracted siege against the stout defenses that the volunteers had built at Goliad. And ultimately, it is exactly what happened, although there is nothing in the records to suggest that it occurred by design. Modesty was not a quality that was ever attributed to Urrea, and it is certain that if he had been so crafty as to orchestrate the subsequent events in which he emerged victorious he definitely would have recorded it and taken credit, yet he did not do so. All accounts suggest that the Mexican pickets simply let Fannin and his men slip away unnoticed.

It did not take Urrea long to react. By eleven that morning, approximately two hours behind Fannin, he gave pursuit with a force that he tallied at eighty cavalry and 360 infantry.

Fannin's mindset at this point is incomprehensible. He knew that the countryside was filled with Mexican troops and that many of them were mounted. He was moving, at best, about two miles an hour, and Victoria was almost thirty miles north of Goliad, meaning he had more than fifteen hours of travel in front of him. He had to know that, moving as slowly as he was, an engagement with Urrea's men was inevitable.

Perhaps he felt he had no good options. Houston had ordered him to bring the cannon when he abandoned Goliad. Fannin may have felt that, if he was bound by Houston's orders to bring at least two or three pieces, he might as well bring enough guns to enable him to prevail in the fight that was sure to come when he was chased down. Considering all of this, it is quite likely that Fannin knew the coming battle was a certainty before he even left the presidio.

And it evidently did not bother him. This attitude might be attributable to his personal experience fighting against regular Mexican army units. He had been at Gonzales the previous October when the Anglo civilians there had roundly defeated the Mexicans. Two months later, he had helped lead the defensive effort at Concepción when he and James Bowie and a contingent of ninety men had not only defeated a much larger attacking Mexican force, but had absolutely decimated them, even taking their cannon from them. If Fannin was unimpressed by the fighting prowess of his adversary, it was because his experiences fighting against Mexican *soldados* had made him so.

CHAPTER 10

Battle on the Prairie

I f James Walker Fannin's decisions to this point had been late, or ill considered, or unpopular, or even just plain wrong, they still had not necessarily doomed his men to death. His next decision did. Shortly after crossing Manahuilla Creek on the way from Goliad to Victoria on March 19, 1836, he stopped the column in the middle of the prairie approaching Coleto Creek so that the men and animals could eat and relax.

The fog that had shrouded the escape from Goliad just a few hours earlier had lifted, and visibility on the tree-rimmed grassland was good. Fannin's scouts, Colonel Albert Horton's horsemen, reconnoitered the route ahead while also keeping watch on the column's flanks. They reported no sign of the Mexicans. Fannin himself, from where he was halted in the prairie grass, could see no sign that the Mexican army was hot on his trail. He did not know that General José Urrea's men had discovered the presidio was empty, and that they were not far behind him.

Jack Shackelford, the leader of the Alabama Red Rovers, was distressed with the decision to stop. Immediately after Fannin called the halt, Shackelford pressed him to change his mind and to keep moving because the open prairie was not good terrain from which to fight a defensive battle. There was no cover, and if the Mexicans attacked they would do so with the advantage of numbers. Shackelford was insistent in his protestations to Fannin: "I remonstrated warmly against this measure and urged the necessity of first reaching the Coleta [Creek], then about five miles distant."[1]

Enemy cavalry worried Shackelford more than the more numerous Mexican infantry. Open ground was ideal cavalry terrain, and Horton's men, as skilled as they might have been, were too few to counter Urrea's formations. Better to push ahead, Shackelford insisted, until they reached the relative safety of Coleto Creek and its timbered—and defensible—banks.

Fannin dismissed these concerns. He believed that the Mexican forces in the area numbered no more than five hundred, and he was confident that they could manage such a force. Probably his low opinion of the Mexicans decided the matter. He believed, as did many of his staff, that Shackelford was being too cautious or was overly interested in saving his own skin. Shackelford noted this in his recollections:

> In this matter I was overruled, and from the ardent manner in which I urged the necessity of getting under the protection of timber, I found the smiles of many, indicated a belief that at least I thought it prudent to take care of number one. Here let me state one thing, lest I may be misunderstood: Col. Fannin and many others could not be made to believe that the Mexicans would dare follow us. He had too much contempt for their prowess, and too much confidence in the ability of his own little force. That he was deficient in that caution which a prudent officer should always evince, must be admitted; but that he was a brave, gallant, and intrepid officer, none who knew him can doubt.[2]

Shackelford was not alone in his objection to the halt. Burr H. Duval of the Kentucky Mustangs and Ira Westover, one of the few regular Texas army officers with Fannin, also wanted the march to continue. The pause simply did not make sense when the same benefits could be realized, and in relative safety, if they simply continued the march for just a bit longer.

Fannin was unmoved. The animals were freed from their traces to graze while the men rearranged gear, ate, and relaxed. The officers met and conferred, and in the end, perhaps because of the strident objections of Shackelford, Westover, and Duval, the halt was not overly long. After an hour, the oxen were back at the yoke and the men back in column. The volunteers pressed toward Victoria once more. Horton and his men continued to scout ahead, while Fannin sent four horsemen back to watch the rear.

Fannin's demeanor on this particular morning is unknown. He may very well have been relaxed and confident. As for his prejudices toward the Mexican army, they were typical of Americans at that time, and he made no effort to conceal them. He believed that, man-for-man, his volunteers were much better in a scrap and that the Mexicans would have no stomach for tangling with so many of his men.

In fact, Urrea had plenty of stomach for just that. He was a professional officer who had yet to be defeated in Texas—notwithstanding the losses he had sustained at Refugio. Fannin's force merited caution, but it was not invincible. Urrea planned to defeat it decisively.

During the chase, Urrea's advance patrols informed him that the revolutionary force was smaller than he had supposed; earlier reports had led him to believe that Fannin had at least five hundred fighters under his command. With this new information, Urrea sent a hundred of his infantrymen back to Goliad to secure the presidio.

In the meantime, Horton's riders continued to scout the surrounding area. The bulk of them swept the route in front of the column. For some reason, Fannin believed that any Mexican threat would come from the column's front. Still, the four horsemen he had earlier sent to guard the tail of the column should have provided some measure of protection against being surprised from behind.

Accounts differ about the conduct of those four riders. One of them was Herman Ehrenberg. Although he was young, he was also experienced. He had volunteered the previous October, but had already participated in the fight for San Antonio and the abortive Matamoros Expedition. On this day, he and the three other men watched for any Mexican forces that might be in pursuit. Yet, young Ehrenberg and his comrades seemed more enchanted by the countryside than they were fearful of the Mexicans:

> Our route led us through one of those charming landscapes where little prairies alternate with thin forests of oak without any undergrowth. Frequently we saw herds of cattle grazing on the luxuriant grass; and immense herds of deer looked with amazement at the little army wending its way through the stillness of the west. . . . Since not the least trace of an enemy had shown itself so far we rode carelessly along until we accidentally turned around and noticed at a distance of about four miles a figure in the part of the forest through which we had just come that looked like a rider on horse back. Since, however, it did not move, we came to the conclusion that it was a tree or some other lifeless object.[3]

As it happened, what they saw was nothing like a "tree or some other lifeless object": it was one of Urrea's scouts. After dismounting and setting their animals to graze, the horsemen made out in the distance what they first thought was a large herd of cattle being driven by displaced settlers. On careful scrutiny, they noted that a portion of the stream was moving at a fast gallop. As soon as they saw that, they realized that Urrea's cavalrymen were coming hard. Behind them a formation of several hundred infantrymen hurried. Caught off guard, Ehrenberg and the other three scouts flew to their horses and raced to warn Fannin.

Shackelford's worst fears were realized while the volunteers were still well short of the trees lining Coleto Creek. Behind the column, and ahead and to its left, there came lines of Mexican cavalry. Men shouted the alarm and a ripple of excitement, anxiety, and fear swept through the volunteers. The enemy horsemen moved quickly to encircle Fannin's men. Most of the volunteers had never seen so many mounted troops; their estimates of exactly how many Mexican cavalry there actually were varied wildly—from several hundred to a thousand or more. Even Shackelford, an educated man and a veteran of the War of 1812, described a cavalry force of several hundred. Mexican accounts hold the number at about eighty.

Whatever the number of cavalry, Mexican infantry soon appeared as well. Its arrival warned the volunteers to expect a real battle rather than slashing cavalry attacks. Although cavalry was fast and maneuverable—and provided tremendous shock value—it was infantry that performed the close, dangerous work.

Ehrenberg and the other three horsemen then swept back into Fannin's column atop their exhausted animals. Some accounts state that the small party raced past the line of troops and through the encircling Mexicans to where Horton's band of scouts were safely gathered. Their brethren on foot shouted curses at them, damning them for their seeming cowardice. Ehrenberg said later that he had rejoined Fannin. His subsequent capture with the rest of the volunteers certainly validates his claim that he, at least, rejoined the formation.

Fannin started his men off the track and toward the trees that lined Perdido Creek to the column's left front and about a mile distant. The sound of shots rang from the direction of the Mexican formations, and Fannin was heard to declare, "That's the signal for battle, I won't retreat another foot."[4] He subsequently formed his troops into a moving hollow square with ranks three men deep, distributing the nine cannon to the square's four corners.

At the first sound of the shooting, Horton and his scouts raced back toward the column. Before they could rejoin their comrades, Urrea's men put themselves in Horton's path, and they were forced to pull up short. The Mexican cavalry outnumbered their small group several times over, but Horton is reported to have been willing to try to cut his way through. That effort would probably have been fatal, and his men recognized it. Before he could make the argument, his lieutenant cut the debate short by declaring the notion folly and dashing away from the fight. The rest of Horton's men followed, as did Horton himself. He had no other choice.

Almost every account of the battle states that the volunteers formed a hollow square, but few note that this was a difficult accomplishment, especially for undisciplined troops. A column of three hundred men, nine pieces of animal-drawn artillery, and several wagons may have stretched up to a quarter mile or more. Getting the men and the unruly animals to close ranks and take their positions evenly on each side of the square, while getting the artillery pieces into the corners, could have gone badly wrong. That it did not is a credit to Fannin and his men.

In the center of the mass were carts, wagons, and oxen. In the tumult before the Mexican attack, many of the animals broke loose and fled, ironically, for the enemy lines. Sometime during the confusion the ammunition wagon broke down. Nearly helpless without it, the volunteers had to wait in place until it could be moved. Shackelford later described the disposition of the two forces:

> The prairie, here, was nearly in the form of a circle. In front was the timber of the Coleto [Creek], about a mile distant; in the rear, was another strip of timber, about six miles distant; whilst on our right and left, equi-distant, four or five miles from us, there were, likewise bodies of timber. The order of battle was that of a hollow square. But, unfortunately for us, in endeavoring to reach a commanding eminence in the prairie, our ammunition-cart broke down, and we were compelled to take our position in a valley, six or seven feet below the mean base, of about one fourth of a mile in area. I have said the order of battle was that of a hollow square; I should more properly say an oblong square.[5]

Finally, the formation was stabilized. It was defensible but terribly unwieldy and difficult to move at any pace other than a crawl. Fannin's command—awkwardly configured as it was—started for cover. Progress was agonizingly slow, and it must have seemed to the men that they would never reach the line of trees.

It was sometime during this initial flurry and commotion that the volunteers unlimbered one of their artillery pieces and sent three rounds at a Mexican position. Accounts suggest that this was not done at Fannin's orders, and that the shots fell harmlessly short of their targets. This otherwise uninteresting

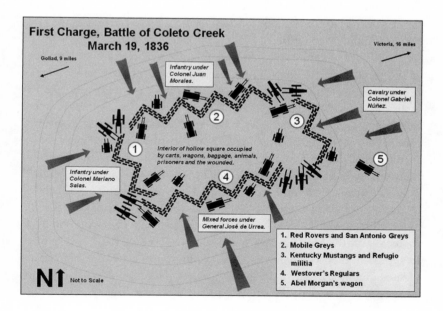

First Charge, Battle of Coleto Creek
March 19, 1836

Victoria, 16 miles

Goliad, 9 miles

Infantry under Colonel Juan Morales.

Cavalry under Colonel Gabriel Núñez.

Interior of hollow square occupied by carts, wagons, baggage, animals, prisoners and the wounded.

Infantry under Colonel Mariano Salas.

Mixed forces under General José de Urrea.

N↑ Not to Scale

1. Red Rovers and San Antonio Greys
2. Mobile Greys
3. Kentucky Mustangs and Refugio militia
4. Westover's Regulars
5. Abel Morgan's wagon

event underscores the fact that the men who made up the volunteer force—despite their fighting spirit and individual martial skills—were not well-disciplined, professional soldiers. It also highlights the fact that Fannin was not able to exercise the type of control that would have been expected of a competent military commander. Indeed, the New Orleans Greys, desperate to get to the better cover of the tree line along Perdido Creek, threatened what was tantamount to mutiny: they wanted to break from the larger formation. Ultimately, they did not carry out their threat, most likely because Urrea's men blocked their escape.

Andrew Boyle (1818–1871) recalled that Fannin nevertheless recognized the danger: "When Fanning [*sic*] seeing clearly I presume that the main object of the enemy was to cut us off from the timber, ordered us to limber up again and continue the march, we left the road, marching in an oblique direction to the left towards the nearest timber."[6]

Mexican accounts note that their troops were enthusiastic and ready for battle and declare that "the moment that they discovered the enemy, [they] filled the air with loud shouts; their enthusiasm seemed to General Urrea to augur good, and from then on he believed that victory was certain."[7] In preparation for the coming fight, the Mexican commander ordered his men to fix their bayonets.

Urrea's men quickly closed the distance to Fannin's, who were, quite literally, in a bad spot. When Fannin realized that an attack was imminent, he stopped the formation in a slight depression about six or seven feet below the ground held by the Mexicans. Although not a debilitating disadvantage, any attempt to crash through the Mexican lines would require an uphill charge that would slow them and sap their energy. In addition, the volunteers could not see over the surrounding crest of their basin.

The Mexicans continued to close on the Anglos. Their numbers increased as stragglers from the area around Goliad caught up and joined Urrea's columns. Again, accounts vary as to how many Mexican soldiers were present at the start of the battle. Urrea's original complement of nearly three hundred infantrymen and somewhat fewer than a hundred horsemen was augmented through the day by more troops from his main formation to the west.

Virtually all the survivors from Fannin's command estimated one or two thousand or more enemy soldiers, while Mexican tallies were much lower. John C. Duval (1816–1897), part of the Kentucky Mustangs and brother of Burr Duval, was college educated, and his account of the battle is fairly even and reasoned. Yet even he wildly exaggerated when he wrote about the moment that the Mexican cavalry first came into sight: "As they continued to approach, they lengthened out their columns, evidently for the purpose of surrounding us, and in doing so displayed their number to the greatest advantage. I thought there were at least ten thousand (having never before seen a large cavalry force), but in reality there were about a thousand besides several hundred infantry."[8]

Some of the discrepancies can be attributed to the number of animal drivers and camp followers that accompanied the Mexican troops and were counted by Fannin's men. The differing recollections are vexing and they make an exact count difficult to reconcile. Nevertheless, it is not unreasonable to assume that Urrea had at least five hundred soldiers available at the start of the fighting.

Rather than charging Fannin's hollow square in a pell-mell rush, Urrea took the time to plan a professional, coordinated attack. He assigned Colonel Juan Morales to attack the north side of the hollow square and ordered Colonel Mariano Salas (1797–1867) to attack the front (west) side. Urrea himself took the south edge of the square and directed Colonel Gabriel Núñez to lead his cavalry against the rear (east) side.

The Mexicans fired their weapons from several hundred yards before they began their attack in earnest. For the most part, the rounds fell to the ground long before they reached the volunteer positions. A few dropped harmlessly among the men, like tossed stones, without causing any injury. Nevertheless, Shackelford was conscious of the danger and directed his men to sit or kneel. Most of the Anglo formation followed suit. Tall grass provided cover and concealment but no actual protection. Conversely, the same grass that made it difficult for the Mexicans to make out the Anglos' location also made it more challenging for Fannin and his men to see Mexican movements.

Shackelford recorded how Fannin positioned himself behind the Red Rovers and the New Orleans Greys: "The Red Rovers and New Orleans' Greys formed the front line of the square; the Red Rovers being on the extreme right. Colonel Fannin took a commanding position, directly in rear of the right flank. Our orders were, not to fire until the enemy approached in point about a quarter of a mile of us."[9]

Shackelford's Red Rovers had been at the rear of the column, but this was now the front of the hollow square. They shared this side of the square with the San Antonio Greys, a group that in turn was made up primarily of men from the New Orleans Greys. The Mobile Greys held the north side while Westover's regulars manned the south. Burr Duval's Mustangs, previously acting as the van (advance guard) of the column, were now at the rear of the square, along with elements of Hugh Frazer's Refugio militia. The positions of the remaining elements are not well recorded.

Notwithstanding the initial dispositions, men moved from one position to another as the situation dictated. In doing so, they did not have far to move, because their numbers simply did not take up much ground. Captain Benjamin Holland described the formation as a rectangle "49 feet of shortest central diameter, and about 60 feet of longest diameter."[10] This meant that

Fannin's three hundred or so men were packed very tightly together.

Given the circumstances, Holland's measurements could not be completely accurate, but the formation was certainly very compact. The men were shoulder-to-shoulder in their three-deep ranks. This concentrated their fire, particularly at close range. On the other hand, if the Mexicans were able to put a round into the Anglo formation, they were almost guaranteed to hit someone.

The Mexican cavalry led the initial charge sometime in the early afternoon. Amid the blaring of bugles, the snapping of flying pennants, and the cheers of the infantry, Urrea's horsemen spurred their mounts into a rumbling gallop, adding their own shouts and cries to the din. The men waiting in the hollow square felt the ground shudder under the pounding of the animals' hooves, but they held their fire. They knew that musket fire at a distance created a lot of smoke and noise but had little effect on the enemy. Outnumbered as they were, the volunteers could not afford to have little effect. Fannin shouted at the men to hold back.

The men obeyed his command. At last they were doing what they had signed up for—fighting Mexicans. Each of them steadfastly waited for the order to fire. Shackelford recalled the tension as they waited for the Mexicans to close: "The third volley from their pieces wounded the man on my left and several others. About this time, Colonel Fannin had the cock of his rifle shot away by a ball, and another buried in the breech. He was still standing erect, a conspicuous mark, giving orders, 'not to fire yet,' in a calm and decided manner."[11]

Fannin hoped that the effects of his formation's massed fire from short range would devastate the enemy's charge, and his hopes were realized. When the cavalry closed to well within a hundred yards he gave the order, and the corners and sides of his hollow square exploded in gunfire. The combined effects of the rifle and musket rounds and the artillery grapeshot tore in to the Mexicans. Riders were blown out of their saddles and the bloodied limbs of man and beast alike tumbled through the chaos.

Wounded horses panicked and raced out of control in all directions, crashing into each other and the following infantrymen. Downed horsemen were trampled, and tangled collisions of horses and *soldados* careened wildly over the smoke-shrouded field. The collective shrieks of the wounded—both animals and men—were a piercing punctuation to the already horrible clamor. Through it all, the Anglos kept up a heavy volume of artillery volleys and gunfire that made the gruesome scene increasingly awful.

Abel Morgan, the medical orderly that had lived in Kentucky before settling in Texas, was nursing five sick men aboard a wagon at the front of the column. When Fannin put the volunteers into the hollow square formation, Morgan and his wagon of sick men were caught about sixty yards ahead of the rest of the volunteers.

> There was a Mexican employed to drive the oxen, and as soon as he was ordered to halt he let the wild cattle go and ran off to the Mexicans. I was left to head the oxen or let them carry the sick men right into the enemy's ranks. About the time that I got ahead of the oxen, the one of them received a ball that stop[p]ed the wagon. Soon after another one of the oxen was crippled so bad that I knew my wagon was safe. I looked around and found there was no chance of me to get water for the sick ones and saw that I could do them no further service. I walked into the square. I knew we had some new muskets in the ammunition wagon. I selected me one of them and catched up two packs of cartridges and walked out to my wagon again where the balls were whizzing about like bees swarming.[12]

Fannin can be criticized for many things, but not for cowardice. He stalwartly held his position in the square. From there, he directed the fight as best he could, although he did not have much control once the melee began. Fannin had to put his trust in the skill and courage of his men, and hope that their limited drill and training would pay some dividend.

Nor did Fannin's men lack bravery. Several accounts describe the stolid yet ferocious spirit they embodied as they repelled the several Mexican charges that made up the day's battle. Indeed, a Mexican account recalled, "But the enemy, recognizing their critical position, did not falter, rather they defended themselves with bravery and desperation."[13] Fannin's men held their lines under intense attack while inflicting grievous casualties—far more than they sustained.

Urrea did not demean his opponents nor did he disparage the prowess and fighting spirit of Fannin's men. Perhaps he tried to enhance his own professional reputation by painting his enemy as a formidable and ferocious force, but his account agrees with those of the volunteers. Probably he simply recorded his honest observations of the first coordinated engagement:

> The orders were immediately carried out and a determined charge was made on the right and left flanks. In order to obtain a quick victory, I ordered my troops to charge with their bayonets, at the same time that Colonel Morales did likewise on the opposite flank; and, according to previous instructions, the central column

advanced in battle formation, sustaining a steady fire in order to detract the attention of the enemy while we surprised the flanks. Though our soldiers showed resolution, the enemy was likewise unflinching. Thus, without being intimidated by our impetuous charge, it maneuvered in order to meet it; and assuming a hammer formation on the right, they quickly placed three pieces of artillery on this side, pouring a deadly shower of shot upon my reduced column. A similar movement was executed on the left, while our front attack was met with the same courage and coolness.[14]

But the volunteers were not impervious to the Mexican fire. Several men were killed and dozens wounded in the first wave of attacks. Among those hurt was Fannin, who was hit more than once. A bullet buried in his right thigh was the most severe wound. Ehrenberg recorded that it had "penetrated through a waterproof coat, the trousers, a pocket in the overcoat in which he had a silk handkerchief and into the flesh. But strangely enough it did not tear through the handkerchief and as he pulled it out [of his leg], the bullet fell on the ground. Now first he felt the pain of the wound." Heedless of his injury, Fannin remained in command. Ehrenberg recorded that "he did not give up for it, but kept about most of the time."[15]

Several Mexican prisoners, captured before the march from Goliad, were within Fannin's hollow square. The volunteers took grim amusement at watching them try to stay clear of fire from their own countrymen. The Mexicans crawled into holes they scraped into the earth and spent the rest of the day in relative safety. Many of the volunteers envied their protected positions. John Duval later remembered that "I for one, however, did not blame them, as they were non-combatants, and besides to tell the truth when the bullets were singing like mad hornets around me, and men were struck down near me, I had a great inclination to 'hole up' myself and draw it after me."[16]

Abel Morgan was not alone in his wagon with the wounded for long. Four other men reinforced him: an Irishman, George Cash (d. 1836); a Dutchman, Augustus Baker (d. 1836); an unidentified Georgian; and one other man, James Hughes (d. 1836). It was not long, though, before they started going down. Cash took a bullet to the head that did not kill him, while Baker was struck by a round that broke his leg. Another bullet struck him in the torso before he, along with Cash, was finally hustled to the relative safety of the hollow square. Hughes had a rifle and killed three Mexicans before leaving Morgan and the Georgian alone with the sick.

The two of them soon spotted an officer on horseback exhorting his men to attack. As he closed within range, Morgan and the other man fired simultaneously on signal, and the Mexican toppled dead from his horse while his men fell back in alarm. Morgan was astonished when his companion risked life and limb to sprint out to the fallen enemy officer and cut a substantial money purse from his body. Morgan rebuked the other man for his recklessness. The Georgian subsequently took his rifle and his prize into the hollow square, but others came out to the wagon to support Morgan through the rest of the day.

The chaotic and furious nature of the fighting never changed. Thick smoke from the gunfire sometimes made it literally impossible for Fannin's men to see the advancing Mexicans. Not content to passively hold their positions, they often charged forward out of the smoke to get clear shots. Ehrenberg, the young Prussian rider, had dismounted to take a place at the front of the lines. At the height of the clash his aggressiveness took him out among the enemy: "I myself had gotten so far ahead in the general tumult and fired so incessantly that I did not notice how I stood right among the Mexicans. Everything was confusion and it seemed as if we were shooting each other down for pleasure."[17]

Realizing the danger of his situation, and with a weapon that was hopelessly clogged with debris and spent gunpowder, Ehrenberg moved back toward the protection of the hollow square. During his withdrawal he snatched up the muskets of fallen Mexican soldiers and used the loaded ones to help fight his way back.

Ehrenberg's fouled weapon was typical on that battlefield, and in fact was typical on all battlefields of the day. Compared to today's precision-made smokeless propellants, the black gunpowder of 1836 used by the volunteers was exceedingly dirty and packed much less of a punch. Nevertheless, it was factory-made in the United States with some measure of quality control and for its time it was considered quite good.

On the other hand, the Mexicans used stuff that was worse—much of it manufactured in the field. This—in combination with poor marksmanship—accounted for some of the disparity in casualties between the two forces. Many volunteers were struck by musket balls that failed to penetrate their flesh. Rather than creating mortal injuries, the Mexican rounds produced stinging welts. Indeed, John Duval remembered that "there was scarcely a man in the whole command who had not been struck by one or more spent balls, which, in place of mere bruises would have inflicted dangerous or fatal wounds if the powder used by the Mexicans had been better."[18]

Still, some of the Mexican musket balls did cause mortal injury. On one of his forays back into the square, Morgan "was much mortified to see so many fine fellows laid down there with their blankets spread over them." Morgan further noted how the fight "kept that place in a continual tremor. From that time until after sun [went] down our men appeared to be just as much composed and as busy as they had been at no other work." But his observations, like those of others, were off the mark with respect to the number of combatants. He declared that "it seemed like a great odds to see 360 men [Fannin's force numbered closer to three hundred] in a little band surrounded by something like 1900, and 7 or 800 on horseback."[19]

The popular English Brown Bess musket was likely the dominant firearm on the field that day. It was standard issue for the *soldados*, but Fannin's men also used it, as well as significant numbers of much more accurate hunting rifles. Besides these, there were less common types. John Duval carried an *escopette*, which was a short shotgun favored by Mexican cavalry. The *escopette's* heavy charge of powder and numerous balls obviated the need for careful aim. At the same time, it produced a wicked recoil and a blast of fire and smoke that posed a real danger to its user. It was even more dangerous when its user packed it with an excessive load, as Duval apparently did.

Duval kept his *escopette* in reserve for use when the fighting became close and desperate. This occurred during a cavalry charge later in the afternoon: "It was during this charge and when the Mexican cavalry on our side of the square were in a few feet of us, that I concluded that I had got into that 'tight place' and that it was time to let off the 'scopet' I carried. I did so, and immediately I went heels over head through both ranks behind me. One or two came to my assistance supposing no doubt I was shot."[20] Duval recounted that the enemy charge broke up soon after he discharged his fearsome piece. His shoulder was badly bruised from the recoil, and he contented himself with his rifle for the remainder of the battle.

The Mexicans attacked all four sides of the hollow square that afternoon. The cavalry was the most mobile element but also the biggest target. Shackelford described a charge typical of the earlier attacks of the day: "A body of cavalry, from two to three hundred strong, made a demonstration on our rear. They came up in full tilt, with gleaming lances, shouting like Indians. When about sixty yards distant, the whole of the rear division of our little command, together with a piece or two of artillery, loaded with double canister filled with musket-balls, opened a tremendous fire upon them, which brought them to a full halt and swept them down by scores. The rest immediately retreated, and chose to fight on foot the balance of the day."[21]

Urrea formed his men for several charges through the afternoon. His cavalry had started the attack but became less useful as the day wore on, due in no small part to Fannin's artillerists. The defending artillerymen wheeled and fired their big guns into infantry and cavalry assaults alike. The cavalry charges degenerated from full-on orchestrated attacks, to less-coordinated ad hoc forays. Finally, most of the Mexican horsemen climbed down from their mounts and resorted to shooting at Fannin's position from long range.

Urrea's infantrymen were no more eager than their cavalry counterparts to charge into the fire that Fannin's men were pouring from the sides of the hollow square. Numerous accounts describe how they advanced only reluctantly at the points of their officer's swords. Largely conscripted, or in some cases serving in Texas as an alternative to prison, there can be little wonder at their lack of enthusiasm. In truth, if they survived, they had little to gain, regardless of whether the battle was won or lost. Whereas Fannin's men—aside from the fact that they were fighting for their lives—stood to receive land and a stake in a new country, the rank-and-file Mexican *soldados* would receive nothing other than their pay. And with Antonio López de Santa Anna at the head of their country, even that was at risk. Their performance, as recorded by Fannin's men, differs somewhat from Urrea's report following the battle in which he declared "the valor of our army was brilliantly displayed in the engagement."[22]

Just as Fannin had presumed, the heavy guns were proving deadly against Urrea's Mexicans, but they were quickly becoming less and less potent due to a combination of factors. Artillery pieces of the day required that their barrels be swabbed out with water after firing in order to extinguish still burning pieces of debris. Otherwise the gun crews risked creating a bomb when they loaded the next charge: cramming a fresh bag of gunpowder onto a smoldering bit of detritus was a good way to die. The closest water was a mile or more from where Fannin had formed the hollow square for battle, and there was no way to get to it.

In addition, ammunition for the big guns was quickly running out. There was not much left as the afternoon drew toward early evening. And finally, the crews manning the artillery were specially trained and not readily replaceable from the ranks. As such, they were primary targets, and many of them lay dead or wounded around their guns.

Fannin's men were a tired, bedraggled mess by late afternoon. Aside from sweat and blood and dirt, their faces were smudged black with burned gunpowder. Their teeth and gums were likewise stained a pearly black from gunpowder that spilled into their mouths as they bit the ends from their paper cartridges during reloading.

The scarcity of water quickly became a problem for the Anglos. In addition to the lack of water for the artillery, there was none to dress wounds or slake an injured man's thirst. Those men who had lost a lot of blood were particularly desperate. The volunteers, who were fighting for their lives, were exhausted and dehydrated. By dusk their thirst was fearsome, and they had little hope of relief. Although they had held off Urrea's men for most of the afternoon, they could not expect to drive them away or escape to a water source. In short, the water situation was critical.

Water aside, the volunteers' circumstances were becoming worse in virtually every other respect. It did not matter that there were so many

Mexican dead that the volunteers were able to use their bodies for cover. Significant Mexican reinforcements were on their way to the battlefield, and what had been a substantial numerical advantage in favor of Urrea at the start of the engagement would become markedly more so. Artillery was also on the way. When the Mexican pieces arrived, Urrea would be able to fire down into Fannin's thinly protected lines and tear the hollow square to pieces.

Rifle ammunition was also becoming a problem. Unless they had closed to within bayonet range, the Mexican dead and wounded were being killed and wounded at a high cost in ball and powder. Some of the men used rifles of uncommon caliber and often made their own ammunition. Although there were plenty of rounds for the larger-caliber muskets, those balls were too big to be rammed down the smaller barrels of the rifles.

Urrea made one last attempt to break Fannin's formation before the day was done. Like Fannin, the Mexican commander suffered no lack of courage. He formed his men for an assault that would take all four sides of the hollow square under fire at once. Then, at the head of the cavalry, he led the day's final charge. Mexican records recount the action:

> As the fanfare sounded, which was the agreed signal, the forces advanced with great determination and bravery until they were within forty or fifty paces of the enemy ranks. Their efforts were beyond description, the soldiers took the fire of the bullets from the rifles with breasts bared, and consequently the fire began to lessen notably, and their ammunition was being used up. Under such circumstances the general ordered the infantry to fix bayonets and maintain a slow fire. For little better than half an hour both forces remained in this position until the general saw the impossibility of involving the enemy at that time and that the fight was unequal, and he gave the order to retreat.[23]

CHAPTER 11

The Weapons

T he firearms carried by the fighters on both sides were flintlock muskets, rifles, and pistols. The flintlock had been in service in some form or fashion for two centuries by March 19, 1836, when James Walker Fannin and General José Urrea clashed on the scrubby plains of south Texas. It would not become obsolete until the Civil War, twenty-five years later.

The type on the field in greatest numbers was probably a variant of the English-designed Land Pattern Musket, more familiarly known as the Brown Bess. The British had used various forms of the Brown Bess for more than a hundred years, since 1722. Indeed, Fannin's men had grandfathers who fought the Redcoats in the Revolutionary War when both sides carried Brown Bess muskets. Thirty or so years later, their fathers had fought with the same weapon in the War of 1812. Now, more than twenty years later, Brown Bess–carrying Anglos fought Brown Bess–carrying Mexican *soldados*.

The India Pattern—also called Brown Bess—entered service during the 1790s and was a cheaper, lighter, shorter-barreled derivative of the original Land Pattern; its barrel length was reduced from 46 to 39 inches. Despite the diminished length of the India Pattern's barrel, the accuracy of the weapon—as limited as it already was—was not compromised further. Since gaining independence from Spain, the Mexican government had bought large numbers of surplus India Pattern Brown Bess muskets from Great Britain, presumably at a bargain, because the British were acquiring more modern percussion cap weapons.

For its time, the overall design was solid, and it is estimated that more than three million of the India Pattern variant were built. The Brown Bess musket in all its variants continued to see widespread service around the globe until the end of the nineteenth century. It was a heavy firearm; without the bayonet, its mass of wood, iron, and brass weighed slightly less than ten pounds. And it was long. Depending on the model, it approached five feet long, without the bayonet affixed; early versions were longer. But even the India Pattern, when tipped with its one pound, seventeen-inch triangular cross section bayonet, measured more than six feet. Indeed, there were very few Mexican *soldados* that stood taller than their muskets. For that matter, few among the typically larger Texas volunteers could claim they stretched taller than the Brown Bess.

The length of the weapon, as with most contemporary muskets, was one of its most important attributes. With a bayonet on a lug at the end of the barrel, the Brown Bess was especially well suited for reaching out to stab and slash. Heavy and solid as it was, its stock also made a fine club. And it needed to be good for stabbing and slashing and clubbing because, although it fired a huge .75-caliber (three-quarter inch) lead ball, it did so with very little accuracy. Like all muskets, its barrel had a smooth bore, and it could not be relied on to hit targets beyond about fifty yards. If either side waited until the enemy was that close before firing, neither side could count on getting off another shot before the fight became one of close quarters—a bayonet fight—because there simply was not enough time to reload.

Reloading the typical flintlock of the day and readying the primitive collection of articulating hardware that composed its firing mechanism was a time-consuming and complex exercise: After discharging his musket, a soldier would typically huff a breath of air down the barrel to extinguish any leftover debris that might still be smoldering before he started to reload. Sending fresh gunpowder down a barrel with a hot ignition source was a dangerous proposition.

Next, he would pour a premeasured amount of gunpowder down the end of the barrel. This was usually decanted from a small cup or vial rather than straight from a powder horn. The danger from a premature ignition was considerably more in the event that the pound or more of powder in the horn accidentally exploded.

Once the powder had been poured safely into the barrel, a small patch of greased or moistened wadding was laid across the muzzle. In battle, this patch might be moistened with saliva. It could be made of any of several different types of material. Best was some sort of woven cloth—often, salvaged rags or old clothing. Other material might include paper, thinly scraped animal hide, or even, in a pinch, leaves or grass.

Next, he thumbed a lead ball, or "round," into the patch, and pressed it as far into the muzzle as he could. The patch and ball combination helped to ensure a tight fit against the walls of the gun barrel. This tight fit imparted better accuracy and velocity.

After he had started the ball and patch down the barrel, the shooter pulled a wooden or brass ramrod from where it was held in a series of small pipes attached beneath the barrel. He used the ramrod to force the ball and wadding down the barrel. This step was particularly important: a charge of gunpowder not suitably compacted by the ball might blow the musket apart upon ignition.

Once the ball was tamped properly into place, the ramrod was dropped or slid back into its housing underneath the barrel. Next, the shooter would turn his attention to the lock at the other end of the musket. The apparatus there included a depression, called the "pan," into which a small amount of gunpowder was poured to prime the weapon for firing. The pan and its primer of gunpowder were connected to the main charge of gunpowder inside the barrel via a small vent hole.

An L-shaped component called a "frizzen" covered the pan to keep the charge in place and to protect it from wind and rain. Once the frizzen was pulled over the pan, a sharp rap or vigorous shake helped ensure that some small amount of gunpowder traveled into the vent hole. This increased the odds that the main charge in the barrel would ignite.

Next, the entire assembly was readied for firing by pulling the serpentine cock back far enough that it was locked against the pressure of its spring—a position known as "full cock." When the trigger was pulled, the cock sprang down, and the flint that was clamped in its jaws scraped the long part of the frizzen just above the pan; this created sparks while pivoting the frizzen so that the pan was simultaneously uncovered. If everything worked according to design, the sparks ignited the primer in the pan, which in turn created enough flash to travel through the vent hole and ignite the main charge. The resultant explosion sent the ball and its patch rocketing out of the barrel and hopefully into an adversary.

If luck were not with the shooter—as was the case approximately 15 percent of the time—the charge in the pan did not ignite. Or, if it did, it flashed without igniting the main charge. This phenomenon was a defect of the flintlock that produced the colorful phrase, "flash in the pan." It was, in other words, a fiery show with no real substance or result.

Successful or not, reloading took time. The very best of the highly trained British regular soldiers of the era were said to be able to perform the entire procedure in fifteen seconds. That they were able to do so under anything other than perfect parade ground conditions is suspect. Certainly, neither Urrea's *soldados* nor Fannin's volunteers reloaded that fast, as unnerved as they surely were by the smoke, din, and horror of the battlefield.

In addition, most of them took cover, or at least dropped to their knees if not totally to ground, while they reloaded. Wrestling powder and patch and ball in the right quantities and in the right order into a hot, heavy, bayonet-tipped, six-foot long hunk of metal and wood while lying on the ground under fire was certainly no simple task. In the thick of the fight, men jostled each other while they were reloading, often spilling their own and each other's gunpowder and balls on the ground. Very likely, combatants on both sides took a minute or more to reload their weapons.

The rate of fire was slow even though many, if not most, of the combatants on the field that day used paper cartridges. These prerolled paper tubes were tied at one end and crimped at the other; they held measured amounts of gunpowder as well as the ball. This helped reduce the steps in reloading. Rather than measuring powder from a horn into a separate vial and then pouring that measurement down the barrel, the shooter would use his teeth to tear off the top of the paper cartridge, then pour a bit of gunpowder into the pan as primer and the rest down the barrel. All that remained was the ball. Together with the now-empty paper tube—which served as wadding—the ball was rammed down the barrel.

The musket was the most common firearm type in the fight that day. Although its massive lead ball projectile could be deadly if it struck flesh or bone, it most often did not. Inherently inaccurate beyond short ranges, its smooth bore simply did not impart enough stability to the round as it left the barrel. In fact, the builders of the Brown Bess tacitly acknowledged this facet of their popular weapon: they didn't even give it proper sights for aiming.

Because of its inaccuracy, commanders preferred to put their soldiers on line and fire their weapons simultaneously, thus creating a coherent and concentrated wall of fire. This technique was much more devastating than ill-coordinated, inaccurate potshots taken by undisciplined troops. Fannin's men fired their muskets, rifles, and artillery with such intensity that Urrea's officers had trouble getting their troops close enough to shoot within the musket's effective range, much less to fire with any kind of discipline or order.

One means to increase the probability of hitting something was to increase the number of projectiles loaded into the gun. The buck-and-ball load was made up of a standard ball and two or three or sometimes more buckshot pellets. It did increase the odds of hitting something, but at the cost of hitting power. In addition, keeping the load of standard ball and buckshot loaded into a weapon without it dribbling out the end of the barrel was more problematic.

Many of the volunteers carried personal weapons. These were family pieces that sometimes had been pulled off the wall in their homes and taken into the fight. They were of various manufacture, caliber, and type, including shotguns, muskets, rifles, and pistols. This diversity was a constant headache in terms of providing right-sized ammunition.

Surviving accounts declare that Fannin's men carried up to one thousand additional muskets with them. Some versions of the fight allow only five hundred. Regardless, the typical volunteer could have not only his personal weapon, but also at least one, or perhaps two or three, additional weapons. No mention is made of what type of muskets these were. If they were from captured Mexican stores, they were likely India Pattern weapons. If they were from the United States, they quite possibly were U.S. Model 1816s. These

.69-caliber muskets were made in large numbers at the Springfield arsenal in Massachusetts and the Harper's Ferry arsenal in Virginia. Lewis Washington stated that "of arms we had an abundance—good muskets, fine Harper's Ferry yagers, and close-shooting rifles."[1]

These particular muskets, like many American models, traced their lineage to the Charlevilles that the French provided to the United States during the Revolutionary War. Nevertheless, despite their French heritage, they operated and performed in principle almost identically to the British Brown Bess muskets, or indeed any other comparable weapons of the day.

Other possibilities exist, including the Springfield Model 1830 Cadet Musket in .58-caliber. But the fact that the weapons could have originated from so many sources simply makes a positive declaration impossible. Regardless, as flintlock muskets, they were all roughly equivalent in design and effectiveness.

The volunteers also carried more pistols than did their Mexican counterparts. Holsters were not frequently worn, and most pistol carriers tucked one or more of them into their beltlines. Among the most common pistols of the era were the Model 1816 and Model 1819, built by Simeon North of Berlin, Connecticut. They were flintlocks with smoothbore nine-inch barrels that fired .54-caliber balls. At just more than three pounds in weight and only fifteen inches in length, they were much easier to carry than the muskets but were still effective out to about thirty yards. In a close fight, they were handy bludgeons once their load had been discharged.

Compared to the musket, the rifle was much more accurate. Although rifles were present in fewer numbers, they were at hand in numbers great enough to make an impact on the battlefield. Several stories recount the effect of the Kentucky Rifle at long range. Popular literature insists that these weapons were able to reach out accurately to three hundred yards or more. These stories combine wishful thinking with the performance of modern replicas and modern powder and projectiles. Realistically, the Kentucky rifle of the early 1800s was accurate out to no more than 150 yards.

Still, this was no small feat. If Urrea's *soldados* had to close inside of one hundred yards to have any hope of putting balls into the volunteers, they were at an extreme disadvantage against Fannin's rifles. It was no doubt alarming for the Mexican *soldados* to see their comrades dropping from wounds inflicted at ranges that precluded them from getting rounds near their adversaries.

What made the rifle so deadly accurate were the twisted grooves that lined the barrel walls. These imparted a spinning action to the ball that gave it stability and accuracy beyond what the smoothbore could provide. Still, accuracy came at some cost. Taking advantage of the grooves demanded the ball fit tightly against the barrel walls. Ramming a ball with very tight tolerances down a rifle barrel took more time and muscle than stuffing a musket ball home.

And standardization was a problem. Most of the Kentucky rifles were actually custom made by various gunsmiths in Pennsylvania. The calibers usually varied in size from .28 to .45 and were sometimes even larger. The revolutionary government could not supply all the numbers and types of rounds needed to meet the requirements of these personally owned rifles. Consequently, most of the rifle shooters cast their own bullets.

Although they seemed to dominate the long-range fight that day, Fannin's Kentucky rifles were not the only rifles on the battlefield. Some among Urrea's light infantry, and perhaps some of his horsemen, carried British Baker rifles. Some of the Indians that fought for him may also have carried Bakers. Produced in England beginning in the early 1800s, the Baker had been deadly against Napoleon's forces on the European continent. Many considered it as accurate as the Kentucky rifles that the volunteers shouldered. In addition, the Baker fired a larger .625-caliber round. At less than 46 inches long and weighing only slightly more than nine pounds, it was considerably handier than the Brown Bess.

However, the Baker was less effective in Mexican hands than it could have been due to poor training and poorer gunpowder. Mexican gunpowder was of notoriously cheap quality. Black powder of the day was a mixture of sulfur, saltpeter, and charcoal. The mixtures could vary widely and quality diverged a great deal. The Texas volunteers generally shot comparatively excellent factory-made stuff from the eastern United States. The Mexicans usually fired crude "home-grown" blends often manufactured in the field.

The quality mattered for a number of reasons: Most importantly, the gunpowder needed to reliably ignite and produce the explosive power to propel a ball at deadly velocities to decent ranges. Additionally, the gunpowder had to leave behind as little residue as possible. A common drawback of black powder muskets and rifles was that they fouled easily—to the point that vent holes had to be "picked" clean by a special tool. Indeed, barrels became so dirty and clogged that they would not even accept a ball. Rifled barrels by their nature fouled particularly easily; their grooves collected debris as if purpose-made to do so. Some armies countered this problem by issuing smaller balls. This was effective but further decreased the accuracy of already inaccurate weapons—particularly in the case of muskets.

Herman Ehrenberg wrote later of the effects of fouling. During the fight, he sorted through discarded weapons to find one that would fire after his own had failed.[2] Toward the end of the day, most of the volunteers' weapons were in desperate need of cleaning.

That Fannin's men were much more effective with their firearms than their Mexican foes is disputed by no one. Perhaps the primary reason for this fact was the volunteers' expertise and familiarity with firearms. Although Fannin gave them little or no training, most of them did not need it; many of them were raised on farms, or even farther away from civilization on the American frontier where good marksmanship was a way of life. That sort of life was characterized by the need to use a firearm as a tool for filling the larder and as a weapon for fighting Indians. In addition, some of the older men had fought the British during the War of 1812.

Urrea's *soldados*, on the other hand, generally had not been raised with firearms. While under Spanish rule the peasantry had little familiarity with them, and the training that the Mexican government gave its troops lacked rigor, depth, and discipline. In fact, the troops were taught to fire their muskets not from their shoulders, but from their hips. While this technique protected the *soldados* from the punishing recoil, it also produced very poor marksmanship.

It should also be remembered that the volunteers were fighting from a fixed defensive position. Whereas the Mexican soldiers had only the scant protection that the tall grass afforded, Fannin's men were able to take cover behind the hasty defenses they constructed from their wagons and baggage. Although it was not a stalwart set of breastworks, it was more than Urrea's men had.

There is speculation that aside from flintlock weapons, a few of the volunteers may have been carrying rifles that used newer technology. The percussion cap eliminated the need for the more complex and unreliable combination that was made up of the flint, frizzen, pan, and vent hole. It also did away with the requirement to prime the loaded charge.

In the case of the percussion cap weapon, the frizzen, pan, and vent hole were replaced by a bronze tube, called a "nipple," that ran to the main charge in the barrel of the gun. Atop the nipple was placed a copper cap loaded with an explosive mixture that included fulminate of mercury. When the trigger was pulled, the cock, or hammer, sprang down and over the cap, crushing it against the nipple and causing the cap to explode. The resultant detonation was channeled down the tubular nipple and into the barrel, where it ignited the main charge.

The chief advantages conferred by the percussion cap were speed and reliability. The delicate, imprecise, and time-consuming step of filling the pan with loose gunpowder was eliminated. Instead, one only needed to slip a cap over the nipple. In addition, the percussion cap was very much more reliable, particularly in wet weather. Misfires became much less common, compared to the flintlock's 15 percent misfire rate.

The percussion cap had been in fairly widespread use for a decade or more by the time of Fannin's fight with Urrea, but it had not yet gained widespread popularity on the frontier. The problem was that a weapon designed to use percussion caps was useless without them. It was no better than a club and could not be readily converted back to a flintlock. And there were not a great many places on the frontier that percussion caps could be procured. A man was out of luck if he lost his supply of caps, or if they were damaged or stolen. On the other hand, flint could nearly always be found—even on the ground— for a flintlock.

Although there is no specific mention of percussion caps in association with Fannin's men, the technology was available, and it is possible that they were used in the fight. Further buttressing the idea that they were used is the fact that percussion caps were excavated from the ruins of the Alamo. Nevertheless, the flintlock was overwhelmingly the predominant type of weapon in use during the fight between Fannin and Urrea.

CHAPTER 12

Overnight Misery

Indians composed a portion of the Mexican force. Some accounts claim that they numbered a hundred or more, although this tally seems excessive because, if true, they probably would have been mentioned more often and more prominently. Where exactly they came from is not clear. Variously described as Campeachy or Carise Indians, they probably came from the southern Mexican state of Campeche, on the western coast of the Yucatán Peninsula.

They served General José Urrea well, and the volunteers noted their daring and marksmanship. One account holds that they killed four volunteers and wounded another fifty in the space of an hour of so.[1] Experts at cover and concealment, they made good use of the tall grass that blanketed the prairie, approaching as close as thirty paces from the hollow square: "The confusion arising from the smoke prevented our men from discovering the exact position of their dangerous neighbors, who were so well concealed in the grass that they could not dislodge them."[2]

The Indians were deadly effective shots. They shot Harry Ripley (ca. 1817–1836) in the leg, breaking his thigh. The teenager from Louisiana still had plenty of fight remaining and was lifted into the wagon of Ellen Cash. She was the wife of George Cash, who had earlier been shot in the head while fighting outside the hollow square with Abel Morgan. She, with her fourteen-year-old son, helped tend the wounded. Propped up, and with a rifle and a view of the battlefield, Ripley reportedly shot four *soldados* before another ball slammed into his arm. He called out to Mrs. Cash that she could "take me down now mother; I have done my share, they have paid exactly two for one on account of both balls in me."[3]

John Duval described how his brother, Burr H. Duval, dispatched a particularly troublesome group of Indians:

> [The Indians] boldly advanced to the front, and taking advantage of every little inequality of the ground and every bunch of grass that could afford them particular cover, they would crawl up closely and fire upon us, and now and then the discharge of their

long single barrel shot guns was followed by the fall of some one in our ranks. Four of them had crawled up behind some bunches of tall grass within eighty yards of us, from whence they delivered their fire with telling effect. Capt. D- [Burr Duval], who was using a heavy Kentucky rifle, and was known to be one of the best marksmen in his company, was requested to silence these Indians. He took a position near a gun carriage, and whenever one of the Indians showed his head above the tall grass it was perforated with an ounce rifle ball and after four shots they were seen no more. At the moment he fired the last shot Capt. D- had one of the fingers of his right hand taken off by a musket ball. When the Mexicans quit the field, we examined the locality where these Indians had secreted themselves, and found the four lying closely together, each one with a bullet hole through his head.[4]

Both forces were exhausted as dusk gave way to night. James Walker Fannin's volunteers had inflicted many more casualties than they had sustained, but their situation was nevertheless desperate. Urrea's force had taken a beating but still held the advantage. The Mexicans surrounded Fannin's inferior position with superior numbers that continued to increase as the hours passed and new units found their way through the dark to Urrea's position. With those fresh troops came at least two artillery pieces that would make good what had been a serious deficiency earlier that day: the Mexicans had been mauled by Fannin's cannon and had been unable to reply in kind. They would not be fighting with the same disadvantage in the morning.

Urrea had more men, superior terrain, cavalry, and now, cannon. These overwhelming advantages would permit him to decide the timing and tempo of the fight on the following day. Urrea, of course, realized that Fannin's men were trapped and had few good options.

Escape—perhaps into the safety of one of the distant scattered concentrations of trees or to the banks of the Perdido or Coleto—was the American commander's only real hope. Fannin knew that the number of enemy soldiers surrounding him was increasing, and that the Mexicans would almost surely have artillery in place in the morning. Artillery would play havoc with the crude defenses of his hollow square. The heavy cannon balls would shred the ad hoc breastworks that his men had frantically erected since the start of the battle. The Mexicans would be able to fire the balls straight down the sides of the hollow square, shattering anything or anyone in their path.

Successfully breaking away from Urrea would be risky, with at least as much of a chance of failure as success. Darkness could work for both sides. Although night might aid the Anglos to surprise Urrea's pickets and crash through the Mexican perimeter to freedom, it would also make it very difficult to maintain any sort of cohesiveness. Broken into smaller bands, the volunteers would be easier for Urrea's cavalry to chase down and overcome when morning came.

Still, Fannin believed that making a run for cover was better than waiting for a renewed and stronger assault at dawn. Early in the evening he made his argument to the men. John Duval later recorded that Fannin suggested an escape to the timber along Coleto Creek. He argued that the run had a chance, because the enemy fighters were surely demoralized after the whipping they had sustained that day. On the other hand, he pointed out that the Mexicans would surely be reinforced during the night and that fleeing the battlefield during darkness was their best chance at surviving.[5]

Fannin, characteristically, made no actual decision, but called for a vote. He declared that if the majority of the men favored an escape he would order preparations as soon as the darkness was sufficient to hide their intentions. However, the men rejected Fannin's proposal. They knew that an escape attempt would require them to abandon their badly wounded colleagues. The oxen were too slow and balky to move them, and besides, most of them had been lost during the day. Many of them had been killed by Mexican gunfire, and many of the surviving oxen had been killed for cover or had broken loose and escaped. Carrying the wounded on makeshift stretchers in the darkness while trying to fight through enemy lines would be impossible.

In short, the badly wounded would be unable to leave the field, and for this reason many of the men argued against a breakout attempt. They could not know for certain how Urrea's men would treat the wounded, and the bonds of camaraderie were so strong that the friends and relatives of the stricken refused to abandon them.

This rejection of Fannin's proposal to flee without the wounded—and Fannin's failure to order the men to do so—meant that the volunteers were committed to fight or surrender the following day. Outwardly, at least, there was little indication that anyone intended to give in. Although they were surrounded and outnumbered, the prairie around them was littered with Mexican dead and wounded. Those dead and wounded convinced Fannin's men that they were superior fighters.

Albert Horton and his scouts had fled in the direction of Victoria just as the fighting had started that day. If, as they hoped, Horton and his horsemen were able to bring reinforcements in time, the volunteers thought they might still stand a chance. Rumors held that up to six hundred armed militiamen might come to their aid. Victoria was only about fifteen miles to the northeast. Reinforcements—even after making preparations and traveling on foot—could easily cover the distance to their position well before morning.

These hopes were to prove groundless. No reinforcements were coming from Victoria. Horton had found the town essentially abandoned, with another large Mexican force nearby. After delaying only a short time, he and his men had left for Gonzales to find help. There was little they could do for the volunteers, who were even that moment battling for their lives.

Apart from Horton and the nonexistent militiamen at Victoria, Fannin's men, not unrealistically, believed that William Ward and his formation of more than a hundred men that had escaped under Urrea's nose at Refugio might appear out of the darkness in time to join the coming fight. In fact, Ward had indeed heard the booming of the cannon earlier in the day. As luck would have it, though, he was also trapped. A superior Mexican force had cornered him in the lowlands between Refugio and the Coleta Creek battlefield. Unable to do anything other than try to save their own skins, Ward's men slipped through the swampy woods in an effort to lose their pursuers.

Fannin's fighters reinforced their position with the limited means at hand. They scraped a trench along all four sides of the hollow square and threw up an embankment with the excavated dirt. The result was a chest-high fighting position. Dead draft animals, baggage, and stores thrown atop the soft soil barricade increased that protection somewhat. The impromptu breastworks afforded some protection against musket fire or cavalry charges, but the wagon hulks and storage boxes would be chopped into jagged and deadly high-velocity projectiles if the Mexican forces fired heavy artillery at them.

Behind the perimeter, the wounded men were made as comfortable as possible. What was possible was little enough, and their distress was considerable. Adding to the pain and misery of their wounds was the thin, icy rain blowing out of the north. It was just enough to soak and chill them, but not enough to slake their thirsts or cleanse their injuries. There were no fires to warm them. The men had little to burn, and fires would have highlighted their forms and made them easy targets. Several accounts recall the melancholy and despair of the stricken. Dr. Joseph Field believed that he could not do justice in describing the "horrors of that night, which was spent amid the groans of the dying and the incessant cry for water of the wounded."[6] John Duval's report echoes Field's: "I can never forget how slowly the hours of that dismal night passed by. The distressing cries of our wounded men begging for water when there was not a drop to give them were continually ringing in my ears."[7]

Simply saying that Fannin's men were short on water understates the case. Modern military logisticians consider that soldiers require at least a gallon of drinking water each day, and up to three gallons in particularly stressful environments. The battlefield—particularly one that features close combat—is among the most physically taxing environments in the world. Fannin's men had nothing remotely close to a gallon each, but they certainly needed at least that. After hours of sustained and fearsome fighting, Fannin's men must have felt near-unbearable thirst. The agony of the wounded, whose bodies ached for water to replace lost blood, must have been truly horrendous. And physical distress aside, the lack of water must have affected their mental capacities. Tellingly, their want was so fierce that some of the men tried to dig a well overnight within the lines of their hollow square. The grueling work could have only exacerbated their dehydration.

Those who were not tending the wounded kept watch over the hastily scraped earthen parapet that marked their perimeter. There was no guarantee that the Mexicans would not try to overcome their position under cover of darkness. Urrea ordered false bugle blasts throughout the night. If he could keep the volunteers from resting they would be less effective the following day. Morgan recounted, "Many of us had two muskets. We were down on one knee behind our little embankment with one musket in our hands and braced against our knees and the other leaning against the embankment. Our orders were if they came to charge on us that night, to let them come close enough so as to be sure to kill one out of each fire, for every man, and then to use the bayonet. . . . We remained in the position all night and the Mexicans continued to blow bugles."[8]

Not everyone agreed with the majority who wanted to hold the position and stay with the wounded. The New Orleans Greys, especially, were opposed. They recognized the hopelessness of holding out against an enemy force that was growing stronger while waiting for help that probably was not coming. Ultimately, they accepted the rule of the majority, but they did so with reservations. In fact, three men, whose names or affiliations are unknown, tried to break through the Mexican lines. Again, Duval: "Sometime during the night it was ascertained that three of our men (whose names I have forgotten) had deserted, and shortly afterwards as a volley of musketry was heard between us and the timber on the Coleto, they were no doubt discovered and shot by the Mexican patrol."[9]

Mexican records do not mention intercepting and killing the three volunteers who had tried to desert. Perhaps Urrea's men believed they had caught a patrol meant to probe their defenses or a small party sent by Fannin to bring back help. Possibly, too, the Mexicans attached no special significance to the three hapless men.

Urrea had no intention of rejoining the battle until the following morning. Controlling his formations during the day had been difficult enough, and he saw no special need to throw his men against Fannin's hollow square at night. He could afford to wait. Except for strengthening their breastworks, the volunteers could do nothing to improve their situation. At the same time, Urrea fed and watered his men, repositioned them, and made plans for the following day, while continuing to receive reinforcements.

Although Fannin's men had badly mauled the *soldados*, Mexican spirits were high, and they were anxious to destroy their enemy. Urrea claimed "they were burning with desire to undertake a new bayonet charge."[10] This bravado may or may not have reflected reality. It is hard to imagine that, after having sustained many casualties during a five- or six-hour fight, his men would have beseeched him to lead them on another bloody charge. Ultimately, he closed the matter with this short speech to his men: "Let us gather our forces, let us wait for our ammunitions and artillery, let us watch the enemy during the night, and tomorrow I shall lead you to victory. You do not need your cartridges, for you have your bayonets, and your courage is boundless. The enemy is terrified and will not be able to resist any longer the charge of such brave Mexicans. I promise you a complete victory."[11]

It seems contradictory that Urrea would tell his men to wait for ammunition in one sentence then tell them they needed none in the next. Perhaps he was hedging his bets in the event that his expected supplies did not arrive. It also bears remembering that Urrea himself had spent much of the day on the battlefield and was quite likely exhausted. And although he had not been wounded during the day's fighting, he had come close enough: Mexican General Vicente Filisola recorded that a musket ball had pierced a hole in Urrea's hat.[12]

Regardless of Urrea's exhaustion or his freshly ventilated hat, his first responsibility was to the fight. Throughout the evening, he continued to check on his men while tightening the encirclement of Fannin's hollow square. Ultimately, the volunteers were fully surrounded and Urrea had scouts well placed; Fannin's men did nothing of importance that was not reported to him or his officers.

Other than holding a Council of War, not much is known of Fannin's actions or movements during the night. No doubt he was deeply concerned about the events of the day and what was about to unfold in the morning. As the commander, he was responsible for the unit in its entirety. Whatever his men did or failed to do—whether they ultimately succeeded or failed—he would be accountable. In battle, some of his men were bound to lose their lives, but how those lives were spent, and what was gained as a result hinged in large part on Fannin.

Caught in miserably intractable circumstances, wounded in three places, and suffering from acute thirst, Fannin passed through what surely had to be the worst night of his life. Once he accepted the decision to stay on the battlefield, he could do nothing but supervise the construction of the barricade and stiffen the men's resolve. Andrew Boyle, who had taken a musket ball in his right leg earlier that day and found himself laying next to Fannin, noted that his commander also tried to get some rest: "I lay close by him that night and hearing my groans, he kindly offered me his good leg as a pillow."[13]

Despite his earlier described desire to fight or flee, did Fannin's own condition ultimately persuade him to keep the volunteers in place, rather than to make a break for cover, leaving the wounded behind? He had personally sustained at least three wounds, one of them severe. That he could have taken part in a fighting breakout was dubious. Rather, he probably would have been left behind while the rest of the men escaped. In fact, it might have been best for him to stay behind. As the commander, he could have appealed to his Mexican counterpart for the lives of the wounded. On the other hand, we have seen that Fannin did not make good decisions even when alert and unwounded. In the end, Fannin and his men remained where they were.

CHAPTER 13

Surrender

T he miserable night gave way to an equally miserable dawn. James Walker Fannin's men peered through the lessening dark toward the distant tree lines, but their hopes faded along with the night—no relief force galloped through the trees to their aid. The fact remained that they— worn and wretched as they were—made up the most powerful force on the side of the revolution.

General José Urrea's Indians combed the battlefield during the cold, rainy night to carry away the Mexican wounded and dead. Nevertheless, first light showed that they had not been able to finish the task. The lifeless bodies of dozens of *soldados* dotted the prairie in groups and singles. Among them lay the twisted corpses of the cavalry horses that had likewise fallen to the fire of Fannin's men. Ironically, Urrea's cavalrymen had pinned down the volunteers astride these same horses just the day before.

Urrea had withdrawn his formations during the night, allowing some of the volunteers to strike out beyond the safety of the hollow square. Picking among the enemy dead, one group found a Mexican banner that had fallen with those who had charged the field. There was no fanfare when it was brought back inside the perimeter: it was tossed aside and fell among the rubbish that had accumulated since the start of the fight.[1]

Two wounded *soldados* were also hauled up from the wet ground and brought back to the hollow square. The information they offered was anything but heartening. They estimated Urrea's force at nineteen hundred men and declared that reinforcements were due that very morning. On this news, and with hope for reinforcements lost, it is likely that some of the volunteers renewed the call for a fighting retreat to a more defensible position.

Shortly after daybreak, Urrea formed his men for the coming fight. He assigned the volunteer front to his infantry companies while he ordered the cavalry to hit the flanks. Assembling his men out of rifle range but close enough to make an impression, he ensured that even the pack animals and their drivers—estimated at more than three hundred men—were brought into view. He wanted to impress the revolutionary fighters with the strength of his force. The size of the Mexican formations was impressive enough, but it was the appearance of artillery—two four-pounders and a howitzer—that really grabbed Fannin's attention.

Behind their makeshift breastworks Fannin's men would have had some chance of repeating their successes of the previous day as long as the Mexicans were without cannon, but that was not the case. Fannin understood that Urrea, particularly with the advantage of a slight elevation, would be able to blast his position apart with the big guns, and he would be able to do it at his leisure while Fannin's men would be helpless to stop him.

With ample time at his disposal, the Mexican commander, evidently satisfied that his *soldados* were prepared for the coming battle, fed them a breakfast of hard tack and fresh roasted meat. The meat had been cut from the volunteers' oxen that had been shot the previous day. No doubt, the Mexicans washed their meal down with all the water they desired. On the other hand, Fannin's men sat hungry and desperately thirsty behind their dirt and debris fortifications.

Once his men had finished their morning meal, Urrea readied them for the day's first attack. When it was reported that the volunteers were awake and moving about, the newly arrived Mexican artillery was put to work almost immediately. But the loads from the big guns, perhaps by design, whistled harmlessly over the hollow square. Fannin and his staff immediately went into conference.

Ellen Cash was a courageous and compassionate woman. In response to the thirsty volunteer's cries, she and her fourteen-year-old son made their way across the battlefield to the Mexican lines to ask for water. Upon reaching Urrea's lines, Mrs. Cash found an officer whom she knew from Goliad's former Mexican garrison. This officer took her to Urrea. While she made her request to the enemy commander, he turned his attention to her son. He noted the youngster's weapon and powder horn and rebuked the woman for putting a child in such danger. Mrs. Cash's son replied that he was fighting for his rights as a "Texan" and that he was prepared to die for those rights.[2] It is unknown whether Urrea agreed to Mrs. Cash's appeal for water.

Back at the hollow square, Fannin and his staff debated what their next move should be. The notion of surrendering with terms, or a capitulation, had already been discussed—especially since the appearance of the enemy artillery. The veterans among them knew that the Mexican guns alone could blast their position to smithereens. In combination with Urrea's cavalry and infantry, the cannon virtually guaranteed that the volunteers would not survive another fight. Still, Fannin declared, "We whipped them off yesterday and we can do so again today."[3] This statement is curious: surely he understood that the Mexican position was much stronger than it had been the previous day.

Although there likely were holdouts among the volunteers that were vehemently against giving up the fight, the majority must have wanted to at least see what sort of terms might be reached. The wounded were mentioned often as a reason for negotiating some sort honorable truce: a fighting retreat would leave them at the mercy of the Mexicans. Fannin's men knew that there had been no survivors at the Alamo, and that the wounded survivors must have been slain without mercy.

It is extremely difficult to determine with certainty which side raised the white flag first; accounts are at great odds. Vicente Filisola declared that immediately after Urrea ordered the first salvo of artillery fire, "the enemy [Fannin] raised the white flag."[4] Herman Ehrenberg remembered that the volunteers were ready for the coming fight when, "See! Unexpectedly the white flag, the sign of peace, rose before us and halted us in our progress."[5] Dr. Joseph Barnard, as an educated man arguably a better source than Ehrenberg, wrote that Fannin queried his staff in conference and, "finding that all, or nearly all, had made up their minds [to surrender], he ordered a white flag to be hoisted. This was done and was promptly answered by one from the enemy."[6] Jack Shackelford, the commander of the Red Rovers, recalled, "After they had fired a few rounds at us, they raised a white flag which was soon taken down. We then had a consultation of officers, a majority of whom believed we could not save our wounded without a capitulation. . . . We then raised a white flag, which was responded to by the enemy."[7]

Colonel Juan José Holzinger offered perhaps the most contemporary account on June 3, 1836, less than three months after the fight. While a prisoner of Texas following the revolution, he wrote, "On learning from one of our outposts that the enemy was moving [about], orders were given to attack him with the artillery but when on the third time of firing we perceived that he did not return it, ours [artillery fire] was suspended and 1/4 of an hour afterwards he was seen to hang out a white flag."[8]

Holzinger's account supported Urrea's, who later wrote that, when his artillery battery began to fire on the volunteer position, "the enemy, without answering our fire, raised a white flag." Urrea further noted that he ordered, "Lieutenant Colonel [Juan] Morales, Captain Juan José Holzinger, and my aide, José de la Luz Gonzalez to approach the enemy and ascertain their purpose."[9]

John C. Duval of Kentucky offered testimony that agrees with Urrea's: "We expected momentarily that the cavalry would charge us, but after firing several rounds from their nine-pounders, an officer accompanied by a soldier bearing a white flag, rode out towards us, and by signs gave us to understand that he desired a 'parley.'"[10]

Most likely, Fannin's staff went into conference as soon the artillery fire began and put up a white banner immediately after. The Mexicans may very well have immediately replied with a flag of their own. To suppose that many of the volunteers—braced for an enemy charge—would not have noted the flag raised from their own side is not unreasonable. This explains why most of the volunteers insisted that the Mexicans raised the white flag first. Typical of their reports is what Abel Morgan stated in his pension claim after the revolution: "The next morning early they fired a chain shot out of a large cannon at us which made a wonderful whiz[z]ing over our head. Directly they fired another and then quit and hoisted a white flag."[11]

The issue of who first raised the white banner is so contentious because the white flag carries a stigma of weakness. Neither side wanted their comrades remembered with humiliation or dishonor.

Still, the situation of both sides must be considered. On the one hand, the volunteers had plenty of motivation to put up a white flag. Huddling behind their crude barricade while Urrea's big guns blew them to bits was clearly a fearsome prospect. An arrangement to save their lives, secure their honor, and ensure the wounded received treatment merited investigation. Of course, the volunteers knew that a white flag would be interpreted as a symbol of defeat or surrender. Although their situation was precarious, even hopeless, many among them believed, with some justification, that they had not been beaten.

Why would the Mexican commander raise a white banner? Rather than a sign of defeat or surrender, in his situation it would signal a desire to parley or negotiate. And why shouldn't Urrea negotiate? He was certainly in a strong position to do so. The coming battle would start when he decided it would start—or, if he could prevail on Fannin to leave the field, perhaps it would not start at all.

After all, the volunteers had savaged his men the day before. The horrid proof was scattered broken and lifeless across the battlefield. If he could neutralize the revolution's largest standing force right then and there—and without sustaining any further losses—then surely he should do so. A negotiated solution that removed Fannin's force from the field would save him men and resources. Although perhaps not as glorious as a battle of annihilation, it would still be a victory, and Fannin's men would be neutralized just as effectively as if Urrea's men had killed them all.

Whatever the exact timing, flags went up and the two sides met to negotiate. Urrea's *Diario* entry from March 20 declares that "the enemy, without answering our fire, raised a white flag."[12] Immediately, the Mexican commander checked his artillery and sent his delegation toward Fannin's position. Major Benjamin

C. Wallace (d. 1836) of Fannin's staff, along with Captain Francis J. Dusanque and Captain Benjamin Holland and perhaps one or two others, left the hollow square to meet the Mexican party.

The parties met approximately halfway between the two formations. The meeting by all accounts was short. Morales quickly returned to the Mexican side with the message that the volunteers wished to capitulate—presumably with terms. Morales was sent back to the negotiation with the message that Urrea would and could accept nothing other than an unconditional surrender, which meant that the volunteers would have no rights or guarantees.

Several exchanges followed. Fannin had not been among the initial cadre of officers to negotiate with Urrea's men, perhaps due to his wounds. Regardless, the Mexicans insisted that he be part of the negotiations. Shackelford recorded his own distress that he shared with Fannin before he left the lines to negotiate. He was not against a surrender under honorable terms, but if such could not be achieved, then Fannin should "come back—our graves are already dug— let us be buried together."[13] Fannin assured Shackelford that he would accept nothing other than surrender with honor.

There was quite a bit of confusion as to what was actually being put forth by both parties and how what was being put forth was translated and interpreted. It was further complicated because the German, Holzinger, played a major role on the Mexican side. Ehrenberg recounted the problems:

> This German, Holzinger, was the only officer of the three who could speak English. As it was, however, only in a broken manner, it was often necessary first to translate our transactions into German and from there carry them over to the Spanish. After long negotiations, Fannin finally agreed that we should surrender all of our arms, that our private property should be respected, that we ourselves should be shipped through Copano or Matamoros to New Orleans and set free, and that, as long as we were prisoners of war, we should receive the same rations as the Mexican army received. Our obligation was to be our word of honor not to fight hereafter against the present Mexican government.[14]

As previously described, Holzinger wrote his account of the surrender on June 3, 1836, while he was being held captive following the battle of San Jacinto, which was less than three months after the battle at Coleto Creek. He had little to gain by defending or corroborating Urrea's actions, yet he described the meeting in this way:

> When we were informed that they were ready to surrender as prisoners of war, if the Mexican Commander would engage to treat them according to the usage of civilized nations. We were

acquainted with the law [the Tornel Decree] that establishes the penalty of death for those individuals who may come armed for the purpose of carrying on war in Mexican territory and that the door was therefore closed against any agreement; I offered however to Colonel Fannin to make known his disposition to General Urrea which in effect I did, and received for answer, that inasmuch as the law prohibited his entering into such agreements [Urrea] could not enter into any, nor listen to any other proposition [than] a surrender at the discretion of the Supreme Government of Mexico.[15]

Holzinger further stated that Urrea urged him to tell Fannin that he would use his "influence and endeavors" with the Mexican government to mitigate their punishment. Additionally, he promised to treat them as prisoners of war, "according to the right of Nations" until a decision was forthcoming. Holzinger wrote that Fannin and his staff went into conference after receiving Urrea's reply. After "about half an hour," Fannin's reply was that he would agree to surrender on terms. He would capitulate under the stipulation that their "lives and effects" were guaranteed and that their wounded would receive the same care as the Mexican wounded. They further wanted these terms drawn up and signed by Holzinger and ratified in writing by Urrea.[16]

Urrea would have none of it. His record of the surrender negotiations is straightforward and agrees with Holzinger's. In exasperation, he took himself to the rebel position in order to deliver an ultimatum. He understood that he was negotiating from a position of strength:

My reply [to Fannin's first offer to surrender with conditions] restricted itself to stating that I could not accept any terms except an unconditional surrender. Messrs. Morales and Salas proceeded to tell this to the commissioner of the enemy who had already come out from their trenches. Several communications passed between us; and, desirous of putting an end to the negotiations, I went over to the enemy's camp and explained to their leader [Fannin] the impossibility in which I found myself of granting other terms than an unconditional surrender as proposed, in view of which fact I refused to subscribe to the capitulation submitted consisting of three articles. Addressing myself to Fannin and companions in the presence of Messrs. Morales, Salas, Holzinger and others I said conclusively, "If you gentlemen wish to surrender at discretion, the matter is ended, otherwise I shall return to my camp and renew the attack." In spite of the regret I felt in making such a reply and in spite of my great desire of offering them guarantees as humanity dictated, this was beyond my authority.[17]

Urrea's ultimatum apparently spurred Fannin and his officers to hurry to an agreement. After all, the Mexican commander had the upper hand, and Fannin's situation could do nothing but deteriorate. Holzinger wrote that Fannin and his staff conferred for several minutes before Fannin asked Holzinger, "Do you believe that the Mexican Government will not attempt to take away our lives?" Holzinger and the other Mexican officers replied that they could give no guarantees but that "not a single example could be adduced that the Mexican Government had ordered a man to be shot who had trusted to their clemency."

Then, according to the German, Fannin declared, "Well then, I have no water; my wounded need attendance, I particularly recommend to you those unfortunate men and will deliver myself up to the discretion of the Mexican Government."[18] Urrea then ordered Captain Salas Andrade, his secretary, to draw up two copies of the surrender terms, at discretion. Urrea directed him to write one copy in Spanish, to be held by the Mexicans, while the other was to be composed in English for Fannin to hold.[19]

An hour was set aside for the documents to be prepared and for the rebel fighters to ready themselves and their equipment for surrender. At the close of his record of the negotiations, surely mindful of the fact that he was a prisoner when he wrote his declaration, Holzinger made the following statement: "If subsequently General Urrea, had, through his Secretary any further negotiation with Col. Fannin, on the matter, I am entirely ignorant of it."[20] This statement does nothing but cloud subsequent events.

Whether or not the agreement Fannin and his staff believed they reached is the same one that Urrea declared he offered them will probably never be known. Holland and Dusanque were two of the officers present during the negotiations. Holland later wrote, "A copy of it in Spanish was retained by Gen. Urrea, and one in English by Col. Fannin." Holland stated that the documents were signed by Urrea, Morales, and Holzinger "on the part of the enemy," and by Fannin and Wallace "on our part."[21] Although the English copy of the surrender document has since disappeared, Holland's recollection of the terms was specific:

> ARTICLE 1ST: That we should be received and treated as prisoners of war, according to the usages of civilized nations.

> ARTICLE 2ND: That the officers should be paroled immediately upon their arrival at La Bahia, and the other prisoners should be sent to Copano, within eight days, there to await shipping to convey them to the United States, so soon as it was practicable to procure it; no more to take up arms against Mexico until exchanged.

ARTICLE 3RD: That all private property should be respected, and officers [*sic*] swords should be returned on parole or release.

ARTICLE 4TH: That our men should receive every comfort and be fed as well as their own men.[22]

These terms—almost exactly—are the same stipulations that nearly every survivor recalled being described to him following the surrender negotiations. Dr. Joseph Field later remembered "that in consideration of our surrendering, our lives should be ensured, our personal property restored and we were to be treated, in all respects, as prisoners of war are treated among enlightened nations." He also recalled that they were to be sent to the nearest port within eight days and from there embarked to the United States. Field additionally recorded that Urrea made a show of good intentions when he put his arms around Fannin and declared, "Yesterday we fought, but today we are friends."[23]

Aside from Urrea putting his arms around Fannin, Barnard's recollections are almost identical. He wrote that the volunteers were to be treated as prisoners of war "according to the usage of civilized nations." He also remembered that the wounded were to be "properly attended to, and that all private property should be respected." These, Barnard wrote, are the terms that Fannin told his men he had negotiated with Urrea. Barnard, like Field, also referenced a less well-defined promise that they were to be paroled back to the United States.[24]

Shackelford recorded the same articles as Holland had listed except in a different order. He also strongly asserted "that this Capitulation was entered into without which a surrender never would have been made."[25] In other words, without terms, the volunteers would have fought to their deaths.

Charles Shain, a member of Captain Burr H. Duval's company from Kentucky, remembered Fannin calling the officers together at the conclusion of the negotiations. He recounted that Fannin told them that the terms included their treatment as prisoners of war, the respect of their private property, and that after eight days they were to be sent to the United States on "parole of honor." He also remembered that all the officers consented to these terms except for Captain Duval.[26] It was Duval who had written to his father only a short time earlier, saying that the men never thought of retreat or surrender and that they would have to be "exterminated to be whipped."[27] Upon learning of the surrender, he said to Fannin: "Sir! You have not only signed your death warrant, but the death warrants of all of us." He further declared that the others could do as they wished, but that he would never give up.[28] Ultimately, though, he had no choice but to go along with the others.

Other survivor accounts repeat the same basic terms that Holland outlined. Duval's misgivings aside, from a simple and pragmatic perspective Fannin's men would have been foolish to refuse the terms that Fannin described to them. Essentially, in exchange for giving up the fight and for promising to never again bear arms against Mexico, they were going to be returned to the United States. They were going to live, they were going to be treated well, and their wounds were going to be tended. The Mexicans even promised to protect their personal property. And, on deeper reflection, some of the men may have realized that if the rebellion succeeded and the Mexican army was eventually evicted from Texas, they were probably still going to be able to collect their land bounty.

If anything, the promised treatment was a fair and honorable exchange in recognition of their ferocity during the fight the day before. After all, should they decide to continue the battle, they would probably be exterminated—but their extinction would come at a price of many more dead *soldados*. If some or many of the men among the volunteers believed that Urrea's men also stood to gain from this agreement—because they would not be slain—they were not wrong.

But what they understood the terms to be, and what the Mexicans claimed the terms were, did not match. Maybe Urrea had lied to Fannin, or Fannin and the other men who had taken part in the negotiations had lied to the remainder of the volunteers. Maybe, too, poor translations created an enormous mis-understanding; as noted above, Holzinger's English was poor. From the time that the parleys concluded, accounts and records diverge to an extent that there is little hope that the truth of the matter will ever be uncovered.

The primary piece of evidence that runs counter to what Fannin told his men is the Mexican copy of the surrender document, written in Spanish. "Document" is perhaps too formal a word for the awkward little agreement that was hastily scratched on paper. It promised nothing in detail and only generally and vaguely addressed a few of the points that the Anglo fighters believed they were getting in exchange for their surrender:

> Article 1: The Mexican troops having placed their battery at a distance of one hundred and seventy paces from us and the fire having been renewed, we raised a white flag. Colonels Juan Morales, Colonel Mariano Salas and Lieutenant Colonel Juan José Holsinger of Engineers came immediately. We proposed to them to surrender at discretion and they agreed.

> Article 2: The commandant Fannin and the wounded shall be treated with all possible consideration possible upon the surrender of all their arms.

> Article 3: The whole detachment shall be treated as prisoners of war and shall be subject to the disposition of the Supreme Government.

Camp on the Coleto between Guadalupe and La Bahia,
March 20, 1836.

B. C. Wallace, commandant,
J. M. Chadwick, Aide. Approved, James W. Fannin.[29]

The agreement that Fannin's men believed guaranteed their lives comprised only three brief provisions, or articles. The first one did nothing other than describe the surrender in three short sentences (and incidentally declared that Fannin raised his white flag first). The second article was one sentence that promised care for the wounded. The third provision, also one sentence, stated that the men would be treated as prisoners of war and would be "*subject to the disposition of the Supreme Government*" (emphasis added).[30]

There was nothing in the document about the protection of personal property. There was nothing that promised the men their lives. There was nothing that pledged that the men would be paroled and transported back to the United States. There was nothing about food and comforts for them while they were held prisoner.

So what really happened? Possibly, when Fannin and his staff made their demands, Urrea held his ground and told them again that he could make no guarantees whatsoever. He might have emphasized the fact that he did not even have the authority to make promises. Knowing the dictator, Antonio López de Santa Anna, he definitely was not going to put assurances to paper. That he actually promised care for the wounded in the second provision and allowed it to be included in the agreement was a nod to humanity and something that he could defend even to Santa Anna. The third article that acknowledged Fannin's men as prisoners of war meant nothing. It stated that they were prisoners of war subject to the Mexican government. "The Mexican government" meant Santa Anna. In short, Urrea put nothing in the agreement that he could not defend to his mercurial superior.

Although he did not put promises to paper, he promised Fannin and his men that he would try to meet their requests. He later acknowledged that he did indeed make these promises, and Holzinger in his account also confirms that he did. And while the negotiations were taking place, he very well may have alluded to his power and influence, perhaps stating that although he could not officially agree to any terms, he was a man of authority and could make things happen. He almost certainly meant what he said, and Fannin and his staff probably believed him. How much was lost or misunderstood in translation will never be known.

So, in this scenario, Fannin and the other negotiators likely believed that they had secured their lives and their property. Certainly Holland believed so. The men probably treated the Spanish copy of the surrender agreement as a bit of official necessity, but believed that the real contract had been negotiated orally with Urrea and that he would live up to his pledge to advocate for their cause. It may not even have occurred to them to review what had been discussed against the Spanish copy of the agreement that had been signed.

The English copy of the agreement is the only object that can clear the argument. Unfortunately, Fannin held the copy and it is quite possible that it was stolen and purposely destroyed following his death.

It is reasonable to assume, though, that the English copy of the agreement was not different from the Spanish copy. Had it been different, and if it had delineated all the provisions as verbalized by Fannin and outlined by Holland, it is likely that it would have been shared with the rank and file so that they could see for themselves what terms had been negotiated. Nevertheless, no survivor mentioned having actually seen a surrender document of any sort, although Duval—alone among all the accounts—mentioned that Fannin read from a document.[31]

It is possible that Fannin was entirely aware that neither the Spanish nor English versions of the agreement embodied the stipulations he described to his men. Perhaps he was fearful that if the truth were known his men would revolt against him and that the fight would be renewed. Rather than risking the bloody outcome that would likely result from that course of action, he was more willing to risk his fate—and the fates of his men—to Urrea's charity.

Regardless, the possibilities discussed above are only informed conjecture. Rather than having any real interest in meeting the requests of Fannin and his men, Urrea could have simply been pretending in order to expedite his own mission and safeguard his men. He may have had no empathy whatsoever for the revolutionaries.

The case for those who assert that Urrea was disingenuous with Fannin is bolstered by a curious addendum that the general added to the bottom of the Mexican copy of the agreement. It is a sort of qualification; it is unknown whether it was penned in the presence of Fannin and his men, or after the negotiations. That Fannin or none of the other negotiators ever mentioned it lends credence to the notion that it was added subsequent to the event. It is a disclaimer by Urrea that reads, "Since, when the white flag was raised by the enemy, I made it known to their officer that I could not grant any other terms than unconditional surrender and they agreed to it through the officers expressed, those who subscribe the surrender have no right to any other terms. They have been informed of this fact and they are agreed. I ought not, cannot, nor wish to grant any other terms."[32]

In essence, what Urrea was telling anyone who might read the agreement, particularly his superiors, was that even though it did not explicitly say so in the document, he had told Fannin that he had no rights, and Fannin had agreed.

Urrea later claimed that he agreed to nothing except, for all intents and purposes, not to kill Fannin's men on the spot.[33] The only option he gave them was to surrender "at discretion." This meant that they would be wholly and totally at the mercy of the Mexican government.[34] Urrea recorded that he had no choice in the matter and that he was bound by the Tornel Decree. Then again, he really did make assurances that he would work on behalf of Fannin's men to ensure that their lives were spared.[35] There had been no instances of the Mexican government killing those who sought clemency. Surely, with Urrea's patronage and advocacy, they would not be slain.

It is probable that Urrea truly believed that, rather than killing them, some sort of arrangement would be made to send Fannin's men out of Texas. There were several reasons for him to be confident of this. One was that he probably believed that the Mexican government would not dare to slaughter so many Americans and risk the outrage that such a move would surely incite in the United States. Another reason was the nature of the rebels' submission. They had surrendered—albeit at discretion—but had done so while they still had the means to kill many more Mexicans. This was evidence of a measure—if not of goodwill, at least of respect. In reply, he had promised to work on their behalf to preserve their lives. He probably believed, and with some reason, that his reputation and standing carried sufficient weight to gain his new captives some measure of leniency.

Finally, Urrea believed that killing the men would be a moral outrage that his government simply would not undertake. An enlightened nation did not commit such horrors. He did not take into account the fact that the enlightened nation that Mexico was striving to become was essentially embodied in one man: Santa Anna.

Urrea's credibility is damaged by his *Diario* entry that describes his losses during the fight on March 19. Incredibly, he states, "I lost eleven killed, and forty-nine soldiers and five officers were wounded."[36] This claim, taken in the context of every Anglo account and most Mexican descriptions, is preposterously understated. Narratives describing the first charge alone imply that scores of Mexicans were left dead and dying on the field. And although Fannin's men were certainly as susceptible to hyperbole as any others, it is not unreasonable to extrapolate from their claims that any one of them alone might well have killed eleven men. In aggregate, they would have slain many, many more. The account that tells of Duval sharpshooting four Indians through the head in very short order is but one such example.[37]

In a military context, the loss of eleven *soldados* from Urrea's force of at least several hundred would have been of no practical consequence. If those were the only casualties that Fannin's three hundred men were able to inflict from a defensive position with their nine cannon and at least a thousand muskets and rifles during a battle that lasted an entire afternoon and stretched into early evening, then they were beyond inept.

And were that actually the case, Urrea showed ineptitude that was equal or worse. Instead of wasting time ordering attack after attack and then failing to close with the rebel position, he should have overwhelmed Fannin's men at the first charge, killed or captured them all, then pressed ahead with Santa Anna's orders. Instead, under that scenario, he frittered away a day or more.

In truth, Fannin's men were good fighters and had killed many more than eleven *soldados*. Urrea was not an inept general, but he was willing to lie. He did not feel he could truthfully report his losses. His reputation among his countrymen would certainly be judged by his victories, but that judgment would also include consideration of the costs. In his own eyes, he obviously believed that the price on March 19 had been too high.

Regardless of how Urrea counted his losses, other contemporary Mexican accounts tallied them much higher than he did. He responded angrily to accusations by his sometimes defender, Filisola, that he deserved to be tried by a council of war and punished for his actions at San Patricio, Refugio, and Coleto because he "sacrificed hundreds of brave soldiers when similar results could have been obtained, without such a sacrifice."[38] But instead of disputing Filisola's claim that hundreds of *soldados* had been killed in Texas while under his command, Urrea highlighted the fact that, aside from the siege at the Alamo, it was his forces that had done all the fighting in Texas.

The true extent of the Mexican casualties during the fighting on March 19 will never be known. The accounts from Fannin's men vary greatly, but none of them claim that fewer than two hundred *soldados* were slain. Field described a "great slaughter."[39] Surely eleven dead did not make a great slaughter. John Duval wrote, "[The Mexicans] told us after we had surrendered that we had killed and wounded several hundred." He also recorded that Barnard, who was pressed into service to tend the Mexican wounded in the period following the battle, told him "that he was confident that we had killed and wounded between three and four hundred."[40] Certainly Barnard had as good an opportunity to form an estimate as anyone. Shain was no doubt guilty of overestimating Mexican casualties when he wrote that "about 7 or 800 were killed and wounded," but if even half that number had been slain and injured, the losses were tremendous.[41] Abel Morgan wrote, "It was generally supposed that we killed about 200 Mexicans that day."[42]

As an aside, Urrea predictably overstated Fannin's casualties. He tallied the Anglo dead at twenty-seven.[43] This is a curious number: nearly every account from Fannin's command lists the dead at either nine or ten (although none of them include the three men killed while trying to escape on their own during the night following the fight). Filisola's account mention's Urrea's number— probably because it came from Urrea—but it is noted nowhere else and is impossible to reconcile.[44]

After the conditions of surrender were agreed, Fannin's men had to undertake the physical act of giving up. Holzinger was put in charge of this drill. The rebels were marched a short distance out from their ad hoc fortifications under heavy guard, where they put their muskets and rifles in a pile. The officers' weapons were tagged with their names and boxed. This carefully organized procedure was intended to safeguard the personal property of the officers and lends credence to the surrender agreement as Fannin had related it to his men.

Holzinger also lent believability to the surrender terms that Fannin had described to his men. Several accounts recalled Holzinger's cordial, professional demeanor as he mixed among the newly surrendered fighters. He was quoted by more than one source as having bowed to them and declared: "Well, gentlemen, in ten days, liberty and home."[45] This was an obvious reference to the condition, supposedly negotiated, that the men were to be paroled back to the United States in the near term.

The other Mexican officers also acted reasonably. Morgan noted that after he had unbelted and put down a brace of brass pistols he unsheathed his butcher knife. He caught the eye of a Mexican officer and pointed to his own nearly toothless mouth. Morgan went through a little pantomime making it obvious that the one or two teeth he had remaining were not enough to eat with and that he needed the knife. The Mexican motioned for him to keep it.[46]

Not long after the surrender, a considerable number of Mexican officers and men picked their way around the corpses and other battlefield debris to where Fannin's men were gathered. Understandably, they were interested in the men they had just defeated and in their weaponry—particularly the cannon that had been so deadly. The former combatants communicated as best they could with words and gestures. The mood was described as almost friendly.[47]

But some of Fannin's men were still exceedingly bitter at having been surrendered. Ehrenberg wrote, somewhat dramatically, that "inwardly humiliated, which showed itself on our faces, we walked up and down in our camp, casting angry looks at Fannin and the others that had voted for the capitulation. Some sat lost in thought with eyes fixed stark on the ground and envied those who had died during the battle. Despair stood on the features of many of the men, who only too well foresaw our fate."[48]

Many of the men, Mexicans and rebels alike, smoked cigars as they moved around the hollow square. Possibly that was what caused the explosion: a great roar clapped over the men as Fannin's ammunition wagon went up in a sheet of brilliant flame. The grass caught fire and hundreds of unspent cartridges that had been dropped and lost in the grass during the fight now exploded with sharp cracking reports. The first large blast and the subsequent smaller detonations sent men racing across the prairie and away from the fire.

Order was restored soon and none of Fannin's men took the opportunity to escape. A quick investigation revealed that several men had been wounded and one had been killed.[49] The dead man was identified as Johnson and was probably Edward J. Johnson (d. 1836) of Kentucky. Ehrenberg wrote that Johnson had been particularly upset at the surrender and surmised that he had purposely put fire to the ammunition.[50] Morgan remembered, "Of all the mad people ever I saw the Mexicans were the most enrage[d], for they thought that we had done it on purpose."[51]

The mood of the Mexicans understandably darkened following the incident. It was not long before those among Fannin's men who were able were formed for the march back to Goliad. The wounded were set aside; they would not make the trip until enough wagons became available. In the early afternoon of March 20, 1836, approximately 250 of Fannin's men were marched off the battlefield at Coleto in a double file under an armed guard of two hundred Mexican *soldados*.

This closed what became known among the Anglos as the Battle of Coleto. The name came from Coleto Creek which was still some distance to the north and east when Fannin's men were trapped on the prairie. The Mexicans referred to the fight as La Batalla del Encinal del Perdido, or Battle of the Lost Woods.

CHAPTER 14

Return to Goliad

S ometime later on March 20, 1836, the volunteer dead were buried in the trenches that had been dug as a defense only the night before. When the uninjured and ambulatory injured marched back toward Goliad, they left behind several dozen wounded comrades, to be transported by cart. Among the wounded left behind was James Walker Fannin. That he was too badly hurt to walk the nine or so miles back to Goliad is evidence that he would have been hard pressed to lead a fighting escape from the battlefield. Again, whether or not this influenced his decision to surrender the volunteers is unknown.

Two of the medical doctors with Fannin's men—Dr. Joseph Barnard and Dr. Joseph Field—were left behind with him and the rest of the wounded Anglos. Juan José Holzinger headed the Mexican contingent guarding the wounded *soldados*. Whereas the volunteers counted multiple physicians among their number, the Mexicans had none. Antonio López de Santa Anna had insisted that his forces travel light and cheap. Doctors, their orderlies, and their equipment and medicines were neither light nor cheap.

Holzinger approached Fannin on the day after the surrender and asked for his best surgeon. Field later recalled, "As I was standing near, [Fannin] pointed towards me, and said he believed I was as good as any."[1] Field was subsequently ordered to walk behind a carriage carrying two wounded Mexican officers to Goliad. They arrived at the presidio later that same day.

Not much is recorded of the march back to Goliad. For whatever reason—incompetence, spite, neglect, lack of supplies, or expediency—the Mexicans did not give their captives any food or water.[2] The men were formed in double files and were able to slake their thirst only when they waded across the San Antonio River near the fort; there, they drank straight out of the stream.

None of Fannin's men left an account of their emotions at coming back into the presidio. They had done their best to raze the fort and the town only two days earlier and now they were back as prisoners. After they arrived, the *soldados* stuffed them into a church that was far too small; they numbered approximately 250.

The lack of space compounded their misery. Jack Shackelford later wrote, "We reached there a little after sunset, and were driven into the church like so many swine. We were compelled to keep a space open in the center for the guard to pass backward and forward, and under the penalty of having it kept open by a discharge of guns. To avoid this, we had literally to lie one upon another. Early in the morning, their soldiery commenced drawing the blankets from our wounded. I resisted an attempt of this sort near me, and had a bayonet drawn and thrust at me."[3]

Abel Morgan's record corroborates Shackelford's. He recalled that the men were still dripping wet from crossing the San Antonio River when the Mexicans pushed them into the church and forced down to the floor. "One sat and leaned on your back you leaned on another's back. There we sat until next evening."[4]

It wasn't until the evening of March 21 that they were fed for the first time since Fannin had stopped the column on the prairie two days earlier. Their meal, which never varied for the rest of their captivity, was a chunk of boiled beef smaller than a fist. This and the broth that went with it was what they were served once each day. They received no bread, vegetables, or salt.[5]

During the next two days, the wounded were carted in from the battlefield. Although the Anglos were returned to the presidio before the Mexicans, all accounts assert that the Mexicans received first priority for medical treatment once they were brought back to Goliad. Consequently, the fact that the wounded Mexicans were left out in the open for a day longer than their defeated enemies seems odd; the reason for it is unknown. Regardless, the church was turned into a hospital and the uninjured prisoners were consigned to an open area within the fort where they were exposed to the elements. There they were miserable; winter had just ended but the weather was still cold, windy, and wet. Not all the men had blankets, and those that did took little comfort from them when rain turned them into sodden rags.

Morgan's experience as a medical orderly was put to use when the wounded arrived: "On the next day the Mexicans hauled in their wounded. How many there were I cannot say, but they had two hospitals out side of the fort and they placed 57 in the Church where ours were. The wounded Americans filled one side of the Church and the Mexicans filled the other. Our men lay quietly and it was seldom that you would hear them complain; but as soon as the Mexicans came we had musick enough. To me it was tiresome; for there was no end to it day or night."[6]

Morgan also did double duty as a cook. He remembered how a Mexican officer brought him a quartered calf to cook. After removing the feet from the animal, Morgan put the meat into the pot. The hunger of the other men was such that several of them gathered up the calves' feet, then roasted and ate them in their entirety.[7]

It was two days after the bulk of Fannin's men arrived that William Ward and his contingent were led into the fort as prisoners. After successfully slipping out of the mission at Refugio and through General José Urrea's pickets in the very early morning of March 15, Ward and his hundred or so men had wandered lost until daylight. At sunrise, they reoriented themselves and started north for Victoria while keeping to the cover of swampy ground and wooded areas where it would be more difficult for Urrea's horsemen to follow.

Ward could have made a run for Goliad, but he had already received word from Fannin to proceed to Victoria. He also probably believed that Urrea was guarding the route to Goliad. In any event, if he had made a successful run for Goliad there was a real possibility that Fannin would have been gone by the time he arrived. Ward was careful and managed to evade detection while making slow progress toward Victoria. This feat was all the more impressive because Urrea had the local rancheros looking for him. Ward and his men were from the States, while the rancheros had lived in the area for years, yet the volunteers beat the odds and remained undetected.

Still, Ward's force diminished in size daily as the men deserted or became separated from the column in the woods and swamps. For example, during the night of March 16 Ward sent a small party to a nearby thicket of woods to scout for water. Joseph W. Andrews had come to Texas with Ward:

> David Hott, Dick Rutchles, Butler, Bright, & a Dutchman, [were sent] in advance in search of water. They were to go to some timber in sight; and if water was there, they were to hoist a signal. This was 1 or 2 oclk [sic] in the evening. The advance made no signal; but that eveni[n]g the men found water near where they had halted to rest; they remained there all that night. The next being the fourth day, they took up their, [sic] line of march the Dutchman who had gone in search of water; the others went on, & escaped).[8]

In addition to lacking water, the men were traveling light and had nothing to eat. They moved through the difficult terrain under constant threat of being discovered and attacked, and it exhausted them. That exhaustion was dangerous, because it sapped their will and made them less careful than they might otherwise have been. On the third day, March 17, they killed, butchered, and ate some cattle that, according to Samuel T. Brown (b. ca. 1818) "revived us a great deal."[9]

Ward led his men across the San Antonio River on March 19. That afternoon the sound of cannon and gunfire reached across the scattered groves of woods and grassland. The clamor came from where Urrea's men had Fannin's trapped on the prairie. Ward led his men toward the sound of the fighting but turned back as day turned to dark. The gunfire had stopped and the chance of successfully joining with their comrades was greatly diminished, so the wandering column spent the night in the cover of trees along the Guadalupe River.

An incident on the way to Victoria pointedly illustrates that not all the settlers were keen to support the fight against Mexico. The column came across two Irish boys on Nicholas Fagan's (1795–ca. 1852) ranch. Fagan had been an early settler of the region, having arrived with his family in 1829. He had been captured with Fannin on March 20. The two boys indicated that their fathers were located only about a mile away. Ward sent an escort with the boys to fetch the men, and on being brought to Ward, they agreed to help him lead the column to Victoria but begged for time to bid their loved ones farewell. Ward agreed, and the men headed off, promising to return, but they did not do so.[10]

Ward led his men to the approaches of Victoria on March 21. That they had not made contact with Fannin or his men must have been unsettling; that their enemies held Victoria must have been even more so. Ward sent a party to scout the town and to forage for food, but the foray was a disaster. Andrews later wrote, "Sam Mays, Jos Wilson, and Jos Tatum, went up to Mexican houses & Tatum brought some provisions back to Tichnor [Ticknor], the balance, (Mays, Wordsworth, & Wilson) went on to Victoria, & was captured; Wilson being killed in the fight."[11]

Urrea had arrived at Victoria earlier in the day. His accounts are difficult to reconcile with others, but they show that he and his men controlled the entire area: "Two hours after our arrival a party of twenty was seen down the river making their way towards Victoria. I issued orders to cut them off from the woods along the banks of the Guadalupe, and these having been carried out, they were all killed or taken prisoners."[12]

This record only very roughly corresponds to accounts from Ward's men and is another example of Urrea's propensity to overestimate the size of the forces that opposed him. He goes on, "At eleven of the same day an enemy force of about 100 men* was discovered up the river. They were making their way to Victoria also, doubtlessly acting in combination with the party of twenty that had just been destroyed. As they had good guides with them, they succeeded in evading my vigilance and hid themselves in the woods after having exchanged a few shots with our cavalry, detailed to keep them from getting into the woods."[13]

In fact, Ward and his men had little choice but to run back to the cover of the woods. They fired only a few rounds in self-defense, because their ammunition was practically exhausted; many of the men were literally without a single round. With no help in Victoria and Urrea's cavalry dogging their

*Author's note: That figure was accurate, however.

trail, the beleaguered Anglos hunkered down in the swampy river bottom and waited for their leader to craft a plan.

Samuel G. Hardaway (b. 1820), a Georgian, later wrote that "every man was told to take care of himself. We there got scattered, and I never saw Colonel Ward or the company again, but understood that at night while I was asleep in the cane, that he rallied all the men he could, and made his way towards Demit's [sic] Landing."[14]

In fact, Ward did gather his men again, and that same night they headed for Dimmit's Landing on the Lavaca River. They made good time, and on March 22, just a few miles short of their objective, Ward sent two men to reconnoiter the way ahead. Urrea's own men were waiting and the scouts were captured almost immediately. Urrea declared he used fifty cavalry troops and two hundred infantry to surround Ward's position.[15] The two captives were sent within shouting distance of Ward, where they were made to outline the strength and disposition of the Mexican forces. They called on Ward to negotiate with Urrea.

Accordingly, Ward, Warren J. Mitchell, and Isaac Ticknor went forward to parley with the Mexican general. Ward came back from the meeting with terms similar to what Fannin had promised the men on the prairie near Coleto Creek: they would be made prisoners of war, marched to Copano, and paroled back to the United States on their honor not to fight against Mexico again. Or, alternatively, they would be held and exchanged for Mexican prisoners of war. Ward did not believe Urrea. Brown later wrote his recollections of the event:

> [Ward] was opposed to surrendering, that it was the same enemy
> we had beaten at the Mission, only much reduced in numbers,
> and that he thought our chance of escape equally practicable as
> it was then. He proposed that the attack on us might be evaded
> until night, when he might *possibly* [emphasis in original] pass
> the enemy's lines and get out of danger. At all events, he thought
> it best to resist every inch, as many of us as could save ourselves,
> and if we surrendered, he had doubts of the faith and humanity of
> the Mexicans; that he feared we should all be *butchered* [emphasis
> in original].[16]

That Ward came back with terms similar to—and separately from—what Fannin had been given lends credence to the theory that Urrea had duped Fannin. Certainly, it is arguable that Urrea would have wanted to try the same ploy again. Regardless, no documents exist for Ward's surrender and there is little basis for the debate.

What Ward really intended is difficult to ascertain with certainty. His men had virtually no ammunition. His best hope if it came to a fight was to lead the column deep into the swampy brush where Urrea's cavalry would be near useless and where his men might be able to close the fight to bayonet range. That they could actually defeat Urrea's numerically superior and better-armed *soldados* is doubtful. Nevertheless, they might have been able to hold off annihilation until nightfall and make another escape. Perhaps Ward believed that they might stand a better chance at escape if they scattered on their own.

As it developed, there was no close-quarters fight in the swamp. Like Fannin, Ward let his men vote on their fate. Their hunger, thirst, exhaustion, and lack of ammunition—in combination with the attractive terms that Urrea offered—induced them to surrender. Ward was still against surrender, though. He agreed to comply with their wishes but warned them that he would take no blame for treachery on the part of the Mexicans. With Ticknor and Mitchell, he went forward and offered the surrender to Urrea. Brown wrote that terms were put to paper and that two copies were made, one in English and another in Spanish. Again, those documents have never been found.

The moment of their humiliation came and Ward's men marched forward to surrender to Urrea. Brown recorded their mortification: "Then came the hour for us to see all our hopes entirely blasted. We marched out in order and grounded arms, cartouch-boxes [*sic*], and weapons of every kind. Our guns were fired off, the flints taken out, and returned to us to carry. When we left the [Refugio] Mission, on the night of the 14th of March [or early morning 15th of March], we had about a hundred men; at the time of the surrender we had only eighty-five, the others having left us on the route from the Mission to Victoria—a most fortunate thing for them."[17]

The following day, March 23, Ward and his men were marched back to Victoria. There they were put to work for the Mexicans moving supplies and baggage across the Guadalupe River. Two days later, March 25, they were marched to Goliad. Fannin's entire command was back in garrison again.

Although conditions were uncomfortable and crowded and food was scarce, the Mexicans did not regularly bait or harass their prisoners. There was some petty thievery—Shackelford remembered that the *soldados* snatched blankets from many of the men, and Ehrenberg complained that his cloak was stolen.[18] John C. Duval noted only two abusive incidents. During one of these, a *soldado* was escorting a group of Anglos and "pricked" one with his bayonet, apparently believing that the man was not moving with enough spring in his step. The maltreated American turned about and smashed the Mexican with his fist, knocking him down. Duval was fearful for his comrade and for the punishment he would receive. However, a Mexican officer had observed the entire incident and "came up to him and patting him on the shoulder, told him he was 'muy bravo,' and that he had served the soldier exactly right."[19]

Nevertheless, not all the Mexican officers were so fair-minded. Duval rememered that one man complained about his ration at mealtime. The officer in charge of the meal ordered one of his men to gather a collection of discarded and inedible bits. He threw the scraps at the complaining volunteer and told him, "There, eat as much as you want—good enough for Gringos and heretics."[20]

But generally, as allowed by the surrender terms, the volunteers were able to keep their personal belongings and money. There are several references that show the prisoners had cash. Field said that he had more than a hundred dollars. Ehrenberg recorded that the prisoners bought food—albeit at extortionist prices—from *soldados*.

During this period, a Mexican force under Captain Rafael de la Vara captured a contingent of approximately eighty volunteers at the port of Copano. The hapless men had recently arrived from Tennessee; they made up the Nashville Battalion under William P. Miller (1802–1862). Miller had been born in Ireland and had gone to Texas late in 1835 by way of Tennessee. Commissioned as a major of cavalry on December 20, 1835, he wasted little time in traveling back to Tennessee to gather volunteers. In an incredibly short period—just two or three weeks—he recruited his group and made them ready for the journey. He worked quickly, in part because his effort was one of very few that the U.S. government threatened with legal action for violating the Neutrality Act of 1818. Thus motivated, he left Tennessee and set sail with his group from New Orleans by the end of the first week of March 1836. By March 20, they were at the port of Copano.

Details are sketchy, but apparently the Mexican force confronted Miller's men—perhaps while they were bathing in the sea, before they had unloaded their arms. Without weapons, they had few options and surrendered without a fight. They were subsequently marched to Goliad, where they arrived on March 24.

Barnard later recorded that, immediately on arriving, Miller offered his services as a medical aide, as did many of his men. The beleaguered doctor welcomed the assistance, because, as noted above, the Mexicans insisted that their own wounded be tended before any of the wounded volunteers could be nursed. Miller's men eased the workload considerably.[21]

Fannin left with Holzinger and a small party on March 23 for the port at Copano. The purpose of the trip was supposedly to arrange for a vessel to transport the prisoners back to the States. It is further evidence that some among the Mexicans believed that the terms that Fannin and his men had negotiated with Urrea following the battle at Coleto were legitimate. There was no reason for the party to go to Copano otherwise. It is difficult to believe that the trip was orchestrated as a ruse simply to keep Fannin and his men distracted and ignorant of what their true fate was to be.

The excursion calls into question the severity of Fannin's injuries. He was clearly well enough to travel, although it is unknown whether he did so on horseback, in a carriage, or prostrate in a wagon or cart. On his return, however, he went back into the hospital. Perhaps he was using his injury as an excuse to provide himself shelter from the elements. Those among his men who were healthy enough to stay out of the hospital slept unsheltered within the walls of the presidio yard. Or, possibly, the trek to Copano had been grueling, and Fannin absolutely needed to be returned to the "hospital" inside the church.

The trip itself had been a bust. When the party arrived at Copano, the vessel they had hoped to hire was gone. After the group returned to Goliad without event on March 26, 1836, Shackelford remembered that Fannin "was quite cheerful, and we talked pleasantly of the prospect of our reaching the United States."

Shackelford recollected something else that night. He recalled how, as exhausted and hungry as they were, his comrades were keenly anxious to leave Texas and return home. "Many of our young men had a fondness for music, and could perform well, particularly on the flute. In passing by them to visit some wounded, on the outside of the fort, my ear caught the sound of music, as it rolled in harmonious numbers from several flutes in concert. The tune was 'Home, Sweet Home.' I stopped for a few moments and gazed upon my companions with an intense and painful interest."[22]

Urrea charged Lieutenant Colonel José Nicolás de la Portilla (1808–1873) with command of the presidio and the prisoners. Portilla was likely considered by Urrea to be the least capable of his commanders, or he would have kept him on the march rather than relegating him to relatively unchallenging rearguard duty. Since the fight at Coleto Creek, Portilla had dealt with the tiresome tasks of watching over the prisoners, caring for the wounded, putting the presidio's defenses back in order, and performing the sorts of administrative duties typically demanded of a garrison commander.

One of those tasks was ensuring that the prisoners did not escape; to this end, he kept a constant guard, even keeping a loaded cannon trained on them. As to what their final disposition would be, Portilla was not sure. The presidio was not a purpose-made prison, and the captive Anglos were a distraction to the ongoing campaign. At any rate, Portilla continued to perform his duties while he waited for orders.

What Portilla knew about the surrender terms that had been granted—or not granted—to Fannin when he surrendered to Urrea on March 20 is not known for certain. Nor is it certain what he knew about Urrea's exchange with Santa Anna over the fate of the prisoners. After Fannin's surrender, Urrea wrote to Santa Anna from Victoria recommending clemency for the Anglos. Santa Anna replied harshly with a letter to Urrea dated March 23, demanding their deaths.

Urrea's seeming softness toward the Anglos apparently irked Santa Anna. To ensure that the "perfidious foreigners" were eliminated, he bypassed Urrea entirely. On the same day that he wrote Urrea, March 23, he sent a message directly to "Officer Commanding the Post of Goliad," meaning Portilla, ordering him to kill Fannin and his men: "I therefore order that you should give immediate effect to the said ordinance [Tornel Decree] in respect to all those foreigners." Later in the letter he advised Portilla, "I trust that, in reply to this, you will inform me that public vengeance has been satisfied, by the punishment of such detestable delinquents."[23]

Santa Anna's orders reached Portilla during the night of March 26, 1836. The directive—straight from the leader of his country—was clear: Fannin and his men must be slain. Two hours later, another message arrived from Portilla's immediate superior, Urrea. This one directed Portilla to put the prisoners to work repairing the presidio and the town, and to treat them, especially Fannin, with respect. Urrea wrote this letter after having received Santa Anna's explicit command to destroy the Anglos.

Portilla was horrified. He wrote in his diary: "What a cruel contrast in these opposite instructions!"[24] Between the two sets of orders there was no question that Santa Anna's technically overrode Urrea's. As to whose he should obey, Portilla no doubt spent a miserable night debating. He initially shared the orders only with Colonel Francisco Garay, the man who would save many of the Anglos the following day.

Aside from the moral implications of carrying out such a grotesque order, Portilla was also likely concerned about his own welfare. Urrea was a general, and a proven and valued commander, and thus had some latitude to disagree with Santa Anna. On the other hand, Portilla was only a lieutenant colonel and of little consequence. If Portilla disobeyed Santa Anna, the dictator might very well make an example of him to deter others from disobedience. His punishment might even include execution.

Portilla made his decision before the night was finished. In a note dated March 26, he advised Urrea that he planned to comply with Santa Anna's orders: "In compliance with the definitive orders of his excellency the general-in-chief, which I received direct, at four o'clock to-morrow morning the prisoners sent by you to this fortress will be shot."[25]

There was little time to organize the massive slaughter that Portilla had been ordered to undertake. The killing would be difficult to do cleanly and efficiently. From a practical aspect, the butchery of so many men presented the Mexicans with quite a challenge. Muskets were unreliable, and the *soldados* would likely be nervous and ill prepared for such a gruesome task. In addition, the Mexicans were physically smaller than the men they were charged with slaying. If Fannin's men guessed at their captors' intentions, then there was a real chance they might try to overpower their guards. And considering their size and strength advantage, and how desperate they would be, it was quite possible they might have succeeded.

Was it realistic for the Mexicans to be apprehensive? How could unarmed men stand a chance against a greater number of armed men? Actually, their concern was well founded. If the generally larger Anglos acted quickly and the *soldados* did not, especially at close quarters, the Anglos might have been able to wrest some of the muskets from the Mexicans. The long, awkward weapons were difficult to wield against targets only a few feet away. And even if they were brought to bear, there was at least a 15 percent chance that even a musket that was properly loaded and primed with good quality gunpowder would misfire. The Mexican muskets loaded with lesser-grade gunpowder had a greater chance of malfunctioning. And even if the weapon fired properly, there was a chance that the round would miss, or cause only a light wound.

There was also the consideration that some of the Mexicans would lose their nerve when the time came for them to gun down the volunteers. Or, if nerves were not a factor, there was a chance that their consciences might have come into play. After all, the deed they were to perform was cruel and went against basic human nature. Additionally, unlike the volunteers, they had little stake in the fight for Texas. The best they could hope for was to survive. To be paid—and perhaps secure some war booty—would be the limit of their expectations.

Portilla and his officers considered these factors and put safeguards in place to better their odds of success. First, each of the captives was guarded by two *soldados*. This helped negate the size and strength advantage that the Anglos enjoyed over the Mexicans. And the two muskets that the Mexicans would wield against each prisoner greatly increased the probability of successfully slaying their captives.

Mounted men were also posted at selected points around the places where the killings were to take place. Some of Fannin's men were bound to survive the first volley of musket fire and make a run for cover. The horsemen were intended to run them down and kill them. The prisoner might be able to outrun *soldados* on foot, but there was little chance that they would outrun cavalry.

Deceiving the captives as to their real intent was also part of the Mexican plan. This was not too difficult because many of Fannin's men, perhaps most of them, truly believed that the Mexicans were going to return them to the United States. After all, that was what Fannin had told them. Thus, they were easily gulled. In the end, if they were to be killed, why did Urrea go to the trouble of sending them back to the presidio once they had been disarmed? And why were the Mexicans permitting the Anglo wounded to be treated?

At any rate, by the morning of March 27, 1836, Portilla and his officers had a plan for killing Fannin's volunteers. The *soldados* they assembled in the first gray light of dawn were made ready to carry out a slaughter that would forever be a stain against the heritage of their country. That they understood it at the time is doubtful.

CHAPTER 15

The Massacre

A Mexican officer called out and awakened the prisoners in the early morning of March 27, 1836. He ordered the prisoners to form into a file so that they could be counted. Jack Shackelford's first thoughts were that some of the men had made an escape. He didn't think too much about it and prepared for his medical duties. While he was on his way to tend the wounded, he was intercepted by Colonel Francisco Garay. Garay asked him to find his fellow doctor, Dr. Joseph Barnard, and go to his tent outside the fort, where Major William Miller's men were also gathering. Shackelford admired and respected Garay, and was glad to accommodate him. He later noted that the colonel "spoke the English language as fluently as I did myself; and to his honour be it said, he seemed a gentlemen [sic] and a man of feeling."[1]

In company with Barnard, Shackelford passed out of the fort, stopping to talk with some of William Ward's men who were formed in a column, carrying their knapsacks. He asked where they were going and they replied—with great excitement—that they were going to Copano in order to be shipped back to the States. Shackelford must surely have thought that his nightmare in Texas was coming to an end. And although that end was not satisfactory to him, he probably believed that most of the men he had brought to Texas—the Red Rovers—would return safely to their homes.

Dillard C. Cooper (ca. 1815–ca. 1878) was one of Shackelford's Red Rovers. Just after sunrise—5:45—on Palm Sunday, March 27, 1836, the guards rousted him and the other prisoners and ordered them to make ready to leave the presidio. The men initially believed they were being marched to Copano from where they were expected to board a ship to New Orleans. Subsequently, though, they were confused as word circulated that they were being formed to hunt cattle. It seemed odd to Cooper that men would be sent out on foot to do something that could more quickly be accomplished on horseback.

The prisoners were formed into three smaller groups and led out of the presidio's sally port where three hollow squares of dismounted Mexican cavalrymen were waiting. Each group of prisoners was filed into one of the squares. The Mexicans closed off each square as it was filled until every formation was closely guarded. The Mexican officers heading the three groups were Captain Pedro Balderas, Captain Antonio Ramírez, and First Adjutant Agustín Alcérrica. The *soldados* were primarily from the Tres Villas and Yucatán battalions, but were augmented by detachments from the Cuautla, Tampico, and Durango units.

The largest of the groups included Ward's Georgians and the Kentucky Mustangs; these men were sent northwest toward San Antonio. Shackelford's Red Rovers and Ira Westover's regulars were marched south toward San Patricio. The New Orleans and Mobile Greys headed toward Victoria along the San Antonio River. The rest of the men were scattered among the three detachments.

Cooper's group was marched away to the southwest in a double file; each Anglo was guarded by two *soldados*. About a half mile from the fort, the formation was halted on a line parallel to a newly built brush fence. The *soldados* then put themselves in a column on one side of the prisoners and displaced about eight feet away. The fence ran along the other side of the volunteers, also about eight feet away. Cooper remembered that the Mexican commanding the detachment "came up to the head of the line, and asked if there were any of us who understood Spanish. By this time, there began to dawn upon the minds of us, the truth, that we were to be butchered, and that, I suppose, was the reason that none answered."[2]

The commander ordered the Anglos to turn their backs to the guards. None of them complied. He then moved to the first man in the file, grabbed him by the shoulders, and faced him toward the brush fence. Cooper later wrote, "By this time, despair had seized upon our poor boys, and several of them cried out for mercy. I remember one, a young man, who had been noted for his piety, but who had afterwards become somewhat demoralized by bad company, falling on his knees, crying aloud to God for mercy, and forgiveness." The initial cries of a few men became a tumult of beseeching and pleading as the horrible realization of what was about to happen struck all the men. Cooper recounted that another volunteer, Robert Fenner (ca. 1814–1836), called out: "Don't take on so, boys; if we have to die, let's die like brave men."[3]

The desperate cries of the men were for naught, and the Mexicans fired their muskets at point-blank range into the prisoners. At the instant of the first discharge Cooper threw himself to the ground, face down, resting on his hands. Fenner's body—shot through—fell hard on top of him. On his right, Wilson Simpson was untouched and ran for a gap in the fence.

It took a second or two for Cooper to crawl out from under his dead friend and turn to dash after Simpson: "As we ran towards an opening in the brush fence, which was almost in front of us, Simpson got through first, and I was immediately after him. I wore, at that time, a small round cloak, which was fastened with a clasp at the throat. As I ran through the opening, an officer charged upon me, and ran his sword through my cloak, which would have held me, but I caught the clasp with both hands, and tore it apart, and the cloak fell from me."[4]

Cooper looked through the makeshift fence and out on the wide open prairie stretching in front of him to the southwest. He would have to outrun his captors in order to survive; he started at a hard sprint for a line of distant trees. Motivated by self-preservation, Cooper put distance between him and his pursuers. Out in front of him, Simpson had three *soldados* hard on his trail. Anxious not to jump from the frying pan into the fire, Cooper angled away from his friend and the other Mexicans. He soon slowed to a walk, exhausted, as he continued toward the trees that reached out in two fingers toward him.

> There were two points of timber projecting into the prairie, one of which was nearer to me than the other. I was making for the furthest point, but as Simpson entered the timber, his pursuers halted, and then ran across and cut me off, I then started for the point into which Simpson had entered, but they turned and cut me oft [*sic*] from that. I then stopped running and commenced walking slowly between them and the other point. They, no doubt, thinking I was about to surrender myself, stopped, and I continued to walk within about sixty yards of them, when I suddenly wheeled and ran into the point for which I had first started. They did not attempt to follow me, but just as I was about to enter the timber, they fired, the bullets whistling over my head caused me to draw my head down as I ran.[5]

Cooper spotted Simpson beckoning to him almost as soon as he entered the thicket. The two of them ran for what Cooper estimated was another couple of miles until they reached the San Antonio River. At the river they had a hurried argument about the best way to hide themselves. Cooper suggested they climb into a tree but Simpson did not like the idea because they would have no escape route if they were spotted. Their debate was interrupted by the sound of someone crashing through the woods. Cooper jumped into the river while Simpson ran upriver for a short distance before also jumping in.

Rather than Mexicans in pursuit, though, it was Zachariah Brooks (ca. 1810–1888) and Isaac Hamilton (1804–1859) who rushed out of the timber and onto the riverbank. Both of them were wounded. Hamilton had sustained the most severe injuries: one thigh was shot through with a musket ball and the other was pierced by a bayonet. The four men joined together and swam the river until reaching a bluff covered by a dense thicket of bushes. There they spent the rest of the day.

Captain Benjamin Holland was part of the group that was marched up the road toward San Antonio. Just as the Mexicans halted the formation, the sound of shrieks and musket fire belied the slaughter to the southwest. Holland suggested to Major Benjamin C. Wallace "that it would be best to make a desperate rush." Wallace replied that they were too heavily guarded: each prisoner was flanked on each side by a *soldado*. Holland then called on several more of his comrades to make a break, "but none would follow."[6]

Holland was not going to die without a fight. He lashed out with his fist and struck the *soldado* to his right. The Mexican to his left tried to angle his musket around to shoot him but was unable to bring the weapon to bear in such close quarters. Instead, he swung out with it and landed a blow to Holland's left hand. Holland grappled with the Mexican, tore his musket away, then sprinted for the river. Musket balls sang through the air around him and tore up the ground at his feet, but none found its mark.

A "chain of sentinels" waited to intercept Holland as he raced for the river: "They were about thirty yards apart, three of them closed to intercept my retreat, the central one raised his gun to fire—I still ran towards him in a serpentine manner in order to prevent his taking aim—I suddenly stopped—dropped my piece [took aim], fired, and shot the soldier through the head and he fell instantly dead. I ran over his dead body, the other two firing at me but missing, and immediately ran and leaped into the river, and while swimming across was shot at by three horsemen, but reached the opposite banks in safety."[7]

Herman Ehrenberg was part of the detachment that was marched toward Victoria. It came to him gradually that things were not right—that perhaps the Mexicans were lying and they were not headed toward Copano, or in fact toward any port. The silence of the usually talkative Mexicans perplexed him. He also noticed for the first time that their guards were carrying no camp gear. Finally, there was no sign of the rest of the volunteers. He hadn't realized that the detachment wasn't part of the whole. He wanted to call out these disparities to his comrades, but decided to keep quiet and hold to his hopes that they were headed for their parole. Nevertheless, he threw his few remaining personal articles out onto the prairie because he feared being weighted down if he should have to fight or run.[8]

After about fifteen minutes, the detachment was led off the main road and across the prairie for a short distance. There, a halt was called. The prisoners grew more apprehensive because the turn off the road made little sense. The two lines of *soldados* moved to one side. A short distance away, mounted lancers stood ready.

Almost at the same time, the roar of musket fire from about a mile distant reached them. Ehrenberg and his companions were stunned. The Mexican commanding their detachment drew his sword and bellowed orders that none of them could understand. The *soldados*—only a few feet away—pointed their muskets at the disbelieving Anglos.

The Mexican officer in charge ordered the prisoners to kneel. None of them obeyed. Almost simultaneously another crescendo of musket fire rolled across the prairie at them. This volley of fire was accompanied by distant screams and shouts. Now the detachment understood without any doubt that this was no charade or ruse. The Mexicans were an instant away from killing them.

The realization came too late. The sharp, staccato booming of the Mexican muskets momentarily muted the screams of the frenzied prisoners. Lead balls tore into them. Blood and bits of bone and flesh clouded the air. Smoke from the first volley cloaked the carnage and briefly obscured visibility to just a few feet. Ehrenberg, unhurt, looked desperately about him. His clothes were spattered with the blood of his comrades, both dead and dying.

From the tangled and desperate scene, the young German leapt to his feet and rushed toward the San Antonio River. "Then suddenly a powerful saber smashed me over the head. Before me the figure of a little Mexican lieutenant appeared out of the dense smoke, and a second blow from him fell on my left arm with which I parried it." Ehrenberg recorded that he charged unarmed at the Mexican officer, who subsequently fled and left the way to the river open.[9]

Although that Mexican officer had given up, other Mexicans did not. Ehrenberg threw himself into the river and swam toward the far bank as musket balls ripped into the water around him. A dog the men had adopted as their mascot splashed into the water after the young German. Its loyalty was its undoing: the dog was struck by a round and sank beneath the current.

Ehrenberg scrambled out of the river and up the opposite bank. The shrieks of his dying comrades rang in his ears as he huffed great ragged breaths into his lungs. Wary of the mounted lancers that he could see in the distance, the wet, cold, and winded young man made for cover, his goal to put as much distance as he could between himself and the killing ground the area had just become.

John C. Duval was overjoyed on that Sunday morning when a Mexican officer told him and his group to get ready for the march to Copano where there were ships ready to return them to the United States. They were going to be paroled. He hurriedly packed his belongings and was formed into the group that was marched up the road toward San Antonio. He took little notice when he heard words of pity from local women as the column passed by where they were standing. And although it also seemed odd to him that the prisoners had been split into three different groups and sent in different directions, he did not dwell on it.

It was only when a halt was ordered and the *soldados* were assembled on one side of the column that he grew suspicious. The sound of gunfire in the distance confirmed his suspicions. Someone from the column shouted out, "Boys! They are going to shoot us!" Simultaneously, the clicking of musket locks came almost as a singular sound from the line of *soldados*.[10]

The Mexican muskets—more than a hundred of them—thundered in a smoking, disharmonic volley. Immediately, blood sprayed into the air, mixing itself with the smoke of the spent gunpowder. Duval, stunned by the unexpected treachery, fell to the ground under the weight of the dying man who had been walking beside him only seconds earlier. Recovering his wits, he pushed the other man clear, struggled to his feet, and took off at a sprint. Around him other men raced for a line of distant trees.

Like rabbits, the unarmed revolutionaries zigzagged across the field. In and among them the Mexican *soldados* fired, and then knelt to reload. Many of them lunged out at the fleeing Americans with bayonet-tipped weapons. To his left, Duval spied a Mexican coiling for an attack. Just as the enemy soldier lashed out, one of Duval's comrades inadvertently stepped in front of the deadly blade and fell stricken to the ground with the bayonet driven deep into his chest. The weight of the mortally injured body twisted the musket from the Mexican's hands. Duval looked back over his shoulder as he continued to run. The *soldado* had recovered his musket and was pushing with his foot against the fallen man's torso as he tried to wrench the newly bent bayonet free. In the distance, Duval could see other Mexicans finishing off the wounded.

Wasting no time, he raced down the bank of the San Antonio River and plunged into the deep, narrow current. Duval was a strong swimmer; in a short time, he had reached the other side but found he could not scramble up the steep sandy bank. He swam farther downstream to a point where he was able to grab a wild grape vine and "was climbing up it hand over hand, sailor fashion, when a Mexican on the opposite bank fired at me with his escopeta, and with so true an aim that he cut the vine in two just above my head, and down into the water I came again."[11]

Duval splashed down the river another hundred yards or so. There the bank was shallow enough that he was able to haul himself out of the water and up to higher ground and into the timber. He raced as fast as he could before stumbling to a halt where the woods ended and the prairie began.

There were a dozen mounted lancers waiting on the grass to catch men just like him. Duval was sheltered from their view by the closeness of the trees. From where he was hunkered down, he managed to stop John Holliday and Samuel T. Brown before they raced out into the open. Understandably agitated, the three men excitedly argued about what they should do; there were Mexicans behind them and in front of them. While they debated, they were chagrined to see a handful of four or five of their comrades dash out onto the prairie. Duval recorded, "The lancers charged upon them at once [and] speared them to death, and then dismounting robbed them of such things as they had upon their persons."[12]

After a few minutes, the lancers leapt back atop their horses and galloped away—probably after spotting other survivors. Duval and his companions started up a ravine, not wanting to risk being taken from behind. A few minutes later, the lancers returned, passing very close to where they were barely screened by nothing more than grass. Luckily, the men stayed hidden. After the horsemen passed, Duvall and his companions carefully crept away from the killing ground and eventually stopped in a thicket to hide until night. Duval recounted that the sound of sporadic musket fire rang through the entire day and into the night. No doubt the Mexicans were chasing down and killing others who had escaped the initial slaughter.

Among the men shot down that day was William L. Hunter (1809–1887). He was older than most of the men at about twenty-five years old. He had been in Texas longer than most of his comrades, having signed up with the New Orleans Greys. As part of that group, he had taken part in the fight for San Antonio the previous December.

Unlike most of the men who fell to the Mexican muskets outside Goliad that day, Hunter survived. He was shot at the first volley, but not mortally, and resolved to feign death until nightfall when he could crawl away. However, as the *soldados* looted the bodies, one of them came upon him and tried to pull a black silk cravat from around his neck. Hunter took a breath, and the startled soldier realized that his victim had not been killed. The Mexican started shouting, "no muerto, no muerto," and called for his comrades. Immediately they commenced beating, stabbing, and slashing Hunter. He had "thirteen distinct wounds" before his attackers left him for dead.[13]

Hunter regained consciousness at nightfall. He discovered that he had been stripped of his equipment and clothing and was clad in only his underclothes. In addition to the silk cravat, nearly all of his garments and belongings had been plundered from his nearly lifeless, crumpled, bleeding body. Whether the second band of Mexicans did not realize he was alive, or whether they had, but believed he was dead enough, will never be known.

Hunter mustered all his strength to untangle himself from the body of a friend. That ordeal finished, he dragged himself away from the bloody, heaping, half-naked mess that the Mexicans had made of his companions. The bodies were unguarded. No longer a threat and robbed of anything of value, the Mexicans no longer cared about them.

Horribly savaged and near death as he was, it was a near thing, but Hunter finally made it to the San Antonio River where he stumbled down the bank and slipped into the current. The water soothed his wounds and helped him hide from the patrols of *soldados* still hunting those who had managed to escape the massacre. At nightfall, he crossed the river and dragged himself up the far bank. Back on firm ground at last, he struck out for the east.

William P. Miller, the Irishman who had arrived in Texas only days earlier, was spared from the massacre, as were his eighty men. Miller's secretary, identified only as S. H. B., recalled how, on the morning of the slaughter, they were ordered to tie white bands around their arms. They did so without understanding why. As it developed, the white bands distinguished them from Fannin's men; without the mark, they also would have been killed.

On that fateful morning, they were conducted to an orchard from where they had a view of two of the three massacre sites. S. H. B. was eighteen at the time and remarked later in his life that he could never recall the scene with "any degree of composure." He remembered the faces of his companions as they were forced to witness the mass slaying of Fannin's men: "Surprise, horror, grief and revenge were depicted in the most vivid lines. At first all were startled; some became at once horror stricken; others wept in silent agony; still others laughed in their passion, swore, clinched their teeth, and looked like demons."[14]

From their vantage point, Miller's company watched as many of Fannin's men broke away from their slayers and ran for cover. But cavalrymen posted in the same orchard as Miller's men dashed out and slashed them down before they could escape. "Never did I so want to hamstring a horse," S. H. B. recalled.

He also remembered that those of Fannin's men "who weren't killed outright, were deliberately butchered by the Mexicans, men and women, and stripped." This account shows that it was not just *soldados* who took part in the grisly slayings. Aside from combatants, the group of participants likely also included camp followers and local Tejanos. S. H. B. noted that some of these, "even the women," cursed and insulted Miller's men "by the grossest vulgarities." They taunted the prisoners and promised that they would share the same gruesome fate on the following day. Miller's men could do nothing but watch as their tormentors walked past the orchard carrying the plunder they ripped from the corpses of Fannin's slain men.[15]

Shackelford and Barnard were in Garay's tent in the same orchard as Miller's men. Although Garay was away, they conversed "with a little Mexican officer who had been educated at Bardstown, Ky." When the muskets first started to fire, the Mexican responded to their questions with an explanation that, although he was not sure, it was probably just the guards firing their guns.

But at the sound of a subsequent volley of gunfire from a different direction, Shackelford caught sight of the massacre and heard the screams. "It was then, for the first time, the awful conviction seized upon our minds that Treachery and Murder had begun their work."[16]

Garay stepped back into the tent a few minutes later. Shackelford asked "if it could be possible they were murdering our men?" He recorded that Garay answered in the affirmative. The enemy officer also protested that the grisly treachery was not being done on his orders and that, furthermore, he had saved as many of the men as he could and would have saved more had it been within his power to do so.

Abel Morgan watched that morning as the three groups hefted their knapsacks and marched out of the presidio; word was passed that they were going to Copano to build a fort. After they had left, Morgan and the other ten or so orderlies were put to work moving the wounded out of the makeshift hospital and into the yard. The Mexicans told Morgan that another room was being prepared for the stricken men.

Tears streaming down the cheeks of Andrew Boyle, one of his patients, caught Morgan's attention as he worked. Boyle, who had been shot in the leg, understood Spanish and had overheard the *soldados* talking. He told Morgan that all the wounded and their attendants were going to be gunned down. Morgan was a practical man: "I went out and told the rest of the nurses that we had as well cease carrying out the men, for we were all to be shot. We then quit."[17]

Almost at the same time, the sound of gunfire reached the volunteers still in the presidio. Immediately, *soldados* came and took away ten of the nurses but left Morgan and another, William Scurlock (1807–1885), who had come to Fannin's command after escaping James Grant's decimation at Agua Dulce. An officer came and led both of them to the calaboose (local jail) and directed them to hide behind a set of shutters before he went away. Scurlock slid in first, but there was not enough room for Morgan to take cover and he was spotted, as more men were hauled out into the yard: "As an officer passed he saw me, and he stormed out and motioned me to come to him."

Morgan was fearful that Scurlock would also be spotted, and he quickly stepped out of his hiding place to where the officer was standing. He was put at the end of a column of men that were being readied for killing but was fortuitously spotted by the same man who had hidden him earlier: "I suppose he knew me by my hat for I had a hat made in Louisiana that was larger than common and of the natural color of the fur, so that it was different from the hats worn by my comrades."[18] Morgan's protector took time to talk to his would-be slayer, then made his way over to Morgan. He gave the orderly a shove

The Massacre | **183**

and ordered him back behind the shutters. Out in the yard of the presidio, the *soldados* made ready to slay the wounded Anglos and the other nurses.

Boyle, the tearful young patient, recalled the slaughter: "A company of soldiers formed in front of us and loaded their pieces with ball cartridge. Then a file of men under a corporal took two of our number, marched them out toward the company, and after bandaging their eyes, made them lie with their faces to the ground, after which, placing the muzzles close to their heads, they shot them as they lay."[19]

Just after this pair of slayings—with blood and gore spattered on the ground—Garay came forward and shouted in English, asking if there was anyone named Boyle among the prisoners. Boyle had no idea who Garay was, but answered his call. Garay was an immigrant to Mexico from Greece and had fought Boyle's comrades at San Patricio, Refugio, and Coleto. He ordered a *soldado* to take the surprised Anglo to the officer's hospital where his wound could be cared for. In the hospital, Boyle found himself kindly treated by the Mexican officers.

He also found Dr. Joseph Field and John Sowers Brooks—the homesick Virginian, adjutant, engineer, and former Marine who had never received replies to his many letters home. Field was acting as a personal physician to a wounded Mexican officer. His appeals to the kindness of this same officer were successful in getting his friend Brooks into the hospital where he received Field's personal care. Brooks had been badly wounded the week before when a bullet smashed into his thigh. He had no idea that the slaughter was taking place until Boyle arrived and made him aware. He took the news stoically and declared "I suppose it will be our turn next."[20]

After most of the killing had been done, a Mexican officer charged into the room with four *soldados*. One of the conscripts tore Brooks' blanket from him. Field, in turn, ripped the blanket from the Mexican's hands and placed it back over his friend. Nervous for the welfare of his personal caregiver the wounded Mexican officer called Field over to his bedside and ordered him to be quiet.

Field remembered: "When they rudely bore away Capt. B. he extended his arms towards me, imploring my assistance, until his voice was silenced forever." Field and Boyle could do nothing as the Mexicans shot and killed the hapless Brooks, then stripped him of his gold watch and clothing. The body was heaved into a nearby pit.[21]

Garay came calling on Boyle a few hours later. "Addressing me in English he said: 'Make your mind easy, Sir; your life is spared.'" Boyle's curiosity compelled him to ask the officer who he was and why he had saved him from being killed. Garay explained that he had been with General José Urrea as the Mexicans passed through San Patricio several weeks earlier. While there, he had quartered in the home of Boyle's sister, Mary, and had been impressed with her kindness and with the kindness of Boyle's brother, Roderick. When he tried to pay for his board, the two Anglos refused his offer but asked that if Garay ever had a chance to help their brother, Andrew, that he do so. The Mexican officer put paid to that request.

Meanwhile, Morgan and Scurlock remained out of sight. Outside the calaboose but within the walls of the fort, the booming of gunfire punctuated the slaughter of the other nurses and of the wounded comrades they had been treating for more than a week. Not long after the guns stopped, *soldados* began filing into the calaboose where Morgan and Scurlock were hiding. They carried the bloody booty of the men they had just slain with them. The two Americans were discovered and pulled from behind the shutters and made to sit among the gory knapsacks and clothes to face the Mexicans. Morgan remembered that a pack in front of him "had the name of Wingate on it."[22]

At about this time, George Voss (1809–1848) emerged from under a pile of boards. He had secreted himself away that morning when the few words of Spanish that he knew served him well enough to give him an idea of what the Mexicans planned. The *soldados* shouted and cursed but none of them moved to kill him. Rather, he was pushed over to sit alongside Morgan and Scurlock.

Soup was brought to the *soldados* and they began to eat. That is, most of them ate. Morgan noted that some of the officers were unwilling or unable to take their meal. "I noticed several officers who could not eat, but were shedding tears by which I was convinced that there were some human beings among these savages."

There was also a small boy among the group. He took tentative sips from his soup as he watched the Anglo prisoners. After a short while, he rose and made his way over to where they sat and offered his bowl to Morgan. "I shook my head, but he would not desis[t] until I took three [spoonfuls] of it, and handed it to Scurlock. Scurlock took only one spoonful and refused more. The boy, trying to reassure the three men, pointed at their foreheads and shook his head. There were no plans to kill them.[23]

Following the meal, Morgan and Scurlock were told through an interpreter that they had been saved so that they could assist the doctors—Fields, Barnard, and Shackelford—who were tending the Mexican wounded. A Mexican officer took Voss as a servant. "They then brought some bleached domestic and tore it into strips about two inches wide and about two feet long, and tied them round our left arms. They told us that if we lost them, the first soldier who saw us would kill us."[24]

Morgan and Scurlock were next led to the church. In the yard of the presidio, they passed where the wounded volunteers had been killed. The Mexicans were stripping the bodies and throwing them into carts so that they

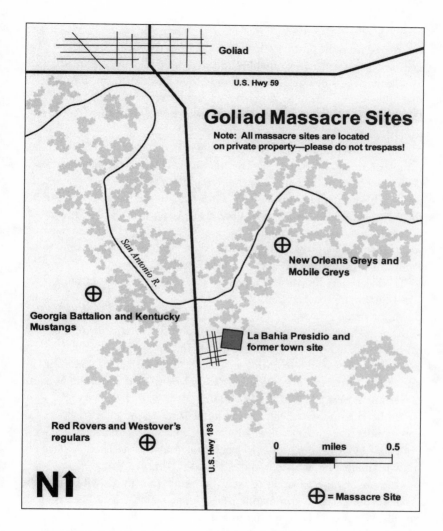

Goliad

U.S. Hwy 59

Goliad Massacre Sites

Note: All massacre sites are located
on private property—please do not trespass!

San Antonio R.

⊕ New Orleans Greys and
Mobile Greys

**Georgia Battalion and Kentucky
Mustangs** ⊕

⊕ La Bahia Presidio and
former town site

**Red Rovers and Westover's
regulars** ⊕

U.S. Hwy 183

0   miles   0.5

N↑

⊕ = Massacre Site

could be hauled clear of the fort. At the church were other volunteers who had been saved to wait on the Mexicans.

At the church, Morgan and Scurlock were given a barrel fixed with ropes and poles for hauling water. They were then sent several hundred yards down the San Antonio River to fetch water. Morgan remembered that there were two or three hundred *soldados* lining the banks and washing the clothes they had pulled from the men they had just massacred. "The edge of the river, where it was about [ankle] deep, was red with blood that had come out of the clothes of the dead men." With their barrel, Morgan and Scurlock went into the deeper, less bloody current before they took on water. On the banks of the river their captors made "signs that we ought to be killed."[25]

Joseph Spohn had proved himself an able interpreter to the Mexicans and was spared from the butchery that morning. Later that summer, the *New York Evening Star* carried his account of Fannin's killing; it was later reprinted in part by a Pennsylvania newspaper on August 9, 1836. The bulk of the information that follows comes from the latter extract, as reprinted in the Web site *Sons of Dewitt Colony Texas.*[26] It is the most complete report of Fannin's death known to exist.

Fannin was among the last prisoners slaughtered that day. The cacophonous rumble of musket fire that marked the massacre of his men brought the broken Georgian out of his bed and into the yard of the presidio. There—across the fort that he once commanded—he made out the rows of his wounded, waiting for their own deaths. At the same time, a Mexican captain ordered Spohn to take Fannin to a point in the northwest portion of the yard. There were six *soldados* with the officer, and Spohn asked outright if they were going to kill Fannin. The officer answered, yes, without hesitating.

The beleaguered former commander asked about the distant musket fire when Spohn approached him. When told that his men were being gunned down, he made no commentary "but appeared resolute and firm." Fannin, with his bad leg, leaned on Spohn for support as the two made their way to the designated spot. On reaching that point, Spohn reported that he was ordered to translate the following statement: "That for having come with an armed band to commit depredations and revolutionize Texas, the Mexican Government were about to chastise him."

On hearing the statement, Fannin immediately asked to see the Mexican commander. The captain refused him but asked why he had made the request. Spohn said that Fannin produced a gold watch that he declared belonged to his wife and that he "wished to present it to the commandant."

One might expect Fannin to want the watch sent to his wife, not to be given to the garrison commander, Lieutenant Colonel José Nicolás de la Portilla. Why would Fannin want to honor the man who had just slain most of his men, and who was about to butcher the rest—including him? Probably Fannin hoped to meet Portilla and negotiate for his life and those of his men who still lived. The force and charm of his personality had carried him farther than most men ever got, and he had nothing to lose by trying.

But the Mexican officer would have none of it. After more stilted exchanges—the Mexican knew a few words of English—Fannin surrendered the watch to the other man on condition that he be buried after he was killed. The captain, "smiling and bowing," promised that it would be done with all the necessary formalities befitting Fannin's rank.

Following this promise, Fannin pulled a "small bead purse containing doubloons" from his right pocket. The clasp on the purse was damaged, and Fannin took time to explain to the Mexican that it had absorbed part of the impact from a musket ball before the round tore into the flesh of his thigh, taking a handkerchief into the leg with it. The purse with the gold was handed over to the captain.

Fannin then reached into the left pocket of his India rubber overcoat and pulled out a canvas-wrapped "double handful of dollars." He also gave this money to the officer. This ritual of handing over his valuables might have been a ploy for time, but it might also have been an attempt to save his body from the ignominy of being stripped and looted.

Once Fannin had exhausted his supply of valuables, Spohn was ordered to blindfold his commander. Fannin passed him his pocket handkerchief to use, but Spohn—obviously distressed—fumbled and was unable to tie it properly. The Mexican tore it from his hands and fashioned the blindfold himself while directing Fannin to seat himself in a nearby chair. He then stepped behind the American commander and tied it into place at the same time confirming with him that it was properly tied.

That task complete, the captain ordered his *soldados* to detach the bayonets from their muskets and come near Fannin. Fannin, ever mindful of his person, told Spohn to ask the Mexicans not to place their weapons so close to his face that they would scorch it when they fired. The Mexican captain directed his men so that their muskets were within two feet of Fannin. On his signal, they fired and "poor Fannin fell dead on his right side on the chair, and from thence rolled into a dry ditch, about three feet deep, close by the wall."[27]

CHAPTER 16

The Survivors, the Butchers, and an Angel

Among all the men marched out of Goliad and slaughtered, only about twenty-seven survived. Many escaped the initial volleys of musket fire only to be chased down and killed, and their stories are lost. The stories of those who survived show the toughness of the men who answered the call to fight for Texas.

Dillard Cooper, Wilson Simpson, Zachariah Brooks, and Isaac Hamilton joined up in the woods soon after escaping the initial volley of musket fire and swam across the San Antonio River. With Brooks and Hamilton wounded—Hamilton badly—they traveled only a short distance before crawling into a dense thicket on a bluff where they spent the rest of that dreadful day.

Late that same night, they left their hiding place, with Cooper and Simpson carrying Hamilton, while Brooks managed to stumble after them. When they were not far from the presidio, they were confused by the sight of several large fires. However, their bewilderment turned to revulsion when the strong smell of burning flesh brought the realization that the fires were actually pyres, with the bodies of their comrades being immolated. Later, Cooper wrote, "I will state what Mrs. Cash, who was kept a prisoner, stated afterwards; that some of our men were thrown into the flames and burned alive."[1]

The small group passed by the fort and found a small spring where they took water before pressing on again into what had become a cold, foggy night. They unwittingly moved in a circle and stumbled back onto the same spring three more times before giving up for the night and hiding themselves again.

For nine days, the four men moved slowly east and north, having only a vague idea of which direction would take them to safety. Frequent close brushes with Mexican *soldados* forced them to take cover—often in swamps or ponds where they shivered with just their heads above water. One morning, a large formation of Mexican troops marched past within a stone's throw of where they were taking cover. Finally, they found an abandoned house on the Lavaca River that was still stocked with corn and other supplies. Eggs were balanced helter-skelter about the place where the free-ranging hens had laid them. They struggled unsuccessfully to spark a fire to cook the eggs, eventually giving up and eating them raw.

Later that day, as they were trying to rest, a large formation of Mexican troops bore down on the house with a detachment of galloping cavalry in the lead. The Anglos dashed to a nearby copse of woods, but the *soldados* spotted them. For the next two days, they hid while the Mexicans searched for them, sometimes coming within just a foot or so of where they were sandwiched between moss-covered logs. Cooper recalled that "six of them came riding quite close, three on each side of us, and leaning down and peering into our hiding place. It seemed to me they could have heard us, for my own heart seemed to raise me almost from the ground by its throbbings."[2]

The men crawled away under cover of darkness on the night of the second day, but Hamilton's severe wounds hampered their progress. He was still unable to walk, and his weak and mostly starved companions were compelled to carry him. Brooks, who was also wounded, urged Cooper to leave him behind, but Cooper's conscience would not permit him to abandon his comrade. Brooks next tried to convince Simpson to leave him behind, while the two were away collecting water. The suffering Hamilton overheard this exchange. Surprisingly, he agreed with Simpson and urged his friends to leave him because his wounds were getting no better, and the others were bound to be caught and killed if they stayed with him: "Boys, Brooks has told you the truth; I can not travel any further, and if you stay with me, all will be killed. Go and leave me, boys; if I have rest I may recover, and if I ever should get off safe, you shall hear from me again."[3] Hamilton called Brooks to him and gave him forty dollars in gold and a gold watch to give to his mother in Alabama.

Cooper, however, still could not bring himself to leave. Simpson and Brooks departed, leaving Cooper and Hamilton behind, but Hamilton was so insistent that he be left alone that Cooper finally bid him farewell and caught up with his two comrades. Eventually, the three of them swam across the Colorado River, where they found friends and food. They had regained their strength and were headed for General Samuel Houston's army when they received word of the victory at the Battle of San Jacinto, on April 21, 1836.

Hamilton stayed put for nine more days and slowly regained his strength while scavenging for anything edible. No longer at death's door, he managed to walk to the abandoned settlement of Texana, and then traveled by a small boat down to Dimmit's Landing, where he was subsequently recaptured. Still suffering terribly from his wounds, he was tied to a mule and taken to Victoria.

After weeks of abuse in the Mexican garrison there, he managed to escape. In the end, he made it home to Alabama in early July that same year.

William L. Hunter survived the initial volley and feigned death, but the *soldados* discovered he was alive as they were looting the bodies. They beat and stabbed him, and again left him for dead. At dusk that same day, very badly wounded, he managed to crawl to and cross the San Antonio River. At daybreak he tried to distance himself from the Mexican patrols that were searching for survivors. He stopped alongside a small stream and—tortured by the pain of his wounds and weakened by hunger—stayed put through much of the rest of the day. After getting as much rest as his injuries would allow, he moved on again but found himself circling back on his tracks. Eventually, the wounded Virginian stumbled across a house on Manahuila Creek not too far from where James Walker Fannin had surrendered him and the rest of the volunteers just a week earlier.

In that small house, Juan Reynea lived with his family. They had previously lived at Goliad, but left—tired of the depredations of the soldiers that passed back and forth through the area. The Mexican family took Hunter under their care, giving him clothes and food and doing what they could to treat his wounds. The kindness of Reynea and his family stood in stunning contrast to the barbarity of the massacre. After Hunter regained his health enough to travel, Reynea took him to the home of Mrs. Margaret Wright who lived on the Guadalupe River near Victoria. There, Mrs. Wright continued to care for him until he regained his health sufficiently to leave.

Having escaped the slaughter, John C. Duval, John Holliday, and Samuel T. Brown pressed on, day and night, toward what they thought was the north and east and safety. Brown had lost his boots when they swam across the river; after the first day his feet were torn and ripped so badly that he could not go on. Duval crafted him a set of crude sandals from the tops of his own boots, and thus shod, Brown hobbled on. Nevertheless, after three days and several near-encounters with both *soldados* and Indians, they found that they had traveled in a circle and were back at the fringes of Goliad.

Dispirited, the men set out again. Holliday, who was older than the other two men but who had grown up in a city, had been leading the way up to this point. When Duval, who had been raised on the Kentucky frontier, recognized that they were veering off course again he tried to correct Holliday. Holliday refused to take Duval's advice and a standoff ensued. After a short argument during which neither man would give way, Duval and Brown started off without Holliday. After a few minutes, Holliday chased them down and joined them, declaring that he would rather "go wrong" than be separated.

Duval's sense of direction was better than Holliday's: they reached the

Guadalupe River five days after the slaughter. Still, by this time, having lived on only meager rations since Fannin had surrendered them and on no rations since they had escaped the massacre, they were exhausted and suffering terribly from hunger. Desperate, they spotted a cow and her calf and tried to chase them over a river bank in the hopes that they would be injured or killed, but "after several ineffectual efforts to force them to take the leap, [the animals] finally broke through our line and made their way to the prairie, taking with them some steaks we stood very much in need of."[4]

Disconsolate and starving, the men bedded down in a pit hidden by a copse of woods. That night, the snuffling of a wild sow and her piglets wakened Duval. Spying the animals, he silently reached out and grabbed a stick and waited anxiously for the hogs to come closer, "and when she and her pigs were in striking distance I suddenly sprang up and began a vigorous assault on the pigs."[5] Roused by Duval's thrashing, Holliday and Brown leapt up and joined the melee. By the time the three men finally fell exhausted to the ground they had killed five of the piglets. They quickly built up a fire and cooked the young animals, eating them on the spot.

Sated by the unexpected meal of tender pork, the men set off the next morning in much better spirits. Two days later they came upon an encampment of rancheros and became separated. Brown was captured. Duval managed to dash away into the woods, and Holliday likewise avoided being seized. During the next several weeks, each of them separately underwent many adventures and close calls with Indians, Mexicans, and wild animals.

Brown escaped his captors only to be captured again. His journeys as a prisoner took him back to Goliad, through Matamoros, and finally to Mexico City. He was eventually released and made his way back to New Orleans in the summer of 1837. In contrast, Holliday successfully made his way to friendly forces but only after being captured by two black men who threatened to kill him as revenge for the suffering that other white men had caused them. He talked them out of that notion—and the idea they had of taking him to a nearby camp of Mexicans. Holliday evidently had a persuasive nature, because the two black men ultimately set him free and gave him provisions and directions to Houston and his army.

Duval later related his adventures in *Early Times in Texas*. His close encounters with Indians, Mexicans, and wild animals illustrate just how dangerous the land was during the period. He described the wild character of the region, particularly the dazzling abundance of animals that included deer, antelope, wild horses, hogs, bears, wolves, and panthers. Like Holliday, Duval also made his way to the army near San Jacinto after the victory over Antonio López de Santa Anna.

After making his getaway, Benjamin H. Holland wandered about for days without food before being recaptured. He escaped again and made it to the revolutionary army almost two weeks before the clash at San Jacinto. Herman Ehrenberg also roamed the countryside for days without food. Fearing that he would starve to death before he found help, he actually turned himself back in to General José Urrea. He stayed with the Mexican army as they retreated and eventually escaped when the army was in Matamoros.

Other of Fannin's men who were not killed in the bloodbath of March 27, 1836, included those who were spared by the Mexicans for various reasons. Most of them had special skills such as medicine or nursing that made them valuable to the Mexican army. Blacksmiths and carpenters were also useful. Similarly, boat builders were in demand because rain-swollen rivers were slowing Santa Anna's advance. These Anglo captives worked, often in miserable conditions, until escaping or finally being released after—in some cases, long after—the victory at San Jacinto.

Abel Morgan and William Scurlock continued to serve as nurses. Their situation was miserable, and the work was filthy and hard. Morgan's description underscores their Spartan conditions and the rudimentary nature of the care that was given to the Mexican wounded: "What time we got to sleep was by turns, for we had but one blanket and had to lay on a stone floor, among wounded Mexicans and they smelled as bad as if they were dead already; for in spite of all that could be done for them, the wounds were full of large worms. They were all allowed to lie out in the prairie until their wounds were fly blown before they were hauled in."[6]

After their charges either recovered or died, Morgan and Scurlock were often given other chores such as gathering wood. The *soldados* ordered them to go after the easy pickings—the pickets that the locals used for fencing. The two men frequently would haul a section of wood nearly all the way back to the presidio only to have an irate rancher order them to take it back to where they had found it.

On one of their wood-hunting trips they came across the field where one group of prisoners had been slaughtered. "I suppose from appearances that about one hundred were shot at that place. Their bones were mostly hanging together, though the flesh appeared to be entirely gone." In only a short time the wolves and coyotes and other creatures had stripped the bones nearly bare. Morgan remembered that "we looked at them in silence a while, and then walked away."[7]

After a few weeks, the surviving Anglos in the presidio were exhausted from overwork, malnutrition, and fear at the constant threat of death. As Morgan nursed one Mexican with "the cholic [abdominal disorder]," two Mexican doctors became agitated at the care he was giving. He learned through an interpreter that he was going to be shot if the man did not recover. Fortunately, the man got well and forced a dollar on Morgan in gratitude for his care. "I made up my mind afterwards that if they all died with cholic, I would do no more doctoring for them, further than to dress their wounds."[8] Later, Morgan again barely escaped being shot when the recovered patient took a turn for the worse and died.

Pete Griffin was another nurse who lost his temper with his captors. Griffin was charged with washing, drying, and folding the almost endless quantities of bandages that the injured men required. Morgan recalled that the Mexicans "worried Pete and made him so mad that he cursed the whole of the Mexican officers and soldiers for a set of blood-thirsty savages, to their faces, in the Spanish language. They took him with the avowed intention of shooting him. Pete defied them, for he felt that his condition could not be made worse."

The Mexicans locked Griffin up in the calaboose rather than shooting him. After a few days, he was taken out and put back to washing bandages. Whether he was saved because his work was valuable or out of a sense of compassion can only be guessed at. Morgan noted that as time went on, Griffin's body odor became especially offensive because he had no change of clothes and "he was careless about keeping himself clean."[9]

News of Santa Anna's defeat at San Jacinto put the Mexicans who were garrisoning the presidio on edge. It wasn't long though before rumors circulated that the remainder of the Mexican forces in Texas had rallied and captured Houston and his army. Morgan recalled how the Mexicans celebrated at the false news: "Three large church bells were placed in the fort, and the Mexicans commenced firing guns and ringing bells with desperate enthusiasm. I heard as much racket that evening as ever I did in the same length of time in my life."[10]

When the Mexican army began its retreat following the fight at San Jacinto, Morgan and Scurlock were split up. The Mexican army took Morgan to Matamoros, while Scurlock escaped, was recaptured and taken to Refugio. Eventually, both of them gained their freedom.

The American physicians Jack Shackelford, Henry Barnard, and Joseph Field had more time available to doctor the Mexican wounded following the Mexican extermination of all the Anglo wounded. We will never know what quality of care they gave their captors, considering what was done to their compatriots. Shackelford recalled the horror of the sight of his slain comrades:

> Had to pass close by our butchered companions, who were stripped of their clothes, and their naked, mangled bodies thrown in a pile. The wounded were all hauled out in carts that evening; and some brush thrown over the different piles, with a view of burning, their bodies. A few days afterwards, I accompanied Major Miller to the

spot where lay those who were dear to me whilst living; and whose memory will be embalmed in my affection, until this poor heart itself shall be cold in death; and Oh! What a spectacle! The flesh had been burned from off the bodies; but many hands and feet were yet unscathed—I could recognize no one. The bones were all still knit together, and the vultures were feeding upon those limbs which, one week before, actively played in battle.[11]

Nonetheless, the physicians had little choice but to practice their profession. Like Morgan, Shackelford deplored the wretched working conditions. He did note, however, that the officers treated them with "evinced great politeness, which they seemed to consider the sum total of their duty."[12] He also recounted that they once invited him and Barnard to dinner but that after being exposed to what the Mexicans called the American appetite, they were not asked again.

Toward the end of April 1836, the Mexican army sent Shackelford and Barnard to San Antonio where more than a hundred *soldados* still needed treatment for the wounds they had sustained fighting for the Alamo. The conditions for the two American doctors improved tremendously in that city, and both the military garrison and the citizens welcomed them "with smiling and pleasant faces."[13] Barnard noted the difference as well. In his journal he wrote, "We meet with much simple and unaffected kindness of heart from the citizens, particularly the females."[14] Both of them were given clean clothes and were boarded with good families in decent homes. Shackelford was very happy at having been "disencumbered of the cannibals which had been preying upon our poor carcasses [at Goliad]."[15]

Still, even after the Mexican army began to evacuate Texas and most of the garrison had left San Antonio, the two doctors could not get permission to leave. Finally, near the end of May, not trusting what the Mexicans might be planning for them, Shackelford and Barnard stole horses and guns and headed east. On their fourth day out, just outside Goliad, they met General Thomas Rusk at the head of a force that was trailing the Mexican army as it retreated out of Texas. Rusk and his men took time over the next few days to inter the bones of Fannin and the other massacre victims.

Fannin's other physician, Field, tried but could find no one among his remaining comrades who would attempt an escape with him. He finally found a co-conspirator in George Voss, the survivor who had been forced to work as a servant for a Mexican officer. The two made good their flight in late April, and Field, who knew the country well from his previous travels, had taken them safely the 150 miles to Velasco by early May.

After being saved by Colonel Francisco Garay because of his sister's kindness to Garay, Andrew Boyle secured a passport from Lieutenant Colonel José Nicolás de la Portilla. Within a few days, he was back in San Patricio with his family. Following its defeat at San Jacinto, elements of the Mexican army passed through that small town during the retreat from Texas. Garay was among these forces; during a brief reunion with Boyle's family, he asked the young Anglo to accompany him to Matamoros.

Boyle agreed, but upon reaching that city was told by Garay that he was, essentially, a prisoner again. After a few weeks, Garay proposed to take Boyle to Mexico City with him. The offer, "which was accompanied with the most profuse offers of friendship and assistance,"[16] was declined by the young Anglo, who was subsequently left by the Mexican colonel to his own resources. After some time and difficulty, Boyle secured a passport to New Orleans under false pretenses and escaped Matamoros via schooner.

He arrived at New Orleans without money, resources, or clothes other than what he had on his back, but found work painting warehouses. After eleven days, he drew his pay and purchased passage back to Texas—he was still technically a volunteer in the service of Texas and wanted proper discharge papers. Upon arriving at the Brazos River, Boyle traveled to Velasco and secured a letter from David G. Burnet, the ad interim president of the provisional government. From Velasco, he walked 150 miles to where Rusk had the army encamped at the Guadalupe River and received a discharge from him.

It is difficult to determine how much consideration Urrea gave to the fate of Fannin's men immediately following the fight on the prairie. After all, he had a military campaign to prosecute. Dealing with the surrendered men was just so much housekeeping, as far as he was concerned. There were many more revolutionary forces on the loose that needed to be dealt with.

This point was punctuated by the capture of William Ward's hundred or so men on March 22. Indeed, Urrea pressed this new batch of prisoners into service at Victoria for three days before sending the majority of them back to Goliad to rejoin Fannin's men on March 25. Those he did not send away were the skilled carpenters and boat wrights. Winning the campaign in Texas would take all the labor and skill he could muster—including that of the captured Anglos.

A statement Urrea made later indicates, at least to some degree, that he was concerned about what Santa Anna would do to the prisoners. In his *Diario*, he referenced his own "conduct in the affair," as "straightforward and unequivocal." He pointed out that Santa Anna's orders that "always seemed to me harsh" were very emphatic.[17] He declared that he did his best to get around Santa Anna's commands as delicately as he could: "I wished to elude those orders as far as possible without compromising my personal responsibility."

He stated that he sent several detailed orders to Portilla directing him to use the prisoners to perform useful work at Goliad, particularly in rebuilding the fort and the town.[18] Possibly, he believed that this act of putting the prisoners to work furthering the Mexican cause would blunt Santa Anna's desire to have them slain.

Urrea also detailed how he deliberately returned prisoners to Goliad. Ward's men were among these, as were William P. Miller's. He said that he did it "in the hope that their very numbers would save them, for *I never thought that the horrible spectacle of that massacre could take place in cold blood and without immediate urgency, a deed proscribed by laws of war and condemned by the civilization of our country*" [emphasis added].[19]

This quote of Urrea's is the most compelling statement about the killings to come from an official, ranking, contemporary Mexican. It is an outright and unqualified admission by Mexico's most successful general that the killing of Fannin's men was a horrible wrong. He—a ranking combatant commander in Santa Anna's army—used the word "massacre,"* and declared that the act was "a deed proscribed [forbidden] by laws of war, and condemned by the civilization of our country."[20] So, regardless of how anyone then—or now— might wish to justify the slaughter, she or he must first explain away Urrea's denunciation of that event.

In his *Diario*, Urrea went on to explain that the bloodbath was difficult for him, particularly because Fannin's men had "doubtlessly surrendered confident that Mexican generosity would not make their surrender useless," and that had they not expected that generosity, "they would have sold their lives dearly, fighting to the last."[21] That Urrea played a part in making them believe in the generosity of Mexico no doubt also weighed heavy on his conscience.

Urrea also indicated that he used his influence with Santa Anna to try to get some sort of clemency for the volunteers. Obviously, his influence was not enough: he received a stern rebuke from his commander-in-chief rather than consideration for the prisoners. But, strangely, he seemed to let Santa Anna off the hook, stating that the general's orders were "doubtlessly dictated by cruel necessity."[22] It can only be conjectured at what "cruel necessity" this could have been. Santa Anna was the commander-in-chief of the Mexican army and the dictator of Mexico. In the field, nothing threatened him. He was under the pressure of no cruel necessities other than his own.

Probably, Urrea simply did not want to push the issue with Santa Anna any farther. He was willing to press the case to a point, but not to the point where

---

*Author's note: I have relied heavily on Carlos E. Castañeda's 1928 translation of Urrea's *Diario*. All attributions to Urrea are based on this translation. An esteemed historian and professor, Castañeda's translation has proven accurate and is widely accepted and quoted in scholarly circles. Castañeda uses the word "massacre" in *The Mexican Side of the Texan Revolution*, which is his English translation of Urrea's written *Diario* and other writings. Most of the scholarship on this topic refers to the incident as a "massacre," so that is the word I use.

it could jeopardize his career. It boiled down to this: the lives of the volunteers were important to Urrea—in large part because he had promised to do his best to save them—but they were less important than his position in the Mexican army. After all, he almost certainly reminded himself, Fannin and his men were the enemy.

On March 21, the day following Fannin's surrender, Urrea dispatched a report to Santa Anna. Probably the most important debate associated with this information is that some copies of this report (copies were routinely made for archival purposes) describe Fannin's men as those "who capitulated," whereas others portray them as "those who describe themselves as such [capitulated]."[23] It should be borne in mind that a *capitulation* was a surrender under terms, while *giving up at discretion* was an unconditional submission.

This discrepancy between the different copies begs a very basic question: Why would the volunteers call themselves capitulated rather than acknowledging that they had given up at the discretion of Mexico? And furthermore, why would Urrea even bother to mention Fannin's men as anything other than prisoners, if there was any question about their true status? The likely answer is that Urrea knew that the true terms that he had negotiated with Fannin were ambiguous. That ambiguity tormented his conscience, and he believed that he had to suggest to Santa Anna that some sort of terms were certainly part of the surrender, even if not explicitly promised in writing. Otherwise there was no reason to even mention capitulation in the document.

If Urrea intended to provide subtle hints, it did not work. Santa Anna later stated that if a capitulation had been arranged, he would have considered it when he decided the fate of Fannin's men. He wrote, "Had any such [capitulation] existed, even though General Urrea had no authority to grant it, it would have afforded me an opportunity to petition, in the name of humanity, the indulgence of Congress for Fannin and his soldiers."[24]

Santa Anna was a liar. The Tornel Decree was his own doing. Aside from that, he knew that the Mexican Congress would not oppose him if he spared the men. He was the dictator of Mexico and the commander-in-chief of its army. He had financed a significant portion of the Texas campaign with his own money. He could do whatever he wanted with Fannin's men, and he chose to slaughter them.

Santa Anna's secretary during the Texas campaign, Ramón Martínez Caro, noted that Urrea recommended "the unfortunate prisoners," to "the clemency of his Excellency [Santa Anna]." Caro recorded that Santa Anna strongly upbraided Urrea and ordered him "not to soil his triumphs with a mistaken display of generosity."[25] That missive came with orders to slay all of the prisoners.

His cruelty notwithstanding, Santa Anna could be prevailed upon when confronted. The final order that he drafted directing the killing of all the prisoners at Goliad originally included Miller's men. These men had surrendered to Colonel Rafael de la Vara without a fight on hearing of Fannin's surrender. Santa Anna knew this and nevertheless included them in the order. When the courier for this death sentence, Captain D. N. Savariego, learned of this, he asked for and was granted an audience with Santa Anna.

At the meeting, Savariego explained that de la Vara desired Santa Anna to grant clemency to Miller's men because they had given up their arms voluntarily. Santa Anna blustered and fumed and loudly denigrated Savariego, but he directed Caro to change the order. Miller's men were to be kept alive until an investigation was completed.[26] Ultimately, they were spared. When it is considered what Savariego, a mere captain, was able to do, one wonders what Urrea, a respected and competent general, could have done for Fannin's men if he had only pushed forcefully for clemency.

Yet he did not, nor did the unimaginative and frightened Portilla, who followed Santa Anna's orders and ordered the killing of the Anglos. In later years, Santa Anna sought to blur his association with the slaughter, preferring to blame others. In fact, he declared—incredibly—that Portilla "was responsible for the cruel and inhumane manner of carrying out the execution to the nation, to the world, and to God."[27]

Immediately following the massacre, Portilla sent a message to Urrea, addressing him as "My Beloved General." His distress was evident: "I am most wretched, because today, in cold blood, a scene has been enacted that has horrified me." Of course, he had a major role in the slaughter that had just "been enacted," and he attempted to justify it as best he could. In his note he described his previous service in a self-deprecating manner before stating, "Nevertheless, I will always do what I am ordered, since I have the pleasure of being one of the most disciplined officers that there could be in our army, and I always do my duty, even against my natural sentiments."[28]

In this note, Portilla obliquely rebuked Urrea for putting him in such a difficult position. He declared, "You have left me here, my General." That he hoped to never again be put in such a position is indicated in the note. Although the sheet is torn and the leading portion of the sentence is missing, Portilla wrote, "less to serve as an executioner, and be ordered to kill more people."[29] We can assume that the missing portion stated that he never wanted to be forced again to commit such an atrocity.

Urrea recorded in his *Diario* that he and his own men were taken aback when word reached them that Fannin's men had been slain: "All the members of my division were distressed to hear this news, and I no less, being as sensitive as my companions who will bear testimony of my excessive grief. Let a single one of them deny this fact!"[30] In the next sentence, as if to affirm his innate goodness, he pointed out that the prisoners that were with him in Victoria had escaped death.

Those who argue today that the Tornel Decree actually provided a legal and technical instrument for slaying Fannin's men—despite such an action's moral implications—are treading on slippery ground. The proclamation was directed against foreign adventurers and pirates, and not Mexican citizens. True, most of the men were not Mexican citizens, but no one established the citizenship of each man that was killed.

In addition, Fannin's command was technically organized and serving under former Mexican citizens—albeit, largely of American origin—who had declared themselves to be a republic independent of Mexico and the United States. Certainly Mexico City did not recognize this new nation, but nevertheless there is an arguable case that Fannin and many of his men were not pirates. Instead, they were citizens in rebellion against their government. Neither were the newly arrived volunteers pirates, but rather they were sympathetic foreigners who had come to fight under the flag of the rebellion, and later, the newly declared republic. It could be argued, then, that they were de facto citizens of Texas, and not pirates.

Admittedly this logic would likely not have been ironclad in the context of Mexican law, but it does have some merit. Indeed, it would have been arguments like these that—if the men had been tried in a Mexican court—would have made their conviction uncertain. However, even if they had been found guilty, they almost certainly would not have been slain. As it was, they were killed in near-isolation away from major population centers. Had an official trial been conducted, the United States probably would have created considerable pressure to force Mexico to parole the men.

Additionally, as it developed, the Tornel Decree was rescinded in April 1836—less than a month after the killings—and a general amnesty was granted. And laws and decrees aside, many Mexican citizens were horrified and ashamed of what had happened at Goliad. Given that horror and shame, it is quite likely they would not have condoned the organized slaughter of Fannin's men.

She was just a camp wife, but she had the courage to save several of Fannin's men from being killed. Sadly, her name was never recorded with any certainty. Her first name was variously reported as Francita or Francisca, while her middle (paternal) name was recorded as Pancita or Panchita. Even her surname is a matter of conjecture—it was either Alvarez, Alavéz, or Alevesco. She is commonly thought to have been the common-law wife of one of Urrea's cavalry officers, probably Captain Telesforo Alavéz, who had abandoned a wife and two children in Mexico.

Several accounts declare that she was a beautiful woman. Her hair and eyes—especially her flashing eyes—were noted for their exquisite, dark beauty. She carried herself well and was not afraid to take on anyone, regardless of rank, when she sought to prevent cruelty. Her intolerance for brutality was first noted at San Patricio where she helped Father Thomas Molloy dissuade Urrea from carrying out Santa Anna's orders to slay prisoners taken there. Ruben R. Brown, one of James Grant's men, specifically remembered, "I was then taken out to be shot, but was spared through the interposition of a priest and a Mexican lady named Alvarez."[31]

She left San Patricio, going with Alavéz to Copano, where Miller's men surrendered without firing a shot, as they disembarked. The men were tied together by their wrists, with bindings so tight that they severely restricted circulation and caused excruciating pain. The dark-eyed beauty prevailed on her Mexican countrymen to loosen the cords and to give the Anglo invaders food and drink.

She had been at Goliad for at least a few days on March 27, just before Fannin's men were butchered. The men that Garay saved owed some debt to Francisca Alavéz. If the colonel was inclined to spare as many men as he could, Francisca Alavéz encouraged him further. Barnard wrote, "And when, on the morning of the massacre she learned that the prisoners were to be shot, she so effectually pleaded with Colonel Garay (whose humane feelings so revolted at the order) that with great personal responsibility to himself, and at great hazards at thus going counter to the orders of the then all-powerful Santa Anna, resolved to save all that he could; and a few of us, in consequence, were left to tell of that bloody day."[32]

One of those "left to tell of that bloody day" was a boy named Benjamin Franklin Hughes (ca. 1821–1892). He was only fifteen years old on March 27, 1836, when he was formed in the presidio yard with the rest of Fannin's men before being marched out the gate. He remembered seeing "Madame Captain Alvarez," standing with a young girl and another woman that he identified as Urrea's wife. He noticed that they spied him among the others and subsequently engaged one of the officers, perhaps Garay, in a discussion. No doubt his youth provoked their tenderness. A moment or two later, a *soldado* pulled him from the formation and put him between the two women.

Shortly afterwards his comrades were marched clear of the fort and slaughtered. Later, some of the *soldados* rushed back to the presidio and spotted Hughes, still with the women. He wrote later, "I nudged up to the ladies, and immediately after some of the Mexicans came running back and menacing me with their muskets with bayonets, as if they had bayoneted all who were not killed out right—which they did."[33]

The horror of the killing must have undone Francisca Alavéz later that day. Barnard recalled, "During the time of the massacre she stood in the street, her hair floating, speaking wildly, and abusing the Mexican officers, especially Portilla."[34] Santa Anna's vicious orders and Portilla's failure to defy them had killed hundreds of men and made a mockery of the relatively few lives she had managed to save.

Barnard remembered Francisca Alavéz's reaction a few days later when she learned of the death of Shackelford's son. Shackelford had been tending the wounded almost without pause since the battle of March 19, and his son had been among those slaughtered on March 27. Francisca Alavéz came to Shackelford and burst into tears: "Why did I not know that you had a son here? I would have saved him at all hazards!"[35] Shackelford confirmed the woman's kindness in his own recollections, saying that she did everything possible to lessen their miseries.

After the massacre, she accompanied her common-law husband to Victoria, where he was put in charge of the Mexican garrison. While there, she continued applying her kindnesses to the Anglos, even sending "messages and supplies of provisions" to the prisoners still surviving at Goliad.[36] She was instrumental in saving the life of Hamilton who had been badly wounded in the massacre, and who escaped with Brooks, Simpson, and Cooper, only to be captured again. In Victoria, he was sentenced to be shot, but two women— one of them quite likely Francisca Alavéz—interceded on his behalf and he was spared.

Her final acts of goodness toward the Anglo revolutionaries occurred at Matamoros. She again worked on behalf of Americans imprisoned there, long after the Battle of San Jacinto had essentially ended the fight in the favor of the rebellion. Alavéz subsequently took her to Mexico City with him, where he abandoned her, penniless.

CHAPTER 17

Mayhem, Victory, and Marking the Bones

"Runaway Scrape" is the name given to the massive and panicked flight of Anglo settlers who sought to stay ahead of Antonio López de Santa Anna's advance into Texas in early 1836. It started south of San Patricio and moved north and east ahead of Santa Anna's army. The families that Captain Amon B. King was supposed to evacuate at Refugio were part of that hurried evacuation. The Runaway Scrape picked up momentum as the revolution's fortunes dimmed, particularly after the Alamo was taken. After James Walker Fannin's men were shot at Goliad, the flight became a mad rush.

Settlers abandoned homes and fields and animals. Whole families took to the muddy roads and trails where bandits and Indians preyed on them. Sometimes the revolutionary army snatched their possessions: the fighters were short of horses, draft animals, wagons, and provisions. Many families just starting out in the new land had no real assets or animals, or anything at all worth taking. They simply fled on foot, empty handed. Hunger and disease were common, and many refugees fell sick, died, and were buried on the trail. Noah Smithwick later described the chaos of the hurried flight:

> The desolation of the country through which we passed beggars description. Houses were standing open, the beds unmade, the breakfast things still on the tables, pans of milk moulding in the dairies. There were cribs full of corn, smoke houses full of bacon, yards full of chickens that ran after us for food, nests of eggs in every fence corner, young corn and garden truck rejoicing in the rain, cattle cropping the luxuriant grass, hogs, fat and lazy, wallowing in the mud, all abandoned. Forlorn dogs roamed around the deserted homes, their doleful howls adding to the general sense of desolation. Hungry cats ran mewing to meet us, rubbing their sides against our legs in token of welcome. Wagons were so scarce that it was impossible to remove household goods, many of the women and children, even, had to walk.[1]

The ad interim government fled with the settlers. It left Washington-on-the-Brazos on March 17 as soon as the Convention adjourned, and from there set up shop first in Harrisburg, then on Galveston Island, then in Velasco, and, finally, in Columbia. Other settlements were also affected. Richmond was empty by April 1, and Nacogdoches had been deserted by April 13. Most refugees headed for the Sabine River, where they hoped to cross to the eastern bank and find safety in the United States.

The revolutionary army fled east as well. On the same day that the Convention adjourned at Washington-on-the-Brazos, the army crossed the Colorado River. It continued eastward, its makeup changing as individuals rallied to the cause or deserted to return to their families and move them out of harm's way. By March 30, General Samuel Houston had moved his men to the Brazos River where they stayed for two weeks.

There, Houston assessed Santa Anna's movements while attempting to train and discipline his army, while withstanding criticism. The ad interim president, David G. Burnet, directed him to stand and fight while General Thomas Rusk, the secretary of war, urged similar action. Even his own men wanted to turn and engage the Mexicans. Houston resisted being pushed into a fight until he thought his command was ready. That time had come by mid-April.

On April 21, about a mile from Lynch's Ferry near the present-day city of Houston, Santa Anna camped with more than fifteen hundred men a mile or less from where the revolutionary army bivouacked. The previous day had seen small, inconclusive engagements. Houston gathered six of his leading officers and solicited their counsel. Only two of them advised an attack; the others recommended preparing defenses in anticipation of Santa Anna's expected assault.

Up to this point, Houston had acted with caution, but now he chose to strike first. At mid-afternoon, during the traditional Mexican siesta, he formed his men out of sight of the enemy camp. He recalled in a letter soon after the battle, "Our troops paraded with alacrity and spirit, and were anxious for the contest. Their conscious disparity in numbers [compared to Santa Anna's army] seemed only to increase their enthusiasm and confidence, and heightened their anxiety for the conflict."[2]

Then, between three and four in the afternoon, Houston led them crouching on a broad front across the marshy prairie. As the range to the Mexican camp closed to a few hundred yards, two cannon—known as the Twin Sisters—were swung around and fired. The explosions from those six-pounders ignited the charge that ended the revolution. Full of fury, the motley mob of barely trained colonists and adventurers rushed headlong into the startled Mexicans. Their battle cry was, "Remember the Alamo! Remember Goliad!"

The Mexicans were caught wholly by surprise. Houston recalled that, on his direction, his men held fire until nearly at point blank range. But once it started, the killing was ferocious and passionate. Americans had never slain so many so quickly. It was a spectacular, bloody orgy characterized by an animal-like intensity. Mexicans that fought were shot down or clubbed or stabbed. Mexicans that fled were shot down or clubbed or stabbed. Even some of the Mexicans that tried to surrender were shot down or clubbed or stabbed. The viciousness of the attack stunned men on both sides.

The battle was all over in eighteen minutes. Houston reported that 630 Mexicans were killed and another 730 were taken prisoner. Of the total revolutionary army force of just more than nine hundred men, nine were killed. Another few dozen were wounded, including Houston, who was struck just above the ankle by a musket ball.

Noah Smithwick, attached to a group of rangers protecting citizens during their retreat, arrived at the battlefield just after the killing had stopped. He was chagrined to have missed the fight, but recorded the gory scene and the wretched despondency of the defeated Mexicans: "The dead Mexicans lay in piles, the survivors not even asking permission to bury them, thinking, perhaps, that, in return for the butchery they had practiced, they would soon be lying dead themselves."[3]

Santa Anna was nowhere to be found. While his *soldados* were being cut down, he had run from the Mexican encampment and disappeared into the swampy countryside. It wasn't until the next day that he was found hiding in the grass, clothed as a common *soldado*. His captors did not even know they had snared Santa Anna until he was brought in and the Mexican prisoners cried out, "El presidente, el presidente!"

Santa Anna was taken to Houston to whom he presented himself as "a prisoner of war at your disposition." As crowds of Anglo fighters pressed in around him, he became fearful for his life and entreated Houston for mercy. Houston is recorded to have asked the Mexican president what led him to ask for compassion when he had shown none at the Alamo or Goliad. During this questioning, Rusk took Santa Anna to task. Predictably, the dictator denied responsibility for the butchery of Fannin's men. Rusk would have none of it:

> He did not pretend to deny the existence of the Treaty; but denied that he had given a positive order to have them shot. He said that the Law of Mexico required, that all who were taken with arms in their hands should be shot; that General Ur[r]ea was an officer of the Government, and could enter into no contract in violation of the Laws; and was going on with a course of reasoning, to show the correctness of his position, when I interrupted him, and told him Ur[r]ea had made a Treaty stipulating to extend to Fannin

and his men the usual treatment of prisoners of war; that that agreement alone had induced them to surrender, and that to shoot them in violation of that treaty afterwards, whatever might be the laws of Mexico, was murder of the blackest character; and that if he regarded the preservation of his own life, it would perhaps be well for him to offer no palliation to a crime which would blacken the character of all the officers concerned in it, and would attach disgrace to the Mexican Nation as long as its history should continue to be recorded.[4]

Ultimately, Santa Anna's life was spared despite strident calls for his execution. The revolution's leadership knew that Santa Anna, the president of Mexico, was more valuable alive than dead. If he were executed, even though he richly deserved it, Santa Anna would only be a criminal brought to justice, or, worse, a martyr in whose name the Mexican people might rally and try to retake Texas.

On May 14, 1836, Burnet and Santa Anna signed the Treaties of Velasco. The Mexican army was sent out of Texas. Although the Republic of Texas would experience more Mexican invasions in the coming years, its sovereignty would never be seriously threatened again. It would maintain that sovereignty until joining the United States nine years later, in 1845.

Santa Anna was sent to the United States for an interview with President Andrew Jackson, where diplomatic sensitivities dictated that he receive treatment appropriate for a head of state. To Jackson, also, he protested his innocence in regard to the horror at Goliad. He subsequently returned to a hero's welcome at Veracruz, Mexico, on February 21, 1837, and was never punished for the slaughter of Fannin's men.

It was more than two months after the massacre before the half-burned, animal-gnawed bones of Fannin and his men were collected and buried. Rusk, while dogging the Mexican army out of Mexico, paused in Goliad to inter the remains on June 3, 1836. Overtaken by emotion, Rusk delivered a eulogy that marked the contributions of the men that those bones once were. In it, he noted the idealism that brought many of them into the land: "Without any further interest in the country than that which all noble hearts feel at the bare mention of liberty, they rallied to our standard. Relinquishing the ease, peace, and comforts of their homes, leaving behind them all they held dear, their mothers, sisters, daughters, and wives, they subjected themselves to fatigue and privation, and nobly threw themselves between the people of Texas and the legions of Santa Anna."[5]

At that time, Santa Anna was still being held in Texas. Like many of his contemporaries, Rusk assumed that the Mexican tyrant would be punished for his barbarity: "We can still offer another consolation: Santa Anna, the mock hero, the black-hearted murderer, is within our grasp. Yea, and there he must remain, tortured with the keen pain of corroding conscience. He must oft remember La Bahía, and while the names of those whom he murdered shall soar to the highest pinnacle of fame, his shall sink down into the lowest depths of infamy and disgrace."[6]

Astonishingly, the trench that was the mass grave at Goliad was not permanently marked at that time. Gradually, nature reclaimed the ground and the site was almost lost. More than twenty years after the fact, in 1858, a local Goliad merchant marked the mass grave with a pile of rocks. He did it to keep the cattle and other animals from walking on the spot.

Not for another seventy years was any real attention paid to the site. In 1928, the town of Goliad, on sketchy evidence, purchased two acres encompassing the mass grave. During the next couple of years informal scratching and digging about the area unearthed bone fragments that were identified as human. An archeologist from the University of Texas conducted an investigation in 1932, and he and other experts contributed to the confirmation of the burial site.

Only a short time later, during the Texas Centennial in 1936, the state allocated funds for the construction of a monument to commemorate the final resting place of Fannin's men. On June 4, 1938, a massive, pink granite monument was dedicated to Fannin and his men. Harbert Davenport (1882–1957), the preeminent Goliad historian of the time, gave the memorial address. Davenport's seminal work, *Men of Goliad*, is a sober analysis and critique of the revolution, and of the killings at Goliad. A snippet captures the truth of the event and of the times: "*Forget Goliad!* Would have been a more correct expression of the mingled shame and pride with which early Texans regarded Fannin's men. That anarchy in Texan councils; incompetent Texan leadership and worse; and petty personal prejudices, factional intrigues, and high-handed determination of minor Texan leaders each to have his own way, were responsible for the horrors of Goliad was well known to all Texans in 1836. But Texas had then no time for mortification, and could not afford shame."[7]

Davenport addressed the reasons why the horror of Goliad disappeared from the public consciousness. He took on Texas pride squarely when he declared that

> the Texans had, in another sense, a shame-faced feeling that the men of Goliad had let them down. Texas undertook the unequal struggle with Mexico, sustained by an almost insolent dependence on race pride. That Texans were natural soldiers and brave men, and invincible as against Mexican courage, and Mexican numbers, and Mexico's material and means, were the touchstones of Texan valor and Texan faith.... But if looked to

too closely, the defeat and capture of Colonel Fannin would have to be explained; and the explanation admitted that even Texan valor was not proof against hunger, thirst, and tactical errors, and that Mexicans could be brave.[8]

The reality and veracity of Davenport's declaration was as true in 1938 as it had been in 1836. The tragedy of Goliad—even on the side of the victims—was cloaked in shame.

Epilogue

What did it matter? To the success or failure of the Texas Revolution, Antonio López de Santa Anna's execution of James Walker Fannin's command turned out to be of little consequence. General Samuel Houston and his men defeated the Mexican despot without the slain fighters, and Texas joined the United States in 1845 after almost ten years as an independent republic. It is sometimes stated that the real value of the Goliad tragedy was that it finally opened the eyes of the colonists to the horrors of Santa Anna's invasion. Thus motivated, they supposedly rallied to Houston's army so that he was able to bring battle to the Mexicans on terms that, while not entirely equal, were at least not desperate.

This notion of the massacre as the catalyst that finally united the settlers against Mexico is flawed. The slaughter frightened as many people as it inspired. After word of the massacre got out, the Runaway Scrape developed into a frantic, headlong rush. The makeup of Houston's army during his eastward retreat constantly changed as men deserted to look after their families while others joined, perhaps motivated by the disasters at the Alamo and Goliad, but also perhaps by a compulsory draft. Regardless of the reasons why they joined Houston, the Anglos exploded onto the battlefield at San Jacinto with a ferocity that absolutely devastated Santa Anna's *soldados*. One of Santa Anna's officers recalled that the general himself was so terrified that he "was running about in the utmost excitement, wringing his hands, and unable to give an order."[1] The end result was an independent Texas. And it all happened without Fannin's fighters.

So did their deaths contribute anything to the birth of Texas? And what would have happened had they survived? It is difficult to answer the second without falling into the quicksand of "what if," but the first question is addressed easily. As just discussed, the massacre was probably a wash in terms of inspiring the population to rush to arms against Santa Anna. Possibly the only real impact was the reaction to the massacre in the United States. Although news of it arrived too late for any aid to reach Houston in time to make a difference in the actual fighting, the general horror that the event elicited decisively swung American opinion against the Mexicans. The value of this was significant, although difficult to quantify. In their subsequent forays into Texas, the Mexicans had to realize that rather than trying to bring an intransigent region back into their national fold, they were—in the eyes of the United States—invading an American ally.

It was a consideration that played a role in the events leading up to the Mexican-American War of 1846–1848. Border disputes over Texas ignited a conflict that cost Mexico almost half of its territory. Although it is a tenuous link, the massacre of Fannin's men probably contributed at an emotional level to American arguments in favor of a war with Mexico.

The second question that asks what would have happened if Fannin's men had survived is thornier. If the men had been paroled back to the United States the entire incident would likely have been forgotten. If anything, an amnesty of Fannin and his men may have blunted the anti-Mexico fervor stemming from the defeat at the Alamo.

The discussion becomes more interesting when it dwells on what could have happened if Fannin and his men had been able to escape Urrea and join with Houston. It is perhaps most probable that Fannin would have subordinated himself to Houston and that the army would have continued its measured retreat east until Houston chose a site to stand and fight—much as he did at San Jacinto. Conversely it is not out of the question to consider that Fannin and Houston might have disagreed over command of the army and that the force would have fractured. Houston's dealings with Fannin and the various revolutionary governments had never been wholly satisfactory. Had there been discord, there is a remote possibility that Houston would have given up his command in disgust and left Texas entirely. Whether Texas could have happened with Fannin at the head of the revolutionary army is uncertain.

More realistic is the idea that Houston, augmented by Fannin's men, would have chosen to stop his retreat and engage Santa Anna earlier than he actually did. It can hardly be known whether the army would have been as successful as it was at San Jacinto, but it is difficult to imagine a more complete triumph. A less total victory might not have yielded Santa Anna as a prize. Without Santa Anna as a captive—even if his command had been defeated—the bulk of the much larger Mexican army would have remained in the field as a very real threat.

Speculation is an interesting diversion but it isn't real. What is real is that several hundred men were cruelly killed at Goliad, and then practically forgotten. The reasons they were put out of mind are, in some measure, uncomfortable. First, the settlers never really knew Fannin and his fighters. While they recognized them for the most part as being good men who had come to fight for what they believed was good and right, the majority of the men were in Texas without family or loved ones. To a greater degree than the men at the Alamo, they were complete strangers. After the fighting, with a new nation to tame, it was not difficult to put out of mind outsiders to whom there were no ties of blood or marriage.

The comparison is worn and tired, but still valid: On the one hand, the defenders at the Alamo all died fighting or were put to death immediately after the fight. The garrison never surrendered and the romance of the defenders' dogged audacity in the face of an undefeatable enemy grew into a near-sacred legend. On the other hand, Fannin's incompetence put his men into a situation where they faced the same choice—surrender or death. They chose surrender, and they were killed anyway. Their deaths were ignominious, at the hands of a tyrant, but they came about because they had submitted. Submissions are rarely commemorated by anyone.

Finally, there were the reasons that Harbert Davenport highlighted in his 1938 address. Fannin was destroyed not only because of his own failings, but also because of the shortcomings of the revolutionary leadership. That revolutionary leadership—in the tumultuous period of nation-building that took place after the Battle of San Jacinto—could hardly afford the horror of Goliad to be reviewed in detail, and so it wasn't.

The entire episode was also positive proof that Anglos were not necessarily invincible on the battlefield against Mexicans. This was a difficult truth, particularly because Texas would continue to sporadically fight against Mexico for some years to come. And it was a truth that—perhaps in order to sustain confidence in itself as a nation—early Texas preferred to ignore. This also meant that the men who had died at Goliad came to be ignored. It remains to be seen whether the rediscovery of the slaughter at Goliad by modern popular histories can overcome the pall of humiliation and ignorance that have covered the event since 1836.

Of course, the survivors and the antagonists continued to live beyond the events at Goliad. The lives of some of them reveal examples of both success and failure.

After Herman Ehrenberg escaped from the Mexicans, he returned to Germany to study mining at Freiburg University, and afterward took a position at Halle University teaching English. He also wrote a book, *Texas und seine Revolution*, that survives as one of the most complete accounts of the events at Goliad. The wildness of North America must have exerted a tremendous pull on him: he returned to the United States and traveled with a fur-trapping party from St. Louis to Oregon during 1844–1845. He afterward sailed from Portland and saw much of the Pacific; in fact, he was one of the early surveyors of Honolulu, Hawaii. On returning to the United States, he took part in the Mexican-American War, during which he negotiated the release of a group of American prisoners. Ehrenberg also participated in the California Gold Rush.

He ultimately became a prominent Indian agent, surveyor, cartographer, and mining expert in the Southwest. He was murdered by bandits in 1866 near what is now Palm Springs, California. Ehrenberg Peak in Grand Canyon National Park is named for him. Ehrenberg never collected his land certificate—worth several thousand acres—that he earned as a participant in the Texas Revolution.

Jack Shackelford was disgusted at the decision to spare Santa Anna's life and consequently requested and received an honorable discharge from the revolutionary army. His homecoming from Texas to Courtland, Alabama, was a heartrending event. He had almost single-handedly raised and led sixty of Courtland's best men—the Red Rovers—to Texas. Only he and seven others survived. His heartbreak, sorrow, and feelings of guilt can only be imagined.

Shackelford reestablished his medical practice and his estate while helping the families of his slain men collect the land grants and monies that were due them. His interest in Texas remained strong, and he returned several times, even working to raise volunteers during the Mexican invasion of 1842. He died in 1857. Shackelford County, Texas, was named in his honor.

Dr. Joseph Barnard never returned to Chicago. Instead, he stayed in Texas and held minor offices in the government; he eventually made his home in Goliad and became a primary chronicler of the massacre. His list of the slain was one of the most comprehensive and accurate and formed the basis for later compilations. He was on a trip to Canada when he died in 1861.

John C. Duval studied engineering in Virginia after escaping the massacre. He returned to Texas in 1840 and worked as a surveyor and a Texas Ranger of some repute—serving alongside Bigfoot Wallace and Jack Hays. He became one of Texas' early essayists. His *Early Times in Texas* became a classic in Texas literature, and his later *Adventures of Bigfoot Wallace, Texas Ranger and Hunter* also endures. Duval is said to have been an influence on the renowned writer, O. Henry, during the time that writer spent in Austin.

By all accounts Duval was an intelligent, easygoing, and kind man who had an eye for the natural world and an engaging way of describing it. He served in the Mexican-American War, but was much troubled by the Civil War because he was a southerner at heart but did not support secession. Nevertheless, he was compelled by his roots to enlist as a private in the Confederate army, refusing a commission early in the war. He was a captain when the war ended. His stature in Texas history was such that he became known as "Texas John" Duval even while he lived. He survived almost until the twentieth century; he was eighty-one when he died in Fort Worth in 1897. Before he passed away, he was the last living man to have survived the massacre at Goliad.

Dillard C. Cooper settled in Colorado County, Texas, on the land that the republic granted him following independence. He married and had five children. By his own account, it was years before he could talk of the Goliad massacre without tears coming to his eyes.

William L. Hunter, who had survived the initial slaughter only to be hacked at, stabbed, and left for dead again, moved to Goliad after independence. He served in Texas politics for several years and was a justice of the peace. He died in 1886, fifty years after the massacre, and was buried in Austin with full military honors.

The Mexican army snatched Abel Morgan from Goliad and took him back to Matamoros when it retreated following the defeat at San Jacinto. He worked variously as a boatwright, hatter, and harness mender until 1842 when he was able to obtain a passport back to the United States. Because he had served in the revolution as "Thomas Smith" he experienced difficulty collecting his land grant and back pay, but with the help of fellow veterans he finally received his due. He eventually settled in Fannin County with a second wife. He died there in 1873 at the age of eighty-one.

Young Andrew A. Boyle took up the mercantile life following his time in Texas. He married and took part in the California Gold Rush, eventually moving to San Francisco where he operated a shoe store. He took his business to Los Angeles and also operated a vineyard. Boyle Heights in East Los Angeles is named for him. He died in 1871.

After escaping Goliad, Dr. Joseph Field found friendly forces immediately following the fight at San Jacinto. He subsequently traveled back to the United States and wrote a book, *Three Years in Texas*, which described his experiences. He returned to Texas and after a short stint in the army, practiced medicine for several more decades, but without a deserved pension from the state. He died in obscurity, impoverished and blind, in Clear Water Harbor, Florida, in 1882.

General José de Urrea was adamantly against retreat following the Mexican defeat at San Jacinto. Nevertheless, he followed his orders and left with the rest of the Mexican army. Following his experience in Texas he initiated or was involved in several different unsuccessful revolts against the governments in Mexico City. He spent time in prison for his roles in these various insurrections but was released in time to serve in the Mexican-American war. He died in 1849.

Nicolás de la Portilla, like Urrea, also participated in the Mexican-American War. He sided with the French when they established their empire in Mexico and was awarded with the post of *ministro de guerra y marina*; essentially, he was the secretary of defense. When the French were expelled, he was forced out of the country with them, but he eventually returned to Mexico City where he died in 1873.

As previously discussed, Santa Anna's command was utterly crushed by Houston's army at San Jacinto. After his capture, he spent several months in Texas before being sent to Washington, D.C., in November 1836. During his time in captivity he was under constant threat of harm, primarily because of the Goliad massacre. His secretary, Ramón Martínez Caro, later recorded: "This episode, which after the minutest investigations still remains covered by a mysterious veil, was the chief cause of the infinite hardships and sufferings we endured as prisoners and of the dangers to which we were exposed."[2]

In Washington, Santa Anna interviewed with President Andrew Jackson, who treated him with the official courtesy that was warranted for Santa Anna's position as the Mexican head of state. During this time, Santa Anna offered to sell Texas to Jackson at a discount. Jackson declined and the tyrant was sent home; he arrived in Mexico in February 1837.

The next several decades saw him gain and lose the presidency of Mexico many more times during a period marked by revolts, usurpations, wars, and ceaseless intrigue. He lost his left leg fighting the French during the Pastry War of 1838. Later, he had the limb dug up and interred in Mexico City at an official state event. The Mexican-American war saw Santa Anna hopelessly outmatched by the Americans, who captured Mexico City, destroyed the Mexican army, and took nearly half of Mexico's territory. Later in his career, Santa Anna sold even more land to the United States (the Gadsen Purchase, which ultimately became parts of present-day Arizona and New Mexico) in order to buttress the national treasury, which needed buttressing for the simple reason that he constantly stole from it. Perhaps his most pitiable episode was during a period of exile in 1867 when he traveled to New York and unsuccessfully tried to raise a force to invade his own country.

Had the devil himself been loose in Mexico during the nineteenth century, it is questionable that he could have done more to ruin the country than did Santa Anna. In the end, the Mexican government allowed Santa Anna to return to his homeland in 1874. He died a penniless, extraneous, senile old man in Mexico City in 1876.

Fannin's widow failed in an attempt to assassinate Santa Anna when he was being held in Velasco in June 1836. By 1839, she was dead.

Acknowledgments

My friend Eric Hammel, the accomplished military writer and publisher, was more encouraging than most when I mentioned this project several years ago: "I don't know anything at all about that, but give it a shot if you feel strongly enough about it." It was great advice; thanks, Eric.

Although there are few full-length books on the actions at and around Goliad during 1835–1836, I did benefit from material put together by others who recognized the importance of the events. Harbert Davenport's writings were among the most valuable. He was born in 1882 when there were a few veterans of Texas' fight for independence still alive. He received a degree from the University of Texas in 1908 and became a lawyer, and subsequently a preeminent authority on water and land laws in the southwestern United States. Davenport was also an avid Texas historian and understood the importance of gathering information about the Goliad massacre. It was Davenport who was chosen to speak at the dedication of the memorial to Fannin and his men in 1938. He has been dead for more than fifty years, yet his research remains the single greatest treasure trove on Fannin and his men. A superlative Web site (http://www.tsha.utexas.edu/supsites/fannin/hd_home.html) that features much of Davenport's work is maintained by H. David Maxey.

There are two other resources that I found invaluable. The first is the *Handbook of Texas Online*. It is maintained by the Texas State Historical Association and "is created and maintained by the Texas State Historical Association in partnership with the College of Liberal Arts and the General Libraries at the University of Texas at Austin" (http://www.tsha.utexas.edu/about/). This site is invaluable when it comes to the history of Texas. I can't say enough good things about it.

The second online resource that proved to be virtually indispensable was the *Sons of Dewitt Colony Texas* Web site. It is a "non-profit, privately funded enterprise of Wallace L. McKeehan" (http://www.tamu.edu/ccbn/dewitt/aboutdewitt.htm). It takes only a quick visit to the site to recognize McKeehan's passion for Texas and its history. Particularly valuable were the personal accounts and correspondences that he has collected and posted. His own writing is also interesting, clear, and well considered. I congratulate and thank him for his valuable work.

In the context of the making of Texas, perhaps the greatest single source is *Southwestern Historical Quarterly*. It has been in publication since 1897 and is the premier scholarly journal on Texas history. The pedigree of its contributors and the strength of its editorial staff have ensured the availability of the very best researched material. This book is better because of it.

My friend James David Perry, PhD, graciously took time to help me edit the manuscript prior to submission. He is a critical thinker and provided unambiguous and useful criticism. He wasn't inhibited with his more detailed editing; he believed my initial writing was too loose, whereas I felt he didn't appreciate or understand my style. Fortunately, we reached common ground. If you've already read this book you've benefited from Dr. Perry's temperate treatment of my writing style.

Mark Gatlin, as the former acquisitions editor at Naval Institute Press, recognized the potential of this work as a study in leadership. He believed that it would be valuable regardless of the fact that—aside from lessons in leadership—it has virtually nothing to do with things nautical. Mark has since left to do good things elsewhere, but I thank him and wish him luck. The rest of the staff has been extraordinarily helpful and kind in editing and otherwise preparing the book for release. I am especially grateful for their ever-ready assistance. In addition, my agent E. J. McCarthy did a top-notch job wrestling all the pesky contractual issues that are part of publishing. Thank you, E. J.

My friends and family didn't do much to help me other than remain my friends and family even when I became cranky and antisocial. I've got good friends and family.

Notes

INTRODUCTION
1. "Census and Census Records," *Handbook of Texas Online.*
2. Arnoldo De León, *They Called Them Greasers: Anglo Attitudes Toward Mexicans in Texas, 1821–1900.*
3. Paul D. Lack, *The Texas Revolutionary Experience*, 14.
4. Eugene C. Barker, "Stephen F. Austin and the Independence of Texas," *Southwestern Historical Quarterly Online.*

CHAPTER 1. Bloody Beginnings
1. Donald E. Chipman, "Spanish Texas," *Handbook of Texas Online.*
2. Robert S. Weddle, "San Francisco de los Tejas Mission," *Handbook of Texas Online.*
3. Donald E. Chipman and Patricia R. Lemée, "St. Denis, Louis Juchereau de," *Handbook of Texas Online.*
4. George Klos, "Indians," *Handbook of Texas Online.*
5. Chipman, "Spanish Texas."
6. Robert L. Scheina, *Santa Anna: A Curse Upon Mexico*, 90.
7. Ibid., 6.
8. Ibid., 12.
9. Ibid., 14.
10. Ibid., 21.
11. Ibid., 26.
12. Jack Jackson, "Nolan, Philip," *Handbook of Texas Online.*
13. Harris Gaylord Warren, "Gutiérrez-Magee Expedition," *Handbook of Texas Online.*
14. Robert Bruce Blake, "Magee, Augustus William," *Handbook of Texas Online.*
15. Harris Gaylord Warren, "Long Expedition," *Handbook of Texas Online.*
16. Warren French, "Aaron Burr," *Handbook of Texas Online.*

CHAPTER 2. Americans in Texas
1. David B. Gracy II, "Austin, Moses," *Handbook of Texas Online.*
2. Eugene C. Barker, "Austin, Stephen Fuller," *Handbook of Texas Online.*
3. Margaret Swett Henson, "Anglo-American Colonization," *Handbook of Texas Online.*
4. Noah Smithwick, *The Evolution of a State*, Chapter 1.
5. Ibid.

6. Ibid.
7. Archie P. McDonald, "Edwards, Haden," *Handbook of Texas Online.*
8. Barker, "Austin, Stephen Fuller."
9. Thomas H. Kreneck, "Houston, Samuel," *Handbook of Texas Online.*

CHAPTER 3. James Walker Fannin and the Texas Revolution
1. Gary Brown, *James Walker Fannin: Hesitant Martyr in the Texas Revolution*, 4.
2. Ibid., 7.
3. Ibid., 13.
4. Ibid., 21.
5. Ibid., 29.
6. Steven L. Hardin, "Gonzales, Battle of," *Handbook of Texas Online.*
7. Lack, *The Texas Revolutionary Experience*, 187.
8. Smithwick, *The Evolution of a State*, Chapter 7.
9. Ibid.
10. Ibid.
11. Stephen Austin, "Austin to President of Consultation, November 4, 1835," *Sons of Dewitt Colony Texas.*
12. William Wharton, "William H. Wharton to Stephen F. Austin, November 8, 1835, November 4, 1835," *Sons of Dewitt Colony Texas.*
13. James W. Fannin, "J. W. Fannin Jr. to S. Houston, November 18, 1835," *Sons of Dewitt Colony Texas.*

CHAPTER 4. The Volunteers
1. Alexis de Tocqueville, *Democracy in America*, 1835/2000 & 1840/2000, 511.
2. Emily Zimmerman, "European Travelers in the United States."
3. Mark A. Vargas, "The Progressive Agent of Mischief: The Whiskey Ration and Temperance in the United States Army," *The Historian*, paras. 3–9.
4. Andrew Jackson, "President Andrew Jackson's Case for the Removal Act, First Annual Message to Congress, December 8, 1830."
5. *New York Courier* article copied by the *Richmond Enquirer* of July 17, 1835, and quoted in James E. Winston, "Virginia and the Independence of Texas," *Southwestern Historical Quarterly Online.*
6. U.S. Congress, "A Century of Lawmaking for a New Nation: U.S. Congressional Documents and Debates, 1774–1875," Statutes at Large, 15th Cong., 1st sess.
7. A. Houston and R. R. Royall, "To the Citizens of the United States of the North,"*Southwestern Historical Quarterly Online.*
8. Claude Elliot, "Georgia and the Texas Revolution," *Georgia Historical Quarterly.*
9. Ibid.
10. James L. Noles Jr., "Doctor Jack Shackelford and the Red Rovers," *Rovers History.*
11. Claude Elliot, "Alabama and the Texas Revolution," *Southwestern Historical Quarterly Online.*
12. Edward L. Miller, *New Orleans and the Texas Revolution*, 78.

13. Henry J. Barnard, "The Journal of Dr. Henry Joseph Barnard," *Sons of Dewitt Colony Texas*, introduction.
14. Ibid.
15. Ibid., entry for December 22.
16. G. Gómez, "G. Gómez to Inhabitants of Santa Ana de Tamaulipas, October 17, 1835," *Sons of Dewitt Colony Texas.*
17. "Notes and Fragments," *Southwestern Historical Quarterly Online.*
18. Elliot, "Georgia and the Texas Revolution."
19. Paul D. Lack, "Consultation," *Handbook of Texas Online.*
20. Ralph W. Steen, "Provisional Government," *Handbook of Texas Online.*

CHAPTER 5. The Matamoros Expedition
1. Craig H. Roell, "Matamoros Expedition of 1835–36," *Handbook of Texas Online.*
2. Ibid.
3. Ibid.
4. Ibid.
5. Ibid.
6. Ibid.
7. Ibid.
8. Ibid.
9. Smithwick, *The Evolution of a State*, Chapter 8.
10. J. S. Brooks, "J. S. Brooks to A. H. Brooks, January 20, 1836," *Sons of Dewitt Colony Texas.*
11. James W. Fannin, "J. W. Fannin to J. W. Robinson, January 31, 1836," *Sons of Dewitt Colony Texas.*
12. R. C. Morris, "R. C. Morris to J. W. Fannin, February 6, 1836," *Sons of Dewitt Colony Texas.*
13. Ibid.
14. James W. Fannin, "J. W. Fannin to J. W. Robinson, February 7, 1836," *Sons of Dewitt Colony Texas.*
15. Ibid.
16. Ibid.
17. Ibid.
18. Scheina, *Santa Anna: A Curse Upon Mexico*, 21.

CHAPTER 6. Fannin at Goliad
1. Barnard, *Journal*, January 8, 1836.
2. Ibid.
3. Ibid.
4. Craig H. Roell, "Chadwick, Joseph, M.," *Handbook of Texas Online.*
5. John E. Roller, "Capt. John Sowers Brooks," *Southwestern Historical Quarterly Online.*
6. J. S. Brooks, "J. S. Brooks to M. A. Brooks, February 25, 1836," *Sons of Dewitt Colony Texas.*
7. B. H. Duval, "B. H. Duval to W. P. Duval, March 9, 1836," *Sons of Dewitt Colony Texas.*

8. A. J. Ferguson, "A. J. Ferguson to J. G. Ferguson, March 2, 1836," *Sons of Dewitt Colony Texas.*

9. James W. Fannin, "J. W. Fannin to J. W. Robinson, February 28, 1836," *Sons of Dewitt Colony Texas.*

10. John C. Duval, *Early Times in Texas.*

11. Fannin, "J. W. Fannin to J. W. Robinson, February 28, 1836."

12. Ibid.

13. Ibid.

CHAPTER 7. Urrea's Invasion

1. "The Texas Declaration of Independence: March 2, 1836," *The Avalon Project at Yale Law School.*

2. Ibid.

3. Ibid.

4. Clarence Wharton, "The Life of Santa Anna," *Sons of Dewitt Colony Texas.*

5. "The Constitution of the Republic of Texas," March 16, 1836.

6. Ruben R. Brown, "Eyewitness Account of Johnson and Grant Defeat by Survivor Reuben R. Brown," *Sons of Dewitt Colony Texas.*

7. Carlos E. Castañeda, *The Mexican Side of the Texan Revolution*, 245.

8. Smithwick, *The Evolution of a State*, Chapter 9.

9. Lewis T. Ayers, "Report of Lewis T. Ayers on the fate of Capt. King's Group at Refugio," *Sons of Dewitt Colony Texas.*

10. Lewis M. H. Washington, "Fannin's Command," *Sons of Dewitt Colony Texas.*

11. James W. Fannin, "J. W. Fannin to J. W. Robinson, February 22, 1836," *Sons of Dewitt Colony Texas.*

12. J. S. Brooks, "J. S. Brooks to M. A. Brooks, March 4, 1836," *Sons of Dewitt Colony Texas.*

13. Brooks, "J. S. Brooks to A. H. Brooks, February 25, 1836."

14. Barnard, *Journal*, March 11, 1836.

15. Sabina Brown Fox, "Ward and King at Refugio," *Sons of Dewitt Colony Texas.*

16. L. T. Pease, "Narrative on Ward's Battle at Mission Refugio," *Sons of Dewitt Colony Texas.*

17. Ayers, "Report of Lewis T. Ayers on the fate of Capt. King's Group at Refugio."

18. Pease, "Narrative on Ward's Battle at Mission Refugio."

19. Fox, "Ward and King at Refugio."

20. Joseph W. Andrews, "Account of Ward and King at Mission Refugio," *Sons of Dewitt Colony Texas.*

21. Washington, "Fannin's Command."

22. Andrews, "Account of Ward and King at Mission Refugio."

CHAPTER 8. Clash at Refugio

1. Castañeda, *The Mexican Side of the Texan Revolution*, 225.

2. Pease, "Narrative on Ward's Battle at Mission Refugio."

3. Ibid.
4. Castañeda, *The Mexican Side of the Texan Revolution*, 226.
5. Pease, "Narrative on Ward's Battle at Mission Refugio."
6. Castañeda, *The Mexican Side of the Texan Revolution*, 226.
7. Pease, "Narrative on Ward's Battle at Mission Refugio."
8. Fox, "Ward and King at Refugio."
9. Ibid.
10. Andrews, "Account of Ward and King at Mission Refugio."
11. Francisco Garay, "Diary of Col. Francisco Garay," *Sons of Dewitt Colony Texas.*
12. Castañeda, *The Mexican Side of the Texan Revolution*, 227.
13. Ibid.
14. Ayers, "Report of Lewis T. Ayers."
15. Ibid.
16. Elliot, "Georgia and the Texas Revolution."
17. Fox, "Ward and King at Refugio."
18. Pease, "Narrative on Ward's Battle at Mission Refugio."
19. Castañeda, *The Mexican Side of the Texan Revolution*, 227.
20. Henry Scott, "At Mission Refugio," *Sons of Dewitt Colony Texas.*
21. Ayers, "Report of Lewis T. Ayers."
22. Fox, "Ward and King at Refugio."
23. Ayers, "Report of Lewis T. Ayers."
24. Molly Evelyn Moore Davis, *Under Six Flags: The Story of Texas*, 90.

CHAPTER 9. Flight from Goliad
1. S. Houston, "S. Houston to J. W. Fannin, March 11, 1836," *Sons of Dewitt Colony Texas.*
2. Duval, "B. H. Duval to W. P. Duval, March 9, 1836."
3. Castañeda, *The Mexican Side of the Texan Revolution*, 228.
4. Ibid.
5. Ibid.
6. Vicente Filisola, "Massacre at Goliad—Mexican Centralista Descriptions," *Sons of Dewitt Colony Texas.*
7. Noles, "Doctor Jack Shackelford and the Red Rovers."
8. Jack Shackelford, "Massacre at Goliad—Captain Jack Shackelford's Account," *Sons of Dewitt Colony Texas.*
9. Ibid.
10. Castañeda, *The Mexican Side of the Texan Revolution*, 229.
11. C. B. Shain, "Narrative of C. B. Shain of Louisville: A Volunteer in the Cause of Texas," *Sons of Dewitt Colony Texas.*
12. Abel Morgan, "Abel Morgan's Account & Pension Claim," *Sons of Dewitt Colony Texas.*
13. Herman Ehrenberg, "Battle of Coleto Creek and Massacre at Goliad," *Sons of Dewitt Colony Texas.*
14. Joseph Field, "Dr. Joseph Field's Account of the Events at Goliad," *Sons of Dewitt Colony Texas.*
15. Shackelford, "Massacre at Goliad."

16. Ehrenberg, "Battle of Coleto Creek."
17. Castañeda, *The Mexican Side of the Texan Revolution*, 229–30.

CHAPTER 10. Battle on the Prairie
1. Shackelford, "Massacre at Goliad."
2. Ibid.
3. Ehrenberg, "Battle of Coleto Creek."
4. Andrew A. Boyle, "Reminiscences of the Texas Revolution," *Southwestern Historical Quarterly Online*.
5. Shackelford, "Massacre at Goliad."
6. Boyle, "Reminiscences of the Texas Revolution."
7. Filisola, "Massacre at Goliad—Mexican Centralista Descriptions."
8. Duval, *Early Times in Texas*, 40.
9. Shackelford, "Massacre at Goliad."
10. Benjamin Holland, "Account of Capt. Benjamin Holland," *Sons of Dewitt Colony Texas*.
11. Shackelford, "Massacre at Goliad."
12. Morgan, "Abel Morgan's Account & Pension Claim."
13. Filisola, "Massacre at Goliad—Mexican Centralista Descriptions."
14. Castañeda, *The Mexican Side of the Texan Revolution*, 231.
15. Ehrenberg, "Battle of Coleto Creek."
16. Duval, *Early Times in Texas*, 44.
17. Ehrenberg, "Battle of Coleto Creek."
18. Duval, *Early Times in Texas*, 46.
19. Morgan, "Abel Morgan's Account & Pension Claim."
20. Duval, *Early Times in Texas*, 42.
21. Shackelford, "Massacre at Goliad."
22. Castañeda, *The Mexican Side of the Texan Revolution*, 57.
23. Filisola, "Massacre at Goliad—Mexican Centralista Descriptions."

CHAPTER 11. The Weapons
1. Washington, "Fannin's Command."
2. Ehrenberg, "Battle of Coleto Creek."

CHAPTER 12. Overnight Misery
1. Ellen Cash, "Ms. Cash's Account of Fannin's Retreat and the Battle of Coleto," *Sons of Dewitt Colony Texas*.
2. Ibid.
3. Ibid.
4. Duval, *Early Times in Texas*, 44.
5. Ibid.
6. Field, "Dr. Joseph Field's Account of the Events at Goliad."
7. Duval, *Early Times in Texas*, 46.
8. Morgan, "Abel Morgan's Account & Pension Claim."
9. Duval, *Early Times in Texas*, 47.
10. Castañeda, *The Mexican Side of the Texan Revolution*, 233.
11. Ibid.

12. Filisola, "Massacre at Goliad—Mexican Centralista Descriptions."
13. Boyle, "Reminiscences of the Texas Revolution."

CHAPTER 13. Surrender
 1. Ehrenberg, "Battle of Coleto Creek."
 2. Cash, "Ms. Cash's Account of Fannin's Retreat and the Battle of Coleto."
 3. Hobart Huson, "Refugio," *Sons of Dewitt Colony Texas*.
 4. Filisola, "Massacre at Goliad—Mexican Centralista Descriptions."
 5. Ehrenberg, "Battle of Coleto Creek."
 6. Barnard, *Journal*, March 20, 1836.
 7. Shackelford, "Massacre at Goliad."
 8. Juan José Holzinger, "J. J. Holzinger to W. H. Wharton, June 3, 1836," *Sons of Dewitt Colony Texas*.
 9. Castañeda, *The Mexican Side of the Texan Revolution*, 235.
10. Duval, *Early Times in Texas*, 47."
11. Morgan, "Abel Morgan's Account & Pension Claim."
12. Castañeda, *The Mexican Side of the Texan Revolution*, 235.
13. Shackelford, "Massacre at Goliad."
14. Ehrenberg, "Battle of Coleto Creek."
15. Holzinger, "J. J. Holzinger to W. H. Wharton, June 3, 1836."
16. Ibid.
17. Castañeda, *The Mexican Side of the Texan Revolution*, 235.
18. Holzinger, "J. J. Holzinger to W. H. Wharton, June 3, 1836."
19. Ibid.
20. Ibid.
21. Holland, "Account of Capt. Benjamin Holland."
22. Ibid.
23. Field, "Dr. Joseph Field's Account of the Events at Goliad."
24. Barnard, *Journal*, March 21, 1836.
25. Shackelford, "Massacre at Goliad."
26. Shain, "Narrative of C. B. Shain of Louisville."
27. Duval, "B. H. Duval to W. P. Duval, March 9, 1836."
28. John B. Thomas Jr., "Kentuckians in Texas: Captain Burr H. Duval's Company at Goliad," *Register of the Kentucky Historical Society*.
29. Castañeda, *The Mexican Side of the Texan Revolution*, 62.
30. Ibid.
31. Duval, "B. H. Duval to W. P. Duval, March 9, 1836."
32. Castañeda, *The Mexican Side of the Texan Revolution*, 62.
33. Ibid., 235.
34. Holzinger, "J. J. Holzinger to W. H. Wharton, June 3, 1836."
35. Castañeda, *The Mexican Side of the Texan Revolution*, 236.
36. Ibid.
37. Duval, *Early Times in Texas*, 44.
38. Castañeda, *The Mexican Side of the Texan Revolution*, 237.
39. Field, "Dr. Joseph Field's Account of the Events at Goliad."
40. Duval, "B. H. Duval to W. P. Duval, March 9, 1836."
41. Shain, "Narrative of C. B. Shain of Louisville."

42. Morgan, "Abel Morgan's Account & Pension Claim."
43. Castañeda, *The Mexican Side of the Texan Revolution*, 236.
44. Filisola, "Massacre at Goliad—Mexican Centralista Descriptions."
45. Huson, "Refugio."
46. Morgan, "Abel Morgan's Account & Pension Claim."
47. Ehrenberg, "Battle of Coleto Creek."
48. Ibid.
49. Ibid.
50. Ibid.
51. Morgan, "Abel Morgan's Account & Pension Claim."

CHAPTER 14. Return to Goliad
1. Field, "Dr. Joseph Field's Account of the Events at Goliad."
 2. Morgan, "Abel Morgan's Account & Pension Claim."
 3. Shackelford, "Massacre at Goliad."
 4. Morgan, "Abel Morgan's Account & Pension Claim."
 5. Ibid.
 6. Ibid.
 7. Ibid.
 8. Andrews, "Account of Ward and King at Mission Refugio."
 9. Samuel T. Brown, "Fannin's Massacre—Account of the Georgia Battalion," *Sons of Dewitt Colony Texas*.
10. Andrews, "Account of Ward and King at Mission Refugio."
11. Ibid.
12. Castañeda, *The Mexican Side of the Texan Revolution*, 238.
13. Ibid.
14. Samuel G. Hardaway, "With the Georgia Battalion," *Sons of Dewitt Colony Texas*.
15. Castañeda, *The Mexican Side of the Texan Revolution*, 238.
16. Brown, "Fannin's Massacre."
17. Ibid.
18. Ehrenberg, "Battle of Coleto Creek."
19. Duval, *Early Times in Texas*, 52.
20. Ibid.
21. Barnard, *Journal*, entry for March 24, 1836.
22. Shackelford, "Massacre at Goliad."
23. A. L. Santa Anna, "A. L. Santa Anna to J. N. Portilla, March 23, 1836," *Sons of Dewitt Colony Texas*.
24. Nicolás de la Portilla, "Extract from the Diary of Nicolás de la Portilla," *Sons of Dewitt Colony Texas*.
25. J. N. Portilla, "J. N. Portilla to J. Urrea, March 26, 1836," *Sons of Dewitt Colony Texas*.

CHAPTER 15. The Massacre
The author created the map in this chapter using information found on the Presidio la Bahia Web site: http://www.presidiolabahia.org/massacre.htm.

1. Shackelford, "Massacre at Goliad."
2. Dillard C. Cooper, "Escape of the Four Alabama Red Rovers," *Sons of Dewitt Colony Texas.*
3. Ibid.
4. Ibid.
5. Ibid.
6. Holland, "Account of Capt. Benjamin Holland."
7. Ibid.
8. Ehrenberg, "Battle of Coleto Creek."
9. Ibid.
10. Duval, *Early Times in Texas*, 54.
11. Ibid.
12. Ibid.
13. Francis Richard Lubbock, *Six Decades in Texas*, 119.
14. S. H. B., "Account of Major Miller's Secretary," *Sons of Dewitt Colony Texas.*
15. Ibid.
16. Shackelford, "Massacre at Goliad."
17. Morgan, "Abel Morgan's Account & Pension Claim."
18. Ibid.
19. Boyle, "Reminiscences of the Texas Revolution."
20. Ibid.
21. Ibid.
22. Morgan, "Abel Morgan's Account & Pension Claim."
23. Ibid.
24. Ibid.
25. Ibid.
26. Joseph H. Spohn, "Colonel James W. Fannin's Execution at Goliad," *Sons of Dewitt Colony Texas.*
27. Ibid.

CHAPTER 16. The Survivors, the Butchers, and an Angel
1. Cooper, "Escape of the Four Alabama Red Rovers."
2. Ibid.
3. Ibid.
4. Duval, *Early Times in Texas*, 118.
5. Ibid., 119.
6. Morgan, "Abel Morgan's Account & Pension Claim."
7. Ibid.
8. Ibid.
9. Ibid.
10. Ibid.
11. Shackelford, "Massacre at Goliad."
12. Ibid.
13. Ibid.
14. Barnard, *Journal*, entry for April 27, 1836.

15. Shackelford, "Massacre at Goliad."
16. Boyle, "Reminiscences of the Texas Revolution."
17. Castañeda, *The Mexican Side of the Texan Revolution*, 241–42.
18. Ibid., 242.
19. Ibid.
20. Ibid.
21. Ibid.
22. Ibid.
23. Ibid., 57.
24. Ibid., 19.
25. Ibid., 107.
26. Ibid., 109.
27. Ibid., 63.
28. N. Portilla, "N. Portilla to J. Urrea, March 27, 1836," *Sons of Dewitt Colony Texas.*
29. "Manuscript Report on the Goliad Massacre by Commander Portilla," *Dorothy Sloan Books.*
30. Castañeda, *The Mexican Side of the Texan Revolution*, 241.
31. John T. Molloy, "Irish Father John Thomas Molloy, O. P.," *Sons of Dewitt Colony Texas.*
32. Harbert Davenport, "The Angel of Goliad," *Sons of Dewitt Colony Texas.*
33. Ibid.
34. Ibid.
35. Ibid.
36. Ibid.

CHAPTER 17. Mayhem, Victory, and Marking the Bones
1. Smithwick, *The Evolution of a State*, Chapter 9.
2. "S. Houston to D. G. Burnett, April 25, 1836," *Sons of Dewitt Colony Texas.*
3. Smithwick, *The Evolution of a State*, Chapter 9.
4. Thomas J. Rusk, "T. Rusk to M. Lamar, April 23, 1836," *Sons of Dewitt Colony Texas.*
5. Thomas J. Rusk, "Memorial Address for Fannin's Command," *Sons of Dewitt Colony Texas.*
6. Ibid.
7. Harbert Davenport, "The Men of Goliad," *Southwestern Historical Quarterly Online.*
8. Ibid.

EPILOGUE
1. Pedro Delgado, "Colonel Pedro Delgado's recollection of Battle of San Jacinto," *Sons of Dewitt Colony Texas.*
2. Castañeda, *The Mexican Side of the Texan Revolution*, 106.

Bibliography

Andrews, Joseph W. "Account of Ward and King at Mission Refugio." *Sons of Dewitt Colony Texas.* http://www.tamu.edu/ccbn/dewitt/goliadsanpat2. htm#ayersreport (accessed May 6, 2007).

Austin, Stephen. "Austin to President of Consultation, November 4, 1835." *Sons of Dewitt Colony Texas.* http://www.tamu.edu/ccbn/dewitt/musterbexar4. htm (accessed May 5, 2007).

Ayers, Lewis T. "Report of Lewis T. Ayers on the fate of Capt. King's Group at Refugio." *Sons of Dewitt Colony Texas.* http://www.tamu.edu/ccbn/dewitt/ goliadsanpat2.htm#ayersreport (accessed August 1, 2007).

Barker, Eugene C. "Austin, Stephen Fuller." *Handbook of Texas Online.* http://www.tsha.utexas.edu/handbook/online/articles/AA/fau14.html (accessed May 4, 2007).

———. "Stephen F. Austin and the Independence of Texas." *Southwestern Historical Quarterly Online* 13, no. 4: 257–84. http://www.tsha.utexas.edu/ publications/journals/shq/online/v013/n4/article_1.html (accessed May 3, 2007).

Barnard, Henry J. "The Journal of Dr. Henry Joseph Barnard." *Sons of Dewitt Colony Texas.* http://www.tamu.edu/ccbn/dewitt/goliadbanard.htm (accessed May 5, 2007).

Blake, Robert Bruce. "Magee, Augustus William." *Handbook of Texas Online.* http://www.tsha.utexas.edu/handbook/online/articles/MM/fma12.html (accessed May 3, 2007).

Boyle, Andrew A. "Reminiscences of the Texas Revolution." *Southwestern Historical Quarterly Online,* 13, no. 4: 285–91. http://www.tsha.utexas. edu/publications/journals/shq/online/v013/n4/article_2.html (accessed May 7, 2007).

Brooks, J. S. "J. S. Brooks to A. H. Brooks, January 20, 1836." *Sons of Dewitt Colony Texas.* http://www.tamu.edu/ccbn/dewitt/goliadletters.htm (accessed July 26, 2007).

————. "J. S. Brooks to A. H. Brooks, February 25, 1836." *Sons of Dewitt Colony Texas.* http://www.tamu.edu/ccbn/dewitt/goliadletters.htm (accessed July 30, 2007).

————. "J. S. Brooks to M. A. Brooks, March 4, 1836." *Sons of Dewitt Colony Texas.* http://www.tamu.edu/ccbn/dewitt/goliadletters.htm (accessed July 30, 2007).

————. "J. S. Brooks to A. H. Brooks, March 10, 1836." *Sons of Dewitt Colony Texas.* http://www.tamu.edu/ccbn/dewitt/goliadofficial.htm (accessed July 30, 2007).

Brown, Gary. *James Walker Fannin: Hesitant Martyr in the Texas Revolution.* Plano, TX: Republic of Texas Press, 2000.

————. *Volunteers in the Texas Revolution: The New Orleans Greys.* Plano, TX: Republic of Texas Press, 1999.

Brown, Ruben R. "Eyewitness Account of Johnson and Grant Defeat by Survivor Reuben R. Brown." *Sons of Dewitt Colony Texas.* http://www.tamu.edu/ccbn/dewitt/goliadsanpat.htm#rrbrown (accessed May 20, 2007).

Brown, Samuel T. "Fannin's Massacre: Account of the Georgia Battalion." *Sons of Dewitt Colony Texas.* http://www.tamu.edu/ccbn/dewitt/goliadbrown.htm (accessed May 8, 2007).

Cash, Ellen. "Ms. Cash's Account of Fannin's Retreat and the Battle of Coleto." *Sons of Dewitt Colony Texas.* http://www.tamu.edu/ccbn/dewitt/goliaddiverse3.htm (accessed June 4, 2007).

Castañeda, Carlos E. (Trans.) *The Mexican Side of the Texan Revolution.* Dallas, TX: P. L. Turner Company, 1928.

————. (Trans.) "Surrender of the Force at Goliad under the Command of James W. Fannin." *Son of Dewitt Colony Texas.* http://www.tamu.edu/ccbn/dewitt/goliadmex.htm (accessed January 14, 2007).

"Census and Census Records." *Handbook of Texas Online.* http://www.tsha.utexas.edu/handbook/online/articles/CC/ulc1.html (accessed May 20, 2007).

Chipman, Donald E. "Spanish Texas." *Handbook of Texas Online.* http://www.tsha.utexas.edu/handbook/online/articles/SS/nps1.html (accessed May 3, 2007).

Chipman, Donald E., and Patricia R. Lemée. "St. Denis, Louis Juchereau de." *Handbook of Texas Online.* http://www.tsha.utexas.edu/handbook/online/articles/SS/fst1.html (accessed May 3, 2007).

"Constitution of the Republic of Texas." Drafted at Washington-on-the-Brazos, adopted there by the convention on March 16, 1836. Tarlton Law Library, http://tarlton.law.utexas.edu/constitutions/text/1836cindex.html (accessed August 15, 2007).

Cooper, Dillard C. "Escape of the Four Alabama Red Rovers." Sons of Dewitt Colony Texas. http://www.tamu.edu/ccbn/dewitt/goliaddiverse.htm#cooper (accessed May 9, 2007).

Davenport, Harbert. "The Angel of Goliad." *Sons of Dewitt Colony Texas*. http://www.tamu.edu/ccbn/dewitt/goliadangel.htm (accessed May 9, 2007).

———. "The Men of Goliad: Dedicatory address at the unveiling of the monument erected by the Texas Centennial Commission at the grave of Fannin's men." *Southwestern Historical Quarterly Online*, 48, no. 1. http://www.tsha.utexas.edu/supsites/fannin/hd_a001.html (accessed May 9, 2007).

Davis, Molly Evelyn Moore. *Under Six Flags: The Story of Texas*. Boston: Ginn and Company, 1897.

de Tocqueville, Alexis. *Democracy in America*. Edited and translated by Harvey C. Mansfield and Delba Winthrop. Chicago: University of Chicago Press, 1835/2000 (Vol. I) & 1840/2000 (Vol. II).

De León, Arnoldo. "They Called Them Greasers." http://www.utexas.edu/utpress/excerpts/exdelgre.html (accessed May 3, 2007).

Delgado, Pedro. "Colonel Pedro Delgado's recollection of Battle of San Jacinto." *Sons of Dewitt Colony Texas*. http://www.tamu.edu/ccbn/dewitt/batsanjacinto.htm (accessed August 15, 2007).

Duval, Burr H. "B. H. Duval to W. P. Duval, March 9, 1836." *Sons of Dewitt Colony Texas*.http://www.tamu.edu/ccbn/dewitt/goliadletters2.htm (accessed July 26, 2007).

Duval, John C. *Adventures of Bigfoot Wallace, Texas Ranger and Hunter*. Macon, GA: J. W. Burke, 1870.

———. "Battle of Coleto, Capitulation and Survival of the Goliad Massacre." *Sons of Dewitt Colony Texas*.http://www.tamu.edu/ccbn/dewitt/goliadduval.htm (accessed February 14, 2007).

———. *Early Times in Texas*. Austin, TX: H. P. N. Gammel, 1892.

Ehrenberg, Herman. "Battle of Coleto Creek and Massacre at Goliad." *Sons of Dewitt Colony Texas*. http://www.tamu.edu/ccbn/dewitt/goliadehrenberg.htm (accessed May 7, 2007).

————. Texas und Seine Revolution. Abridged and translated by Charlotte Churchill. Leipzig: Wigand, 1843.

Elliot, Claude. "Alabama and the Texas Revolution." *Southwestern Historical Quarterly Online*, 50, no. 3. http://www.tsha.utexas.edu/publications/journals/shq/online/v050/n3/contrib_DIVL5423.html (accessed July 25, 2007).

————. "Georgia and the Texas Revolution." *Georgia Historical Quarterly*, 28, December (1944). http://www.tamu.edu/ccbn/dewitt/goliadgeorgia.htm (accessed May 5, 2007).

Fannin, James W. "J. W. Fannin Jr. to S. Houston, November 18, 1835." *Sons of Dewitt Colony Texas.* http://www.tamu.edu/ccbn/dewitt/musterbexar5.htm (accessed March 14, 2007).

————. "J. W. Fannin to J. W. Robinson, January 31, 1836." *Sons of Dewitt Colony Texas.* http://www.tamu.edu/ccbn/dewitt/goliadofficial.htm (accessed July 26, 2007).

————. "J. W. Fannin to J. W. Robinson, February 7, 1836." *Sons of Dewitt Colony Texas.* http://www.tamu.edu/ccbn/dewitt/goliadofficial.htm (accessed July 26, 2007).

————. "J. W. Fannin to J. W. Robinson, February 22, 1836." *Sons of Dewitt Colony Texas.* http://www.tamu.edu/ccbn/dewitt/goliadofficial.htm (accessed July 26, 2007).

————. "J. W. Fannin to J. W. Robinson, February 28, 1836." *Sons of Dewitt Colony Texas.* http://www.tamu.edu/ccbn/dewitt/goliadofficial.htm (accessed July 26, 2007).

Ferguson, A. J. "A. J. Ferguson to J. G. Ferguson, March 2, 1836." *Sons of Dewitt Colony Texas.* http://www.tamu.edu/ccbn/dewitt/goliadletters2.htm (accessed July 26, 2007).

Field, Joseph E. "Dr. Joseph Field's Account of the Events at Goliad." *Sons of Dewitt Colony Texas.* http://www.tamu.edu/ccbn/dewitt/goliadfields.htm (accessed May 7, 2007).

————. *Three Years in Texas.* Greenfield and Boston, MA, 1836. Reprint Austin, TX: Steck, 1935.

Filisola, Vicente. "Massacre at Goliad---Mexican Centralista Descriptions." *Sons of Dewitt Colony Texas.* http://www.tamu.edu/ccbn/dewitt/goliadmex2.htm (accessed May 7, 2007).

Fox, Sabina Brown. "Ward and King at Refugio." *Sons of Dewitt Colony Texas.* http://www.tamu.edu/ccbn/dewitt/goliadsanpat2.htm#sabina (accessed May 5, 2007).

French, Warren. "Aaron Burr." *Handbook of Texas Online.* http://www.tsha. utexas.edu/handbook/online/articles/BB/fbu57.html (accessed May 3, 2007).

Garay, Francisco. "Diary of Col. Francisco Garay." *Sons of Dewitt Colony Texas.* http://www.tamu.edu/ccbn/dewitt/goliadurrea.htm (accessed July 31, 2007).

Gómez, G. "G. Gómez to Inhabitants of Santa Ana de Tamaulipas, October 17, 1835." *Sons of Dewitt Colony Texas.* http://www.tamu.edu/ccbn/dewitt/ musterbexar2.htm (accessed April 22, 2007).

Gracy, David B., II. "Austin, Moses." *Handbook of Texas Online.* http://www.tsha.utexas.edu/handbookÇonline/articles/AA/fau12.html (accessed May 20, 2007).

Hardaway, Samuel G. "With the Georgia Battalion." *Sons of Dewitt Colony Texas.* http://www.tamu.edu/ccbn/dewitt/goliadsanpat2.htm#hardaway (accessed May 8, 2007).

Hardin, Steven L. "Gonzales, Battle of." *Handbook of Texas Online.* http:// www.tsha.utexas.edu/handbook/online/articles/GG/qug3.html (accessed May 5, 2007).

Henson, Margaret Swett. "Anglo-American Colonization." *Handbook of Texas Online.* http://www.tsha.utexas.edu/handbook/online/articles/AA/uma1. html (accessed May 20, 2007).

Holland, Benjamin. "Account of Capt. Benjamin Holland." *Sons of Dewitt Colony Texas.* http://www.tamu.edu/ccbn/dewitt/goliaddiverse3.htm (accessed May 7, 2007).

Holzinger, Juan José. "J. J. Holzinger to W. H. Wharton, June 3, 1836." *Sons of Dewitt Colony Texas.* http://www.tamu.edu/ccbn/dewitt/goliadmex.htm (accessed April 14, 2007).

Houston, A., and R. R. Royall. "To the Citizens of the United States of the North." *Southwestern Historical Quarterly Online*, 7, no. 4, ftnote 17. http:// www.tsha.utexas.edu/publications/journals/shq/online/v007/n4/n17.html (accessed July 25, 2007).

Houston, S. "S. Houston to J. W. Fannin, March 11, 1836." *Sons of Dewitt Colony Texas.* http://www.tamu.edu/ccbn/dewitt/andrew3.htm (accessed August 2, 2007).

————. "S. Houston to D. G. Burnett, April 25, 1836." *Sons of Dewitt Colony Texas.* http://www.tamu.edu/ccbn/dewitt/batsanjacinto.htm (accessed August 14, 2007).

Huson, Hobart. "Refugio." *Sons of Dewitt Colony Texas.* http://www.tamu.edu/ccbn/dewitt/goliadcoletohuson3.htm (accessed May 8, 2007).

Jackson, Andrew. "President Andrew Jackson's Case for the Removal Act, First Annual Message to Congress, December 8, 1830." Cited by Vincent Ferraro, The Ruth C. Lawson Professor of International Politics Mount Holyoke College. http://www.mtholyoke.edu/acad/intrel/andrew.htm (accessed May 5, 2007).

Jackson, Jack. "Nolan, Philip." *Handbook of Texas Online.* http://www.tsha.utexas.edu/handbook/online/articles/NN/fno2.html (accessed May 20, 2007).

Kennedy, William, Esq. *The Rise, Progress and Prospects of the Republic of Texas.* London: William Clowes and Sons, 1841.

Klos, George. "Indians." *Handbook of Texas Online.* http://www.tsha.utexas.edu/handbook/online/articles/II/bzi4.html (accessed May 3, 2007).

Kreneck, Thomas H. "Houston, Samuel." *Handbook of Texas Online.* http://www.tsha.utexas.edu/handbook/online/articles/HH/fh073.html (accessed May 4, 2007).

Lack, Paul D. "Consultation." *Handbook of Texas Online.* http://www.tsha.utexas.edu/handbook/online/articles/CC/mjc8.html (accessed July 25, 2007).

————. *The Texas Revolutionary Experience.* College Station, TX: Texas A&M University Press, 1992.

Lubbock, Francis Richard. *Six Decades in Texas.* Austin, TX: Ben C. Jones & Co., 1900.

"Manuscript Report on the Goliad Massacre by Commander Portilla." *Dorothy Sloan Books.* http://www.dsloan.com/Auctions/A20/lot_144.html (accessed March 22, 2007).

McDonald, Archie P. "Edwards, Haden." *Handbook of Texas Online.* http://www.tsha.utexas.edu/handbook/online/articles/EE/fed4.html (accessed May 4, 2007).

Miller, Edward L. *New Orleans and the Texas Revolution.* College Station, TX: Texas A&M University Press, 2000.

Mobile Daily Commercial Register and Patriot. December 4, 1835. http://www. tamu.edu/ccbn/dewitt/goliadgeorgia.htm (accessed August 21, 2007).

Molloy, John T. "Irish Father John Thomas Molloy, O. P." *Sons of Dewitt Colony Texas.* http://www.tamu.edu/ccbn/dewitt/goliadmolloy.htm (accessed January 16, 2007).

Morgan, Abel. "Abel Morgan's Account & Pension Claim." *Sons of Dewitt Colony Texas.* http://www.tamu.edu/ccbn/dewitt/goliadmorgan.htm (accessed May 7, 2007).

Morris, R. C. "R. C. Morris to J. W. Fannin, February 6, 1836." *Sons of Dewitt Colony Texas.* http://www.tamu.edu/ccbn/dewitt/goliadofficial.htm (accessed July 26, 2007).

Noles, James L., Jr. "Doctor Jack Shackelford and the Red Rovers." *Rovers History.* http://www.wheelerplantation.org/rovers2.htm (accessed May 10, 2007).

"Notes and Fragments." *Southwestern Historical Quarterly Online,* 7, no. 4. http://www.tsha.utexas.edu/publications/journals/shq/online/v007/n4/ back_5.html (accessed July 25, 2007).

Pease, L. T. "Narrative on Ward's Battle at Mission Refugio." *Sons of Dewitt Colony Texas.* http://www.tamu.edu/ccbn/dewitt/goliadsanpat2.htm (accessed May 6, 2007).

Portilla, J. N. "Extract from the Diary of Nicolás de la Portilla." *Sons of Dewitt Colony Texas.* http://www.tamu.edu/ccbn/dewitt/goliadurrea.htm (accessed March 22, 2007).

———. "J. N. Portilla to J. Urrea, March 26, 1836." *Sons of Dewitt Colony Texas.* http://www.tamu.edu/ccbn/dewitt/goliadofficial.htm (accessed March 21, 2007).

———. "J. N. Portilla to J. Urrea, March 27, 1836." *Sons of Dewitt Colony Texas.* http://www.tamu.edu/ccbn/dewitt/goliadofficial.htm (accessed March 21, 2007).

Roell, Craig H. "Chadwick, Joseph, M." *Handbook of Texas Online.* http://www. tsha.utexas.edu/handbook/online/articles/CC/fch2.html (accessed May 6, 2007).

———. "Matamoros Expedition of 1835–36." *Handbook of Texas Online.* http://www.tsha.utexas.edu/handbook/online/articles/MM/qdm1.html (accessed May 6, 2007).

Roller, John E. "Capt. John Sowers Brooks." *Southwestern Historical Quarterly Online*, 9, no. 3. http://www.tsha.utexas.edu/publications/journals/shq/online/v009/n3/article_2.html (accessed May 5, 2007).

Rusk, Thomas J. "Memorial Address for Fannin's Command." *Sons of Dewitt Colony Texas*. http://www.tamu.edu/ccbn/dewitt/goliadmassacre.htm (accessed May 9, 2007).

———. "T. Rusk to M. Lamar, April 23, 1836." *Sons of Dewitt Colony Texas*. http://www.tamu.edu/ccbn/dewitt/adp/history/1836/goliad/page12.html (accessed August 14, 2009).

Santa Anna, Antonio López de. "A. L. Santa Anna to J. N. Portilla, March 23, 1836." *Sons of Dewitt Colony Texas*. http://www.tamu.edu/ccbn/dewitt/goliadframe.htm (accessed March 21, 2007).

———. *The Eagle: The Autobiography of Santa Anna*. Edited by Ann Fears Crawford. Austin, TX: State House Press, 1988.

Scheina, Robert L. *Santa Anna: A Curse Upon Mexico*. Washington, DC: Brassey's, Inc., 2002.

Scott, Henry. "At Mission Refugio." *Sons of Dewitt Colony Texas*. http://www.tamu.edu/ccbn/dewitt/goliadsanpat2.htm (accessed August 1, 2007).

Shackelford, Jack. "Massacre at Goliad---Captain Jack Shackelford's Account." *Sons of Dewitt Colony Texas*. http://www.tamu.edu/ccbn/dewitt/goliadshackelford.htm (accessed May 7, 2007).

Shain, C. B. "Narrative of C. B. Shain of Louisville: A Volunteer in the Cause of Texas." *Sons of Dewitt Colony Texas*. http://www.tamu.edu/ccbn/dewitt/goliadshain.htm (accessed March 22, 2007).

S. H. B. "Account of Major Miller's Secretary." *Sons of Dewitt Colony Texas*. http://www.tamu.edu/ccbn/dewitt/goliaddiverse3.htm (accessed May 9, 2007).

Smithwick, Noah. *The Evolution of a State or Recollections of Old Texas Days*. Austin, TX: University of Texas Press, 1900/1988. http://www.oldcardboard.com/lsj/olbooks/smithwic/otd.htm.

Spohn, Joseph H. "Colonel James W. Fannin's Execution at Goliad." *Sons of Dewitt Colony Texas*. http://www.tamu.edu/ccbn/dewitt/goliadspohn.htm (accessed May 9, 2007).

Steen, Ralph W. "Provisional Government." *Handbook of Texas Online*. http://www.tsha.utexas.edu/handbook/online/articles/PP/mzp1.html (accessed July 25, 2007).

"Texas Declaration of Independence." March 2, 1836. *The Avalon Project at Yale Law School.* http://www.yale.edu/lawweb/avalon/texdec.htm (accessed July 31, 2007).

Thomas, John B., Jr. "Kentuckians in Texas: Captain Burr H. Duval's Company at Goliad." Register of the Kentucky Historical Society, 81 (Summer 1983).

Urrea, José. "Diary of the Military Operations of the Division which under the Command of General José Urrea Campaigned in Texas February to March 1836." *Sons of Dewitt Colony Texas.* http://www.tamu.edu/ccbn/dewitt/goliadurrea.htm (accessed April 22, 2007).

————. "General José Urrea's Report of the Battle of Coleto Creek." *Sons of Dewitt Colony Texas.* http://www.tamu.edu/ccbn/dewitt/goliadmex.htm (accessed April 22, 2007).

U.S. Congress. "A Century of Lawmaking for a New Nation: U.S. Congressional Documents and Debates, 1774–1875," Statutes at Large, 15th Cong., 1st sess. http://memory.loc.gov/cgi-bin/ampage?collId=llsl&fileName=003/llsl003.db&recNum=488 (accessed July 25, 2007).

Vargas, Mark A. "The Progressive Agent of Mischief: The Whiskey Ration and Temperance in the United States Army." *The Historian*, June 22 (2005) paras. 3–9. http://www.encyclopedia.com/doc/1G1–135466403.html (accessed May 5, 2007).

Warren, Harris Gaylord. "Gutiérrez-Magee Expedition." *Handbook of Texas Online.* http://www.tsha.utexas.edu/handbook/online/articles/GG/qyg1.html (accessed May 20, 2007).

————. "Long Expedition." *Handbook of Texas Online.* http://www.tsha.utexas.edu/handbook/online/articles/LL/qyl1.html (accessed May 3, 2007).

Washington, Lewis M. H. "Fannin's Command." *Sons of Dewitt Colony Texas.* http://www.tamu.edu/ccbn/dewitt/goliadwash.htm (accessed May 6, 2007).

Weddle, Robert S. "San Francisco de los Tejas Mission." *Handbook of Texas Online.* http://www.tsha.utexas.edu/handbook/online/articles/SS/uqs15.html (accessed May 3, 2007).

Wharton, Clarence. "The Life of Santa Anna." *Sons of Dewitt Colony Texas.* http://www.tamu.edu/ccbn/dewitt/dewitt.htm (accessed May 6, 2007).

Wharton, William H. "William H. Wharton to Stephen F. Austin, November 8, 1835, November 4, 1835." *Sons of Dewitt Colony Texas.* http://www.tamu.edu/ccbn/dewitt/musterbexar4.htm (accessed May 5, 2007).

Winston, James E. "Virginia and the Independence of Texas." *Southwestern Historical Quarterly Online*, 16, no. 3. http://www.tsha.utexas.edu/publications/journals/shq/online/v016/n3/article_3.html (accessed May 20, 2007).

Zimmerman, Emily. "European Travelers in the United States, 1830–1840." *Tocqueville in America*. http://xroads.virginia.edu/~HYPER/DETOC/europeans/front.html (accessed August 15, 2007).

Index

Fox, Sabina Brown, 92, 99, 105–6
France, and Texas, 2–3
Francis, William, 91
Frazer, Hugh M., 112, 125
Fredonian Rebellion, 21–22
French and Indian War, 4
French Revolution, 5
frizzen, of musket, 135
full cock, 135

G

Gadsden Purchase, 214
Galveston Bay and Texas Land Company, 22
Garay, Francisco: and Boyle, 183–84; and massacre, 174, 181–82; and prisoners, 171; at Refugio, 100–101, 103
Garza, Carlos de la, 92
Garza, Julián de la, 84
Georgia, volunteers from, 47–48
Goliad: characteristics of, 74–79; Collinsworth and, 33; destruction of, 116; Fannin at, 72–83; flight from, 107–18; return to, 163–73; settlement of, 12. *See also* massacre of volunteers
Gómez, Gregorio, 51
Gonzalez, José de la, 150
Grant, James, 61, 63–65, 82, 84, 87–88
gray (grey), term, 49–50
Griffin, Pete, 193
Groce, Jared E., 20
Guerra, Luis, 95, 98
Guerrero, Vicente, 8–9
Guerrero Decree, 28
gunpowder, 129, 134, 138
guns: Brown Bess muskets, 130; at Coleto Creek, 133–40. *See also* artillery
Gutiérrez de Lara, José Bernardo, 12
Gutiérrez-Magee Expedition, 12–13

H

Hall, volunteer, 100
Hamilton, Isaac, 176, 188–89
Hanks, Wyatt, 63
Hardaway, Samuel G., 167
Henry, O., 212
Hidalgo, Father, 80
Holland, Benjamin, 125–26, 152, 154, 177, 191

Holliday, John, 179, 190–92
Holzinger, Juan José, 104–5, 150, 152–54, 161, 163
Horton, Albert C., 112–15, 119–22, 143–44
Houston, Samuel: background of, 23–24; and Barnard, 72; and command, 82, 86; and Fannin, 38–39, 107–8; and Matamoros expedition, 63–65; on Mexicans, xiv; and Native Americans, 66–68; and Runaway Scrape, 203; and Santa Anna, 204; and volunteers, 48
Hughes, Benjamin Franklin, 200–201
Hughes, James, 128
Hunter, William L., 180–81, 190, 213

I

Ildefonso, Third Treaty of, 5
India Pattern Musket, 133–34. *See also* Brown Bess muskets
Iraeta, Mariano, 110
Iturbide, Agustín de, 6, 17

J

Jackson, Andrew, xiv, 23–24, 43–45, 205, 214
Jefferson, Thomas, 5
Johnson, Edward J., 162
Johnson, Francis W., 61, 64–65, 82, 84

K

Karankawa, 4, 66, 92
Kemble, Frances, 42
Kentucky Mustangs, 72, 79, 125
Kentucky Rifle, 137–38
Key, Francis Scott, 24
King, Amon B., 92–93, 95–96, 112, 202; and Refugio, 98–99, 101–2, 104

L

La Bahía. *See* Goliad
Lafitte, Jean, 13–14
Landero, Pedro Telmo de, 9
Land Pattern Musket, 133. *See also* Brown Bess muskets
La Salle, René Robert Cavelier, Sieur de, 2
Law of April 6, 1830, xiii, 23

About the Author

JAY A. STOUT is a retired Marine Corps fighter pilot, an Indiana native, and a graduate of Purdue University. He was commissioned in June 1981 and designated a naval aviator on May 13, 1983, at Naval Air Station Chase Field, Texas—eighteen miles south of Goliad. His assignments included orders to fly F-4 Phantoms and F/A-18 Hornets. During his twenty-year career, he flew more than forty-five hundred flight hours, including thirty-seven combat missions during Operation Desert Storm.

Following his military career, Stout worked for a short time as an airline pilot before being furloughed after the terrorist attacks of September 11, 2001. He subsequently flew for the Kuwaiti air force for a year before returning to the United States, where he now works for a major defense contractor. *Slaughter at Goliad* is his sixth book.

Stout has been married to the former Monica Orelup for twenty-six years. They have two daughters, Kristen and Katherine.

THE NAVAL INSTITUTE PRESS is the book-publishing arm of the U.S. Naval Institute, a private, nonprofit, membership society for sea service professionals and others who share an interest in naval and maritime affairs. Established in 1873 at the U.S. Naval Academy in Annapolis, Maryland, where its offices remain today, the Naval Institute has members worldwide.

Members of the Naval Institute support the education programs of the society and receive the influential monthly magazine *Proceedings* or the colorful bimonthly magazine *Naval History* and discounts on fine nautical prints and on ship and aircraft photos. They also have access to the transcripts of the Institute's Oral History Program and get discounted admission to any of the Institute-sponsored seminars offered around the country.

The Naval Institute's book-publishing program, begun in 1898 with basic guides to naval practices, has broadened its scope to include books of more general interest. Now the Naval Institute Press publishes about seventy titles each year, ranging from how-to books on boating and navigation to battle histories, biographies, ship and aircraft guides, and novels. Institute members receive significant discounts on the Press's more than eight hundred books in print.

Full-time students are eligible for special half-price membership rates. Life memberships are also available.

For a free catalog describing Naval Institute Press books currently available, and for further information about joining the U.S. Naval Institute, please write to:

Member Services
U.S. NAVAL INSTITUTE
291 Wood Road
Annapolis, MD 21402-5034
Telephone: (800) 233-8764
Fax: (410) 571-1703
Web address: www.usni.org